Lecture Notes in Artificial Intellige

Subseries of Lecture Notes in Computer Science
Edited by J. Siekmann

Lecture Notes in Computer Science

Edited by G. Goos and J. Hartmanis

J. P. Martins M. Reinfrank (Eds.)

Truth Maintenance Systems

ECAI-90 Workshop
Stockholm, Sweden, August 6, 1990
Proceedings

Springer-Verlag

Berlin Heidelberg New York
London Paris Tokyo
Hong Kong Barcelona
Budapest

Series Editor

Jörg Siekmann
Institut für Informatik, Universität Kaiserslautern
Postfach 3049, W-6750 Kaiserslautern, FRG

Volume Editors

João Pavão Martins
Instituto Superior Técnico, Departamento de Engenharia Mecânica
Secção de Sistemas, Avenida Rovisco Pais, 1096 Lisboa Codex, Portugal

Michael Reinfrank
Siemens AG, ZFE IS INF 33
Otto-Hahn-Ring 6, W-8000 München 83, FRG

CR Subject Classification (1991): I.2.3

ISBN 3-540-54305-8 Springer-Verlag Berlin Heidelberg New York
ISBN 0-387-54305-8 Springer-Verlag New York Berlin Heidelberg

Typesetting: Camera ready by author
Printing and binding: Druckhaus Beltz, Hemsbach/Bergstr.
2145/3140-543210 - Printed on acid-free paper

Preface

The Truth Maintenance Workshop was held on August 6, 1990 during the European Conference on Artificial Intelligence in Stockholm, Sweden. We received 36 submissions and accepted 10 to be included in this volume; 8 of them were presented at the workshop. In general, the quality of the papers submitted was very good and the majority of the papers were devoted to theoretical aspects rather than application areas. Although all the papers concern Truth Maintenance, they can be grouped into several areas of general interest.

Meta-level Control

The goal here is to specify some (meta-) criteria to control the behavior of the TMS. Under this heading is the paper by Dressler and Farquhar that discusses how to allow the problem solver to specify control over the ATMS, and the paper by Junker that discusses several forms of backtracking.

Extensions of TMSs

In this area people try to incorporate new mechanisms in TMS-like systems, mostly mechanisms which have not been considered by the now classical systems of Doyle or de Kleer. Under this heading, the paper by Dubois, Lang, and Prade extends the ATMS with the addition of uncertainty, and the paper by Tayrac defines ATMS based on a new resolution strategy.

Foundations

TMSs were introduced mostly as a procedural description of systems, with little initial concern about the properties of the resulting system and their relationship with other formalisms. Recently, there has been a considerable interest in providing formal descriptions of TMSs, proving results about them, and relating them with other non-monotonic formalisms. The paper by Fujiwara and Honiden defines a semantics for the ATMS in terms of propositional Horn logic, the paper by Witteveen introduces a 3-valued stable model semantics for TMSs, the paper by Inoue presents a procedural semantics for a variety of TMSs, and the paper by Kakas and Mancarella links abduction with TMSs.

Belief Revision

TMSs can be considered as a formalism providing support to a more general problem called belief revision. The paper by Giordano and Martelli addresses the problem of contradiction resolution and the paper by Jackson and Pais presents a revision-based approach to TMSs.

Acknowledgements

We would like to thank the other members of the program committee: Oskar Dressler (Siemens), Gerald Kelleher (University of Leeds), and Charles Petrie (MCC), for all their help in the process of paper selection. Many thanks also go to Patrick Doherty who acted as our local support person.

We would also like to thank the following institutions that provided financial support for the workshop:

- ECAI - Provided general support in distributing the information and setting up the room for the workshop;
- JNICT (Junta Nacional de Investigação Científica e Tecnológica, Portugal) - Under Grant 87/107 provided support for communication and mailing;
- Siemens - Provided snacks and refreshments to the participants;
- Fundação Calouste Gulbenkian (Portugal) - provided travel support for João P. Martins.

Lisbon and Munich, January 1991

João P. Martins   Michael Reinfrank
IST - Technical University of Lisbon   *Siemens*

Contents

Contents

Putting the Problem Solver
Back in the Driver's Seat:
Contextual Control of the ATMS

Oskar Dressler*   and   Adam Farquhar[†]

SIEMENS AG

Otto-Hahn-Ring 6

D-8000 Munich 83

Germany

(dressler@ztivax.siemens.com)

Department of Computer

Sciences

University of Texas

Austin, Texas 78712

USA

(farquhar@cs.utexas.edu)

Abstract

The ATMS is a powerful tool for automated problem solvers and has been used to support several model-based reasoning tasks such as prediction and diagnosis. It provides an efficient mechanism for maintaining consistent sets of beliefs and recording the assumptions underlying them. This enables the problem solver to switch rapidly between contexts and compare them. Such capabilities are central to diagnositic systems, and are also valuable to design and planning systems. Applications to larger problems have been hampered, however, by the problem solver's inability to maintain control over the ATMS.

We present a new approach, implemented in a system called COCO, which allows the problem solver to maintain tight control over the contexts explored by the ATMS. COCO provides means for expressing local and global control over both normal and nogood consumers. Local control is achieved by attaching guards to individual consumers. These guards express control, rather than logical, knowledge

*This research was supported by *Bundesminister fuer Forschung und Technologie*, project TEX-B, ITW 8506 E4.

†This research was in part supported by a SIEMENS doctoral fellowship, and has in part taken place in the Qualitative Reasoning Group at the Artificial Intelligence Laboratory, The University of Texas at Austin. Research of the Qualitative Reasoning Group is supported in part by NSF grants IRI-8602665, IRI-8905494, and IRI-8904454, by NASA grants NAG 2-507 and NAG 9-200, and by the Texas Advanced Research Program under grant no. 003658175.

and consist of sets of environments. Global control is achieved by specifying a set of *interesting* environments. Consumers are fired only when its antecedents are true in some interesting environment. We also successfully apply the same technique to *limit label propagation* in the ATMS. This ensures that the ATMS respects the problem solver's wishes and only makes derivations in interesting contexts.

We demonstrate the both the dramatic increases in efficiency which are made possible by these techniques, as well as their tremendous expressive power, in four examples.

1   Introduction

The ATMS is a powerful tool for automated problem solvers. It provides an efficient mechanism for maintaining consistent sets of beliefs and recording the assumptions underlying them. This enables the problem solver to switch rapidly between contexts and compare them.

The ATMS, however, has two shortcomings: (1) the existing problem solver–ATMS interface is hard to control, and (2) the ATMS attempts to compute all solutions, even when they are irrelevant or unnecessary. Thus, in problems with large, perhaps infinite, search spaces new techniques must be used to control the ATMS.

We define an expressive, flexible, and efficient problem solver–ATMS interface, called COCO (COntext driven COntrol), to address these problems. Using COCO, the problem solver defines a focus — sets of environments which it finds interesting — which is used to control rule execution, and to restrict the contexts in which the ATMS looks for solutions. COCO ensures that the ATMS respects the problem solver's wishes. This means not only that no rule will be executed unless its antecedents are true in some interesting environment, but that only the interesting environments are propagated. In a sense, our approach makes a philosophical break with the previous ATMS research which has emphasized exhaustivity: COCO ensures completeness *only* with respect to the focus.

COCO has seen extensive use in the GDE$^+$ diagnostic system [11]. The basic ideas have also been adapted for use in the SHERLOCK diagnostic system [4]. In Section 5, we present four additional examples of its use along with empirical results which demonstrate both the dramatic increases in efficiency which are made possible by these techniques, as well as their tremendous expressive power.

2 ATMS Background

The ATMS [1] supports problem solvers that are able to explicitly mark out some of the data that they manipulate as *assumptions*. Belief in all other data is then characterized by the assumptions which support them. These sets of assumptions are called *environments*. Each problem solver datum has an ATMS *node* associated with it. Each node has a *label* which is a list of the environments supporting it. The problem solver interacts with the ATMS by making assumptions and by *justifying* one datum in terms of other data. The primary responsibility of the ATMS is to compute the correct label for each datum. A justification with antecedents x and y for the consequent z is written $[x\ y] \rightarrow z$.

Derivation is naturally defined using justifications. The consequent of a justification is derivable when the antecedents are either assumptions or derivable nodes. Inconsistencies arise when a specific node, $\perp$, is derived. The environments that derive $\perp$ are called *nogoods*. Since derivation is monotonic, the ATMS only needs to represent minimal environments. This applies both to the environments that derive a specific node (its label) and the nogoods. The minimal environment characterized by assumptions $a\ b\ c$ is written $\langle a\ b\ c \rangle$. The set of nodes derivable from a consistent (non-nogood) environment is called a *context*. *Context(E)* denotes the context characterized by the environment E.

Following de Kleer, we are considering problem solvers which are capable of expressing most of their knowledge in the form of rules. The consumer [1] is a device for linking rules to the ATMS nodes. A consumer consists of a set of antecedents which are ATMS nodes (or classes) and a body of code which computes some result given the problem solver data corresponding to the antecedents. Once the antecedents are established, the consumer may be selected and be *fired*; it asserts some consequents which are justified by the antecedents. If the ATMS is to support sound deductions, the consumers must obey certain conventions: they must not use any data not present in the antecedents and they must include all of the antecedents in a justification they add. The consequence of these restrictions is that a consumer need only be executed once for a given set of antecedents. Firing a consumer, therefore, may be viewed as compiling it into a set of justifications. A consumer for antecedents x and y is written $(x\ y \Rightarrow)$, or with a body, $(x\ y \Rightarrow [z := x+y])$. The latter indicates that the consumer compiles into a justification such as $[x=2, y=3] \rightarrow z=5$.

3 The Problem of Control

Two major steps towards controlling the ATMS have been reported in [2] and [6]. This research attempts to control the ATMS by restricting the number of consumers which are executed. Unfortunately, in the ATMS, delaying the execution of a consumer is only half the job – it is like keeping the floodgate closed as long as possible. As soon as the consumer fires, it introduces a justification, and all of the environments in the labels of its antecedents flood through the justification, and flow throughout the justification network. Executing a consumer is a simple constant time operation, propagating environments, however, is worst-case exponential.

Therefore, COCO has two main techniques for expressing control: a consumer focus, which restricts the execution of consumers, and an environment focus, which restricts the propagation of environments.

4 Controlling Consumer Execution

4.1 Context and Data Driven Strategies

Standard rule–based problem solvers maintain a single database of facts which are referred to in the preconditions of rules. Each fact in the database is believed and the rules are fired when their antecedents are in the database. In TMS–based problem solvers, these facts are labeled as in or out depending on their support. Rules may fire because certain data are in or out, or because a datum has changed its label. The ATMS is more expressive. Data are not simply in or out, but belief in them is characterized by sets of environments. A datum may be thought of as being in any context that is characterized by one of these environments. Thus, rules used in conjunction with an ATMS must fire on a combination of *data and environments*. Data and environments can be viewed as two orthogonal axes.

All existing strategies for controlling rule execution in the ATMS can be located somewhere on these two axes. There have been a variety of strategies discussed in the literature. In [6], Forbus and de Kleer review :intern, :in, and :addb, and propose two new ones: :implied-by and :contradiction.

:Intern and :contradiction represent the two extremes of data and context driven strategies. :Intern is purely data driven. A consumer fires as soon as its antecedents are in the ATMS database, regardless of their labels. They need not even be members of the same context. :Contradiction is purely context driven. A :contradiction consumer is associated with a single environment. When that environment becomes a nogood, the consumer fires. This is a simple way for the ATMS to signal inconsistencies to the problem solver. There are no data associated with the contradiction consumer at all. The standard consumer execution strategy is :in, which requires that the antecedents are in at least one common context. Thus, it is mostly data driven, but also puts a weak constraint on when it is interesting to fire the rule.

Both :addb and :implied-by make use of a *control environment*. The control environment is specified by the problem solver, and is used to define the current problem solver task. It is a set of assumptions whose consequents the problem solver is currently interested in.

:Addb (assumption-based dependency directed backtracking) puts more constraints on the contextual part of a consumer's precondition. An :addb rule will be executed only when there is at least one environment E where all of its antecedents hold such that (1) the set of control assumptions in E is a subset of the actual control environment, and (2) the union of the actual control environment and E is consistent. In :addb the problem solver delegates part of its responsibility for control to the ATMS. A fixed scheme is used to aggregate the control environment from so-called control disjunctions that are known in advance.

In the :implied-by strategy, the control environment is used as an upper bound. Whenever the antecedents hold in a subset of the control environment the consumer is fired. Using :implied-by, the problem solver is free to install and retract control environments in any order it wishes.

Figure 1: Using antecedents for controlling the ATMS is inadequate.

Another approach to controlling consumer execution is to provide control antecedent nodes. At some point the problem solver justifies the control node with a control assumption C, and the consumer may then fire, introducing a justification (see Figure 1). If the consumer ascribes to the convention of using all of its antecedents in the justifications it introduces, then the control assumptions will be included in the consequent's label. Thus, then we have achieved a limited amount of control at the price of doing more work after the control condition is satisfied. Labels and environments will become bloated with control assumptions. If control nodes are true in different contexts, their consequents will also become discriminated into many contexts which differ only in their control decisions. There is no way to control the propagation of environments after the consumer has fired and installed a justification, nor is there a way to retract a control decision. One final difficulty with this representation is that the control knowledge and decisions are mixed in with the domain knowledge.

4.2 Control of Consumer Execution in COCO

When using the ATMS, people carefully select the data that will be used as assumptions from the data their problem solvers are going to manipulate. In doing so they implicitly define a set of possible contexts. Therefore, a context is normally associated with an application dependent meaning. For instance, in GDE, a system for model-based diagnosis [3], a context is associated with a set of components that are working correctly. Another application views a context as characterizing a specific perceptual interpretation [9]. [8] uses contexts to represent situations for a planning task. In [10] the framework for assumption-based reasoning as provided by the ATMSis used to represent various structural and behavioral aspects of components in a device. During analysis or diagnosis of the device one wants to focus the problem solver on certain aspects of specific sets of components. These are represented as assumption sets, i.e. contexts. Struß in [10] explicitly expresses the need for a means to convey information about these interesting contexts to the ATMS. In Section 6.3 we discuss an example in which contexts are associated with hierarchical layers in a component model. The same technique can be used to encode aspects of components as needed in [10].

From the preceding discussion, it is clear that a consumer strategy consists of two parts: a specification of which *nodes* it should fire *on*, and a specification of which *environments* it should fire *in*. A third dimension, that is present in none of the strategies above, is spanned by an axis that specifies whether the control information is available locally or globally. Local control information is attached to individual consumers, whereas global control information applies to all consumers.

In COCO, we express all of this information explicitly. As usual, the data are specified by a rule's antecedents. Control information is specified by a local *guard* and a global *focus*. Conceptually, both the guard and the focus are simply sets of environments. These sets of environments can most often be conveniently described by upper and lower bound in the lattice of all environments. For instance, $focus = \{E | \{a, b\} \subseteq E \subseteq \{a, b, c, d, e\}\}$ describes the set of environments above {a,b} and below {a,b,c,d,e}.

The *guarded consumer* may fire only if its antecedents hold in some common environment that is a member of the *guard set*. The guarded consumers allow the problem solver to maintain tight *local* control over consumer execution by restricting the contexts in which an individual consumer fires.

The *global focus* affects all consumers equally. A consumer may fire only if its antecedents hold in a common environment that is a member of the global focus. The :implied-by strategy presented in [6] is a restricted version of the global focus in which there is only a single control environment. It uses focus descriptions of the form:

$$focus = \{E | E \subseteq control\text{-}environment\}$$

There are several examples of focusing using an upper bound in the literature, such as [2] and [6]; we provide one more in Section 6.3.

Although very useful, e.g. reasoning about hypothetical situations, using a lower bound to specify a focus environment leads to a minor complication. The difficulty is that the environments in labels are minimal ones. If a consumer's antecedents hold in the common minimal environment, ⟨a⟩, then they hold in ⟨a b⟩, ⟨abc⟩, and so on. Therefore, even if we specify a lower bound focus, say ⟨ab⟩, there is a non-null intersection between the focus and the minimal environments "below" it — ⟨a⟩ and ⟨b⟩ in this case.

By default, we restrict consumers to apply to the minimal environments where all of their antecedents hold. Thus, in our example a consumer sitting on the environment ⟨a⟩ is not fired on ⟨a b⟩.

4.3 Nogood consumers

By specifying the global focus and guards for the consumers, the problem solver can keep tight control of the problem solving activities as far as consistent environments are concerned. A major part of problem solving, however, is finding out about inconsistencies. When nogoods are discovered, the problem solver must be informed so that it can react appropriately. For this purpose we use *nogood consumers*, a special kind of guarded consumers that is executed on the minimal nogoods contained in the attached guard set. Nogood consumers are prioritized. They are scheduled before all other consumers because the problem solver must immediately be informed about changes of the search space as to avoid useless activities. Often the inconsistency of the focus (or parts of it) will be signaled this way. The "contradiction consumer" from [6] is a specialized nogood consumer with an attached guard set of cardinality one.

5 Focusing Label Propagation

Regardless of how sophisticated our mechanisms for controlling consumer execution are, control will be lost after a consumer fired. Label propagation inside the ATMS still occurs throughout the whole network and for all contexts. It is possible, however, to use the techniques described above to control the propagation of environments through the justifications. A guard set similar to the one for consumers allows a justification to propagate environments only when they fall within the specified range. Justifications that have an attached guard set are called *guarded justifications*. Besides guards for local control information we can also use the global focus to exercise control of label propagation globally.

5.1 Local Control of Label Propagation

If a consumer is controlled by a guard, it will under no circumstances be executed on environments outside of the guard set. However, if it is executed, it will, following the consumer architecture [1], compile into a justification. The advantages of a guarded consumer would be lost once the justification is given to the ATMS, as *all* of the environments in the label of its antecedents would be propagated. Label updating does not respect the guard set. For example, suppose there is a guarded consumer $(x,y \Rightarrow)$ with the guard $\{E | \{a, b, c\} \subseteq E\}$. Initially, let label$(x)$ be $\{\langle d \rangle \langle e \rangle \ldots\}$ and label(y) be $\{\langle e \rangle \langle f \rangle \ldots\}$. The consumer does not fire because the label of its antecedents, label(x, y), is $\{\langle e \rangle \langle d\ f \rangle \ldots\}$, which does not satisfy the guard. If the environment $\langle a\ b\ c\ d \rangle$ is subsequently added to label(x) and label(y), the label(x, y) becomes $\{\langle a\ b\ c\ d \rangle \langle e \rangle \langle d\ f \rangle \ldots\}$, which satisfies the guard. The consumer fires, installing the justification $[x,\ y] \rightarrow z$. Unfortunately, the label(z) now contains the complete label(x, y), including the *un*interesting environments which did not fire the consumer to start with. Even worse, these uninteresting environments will be propagated through the label of every node which z is connected to.

We would like the consumer's guard set to be respected by the ATMS and used to control label propagation. If the principles of the consumer architecture are strictly followed, justifications are nothing but instances of rules. Therefore, we can use the consumer's guard set to control label propagation: a justification will propagate when the guard set allows it to do so. Although the label of the conjunction of antecedents is correctly computed (and recorded in the justification's label), only the minimal environments that represent the lower bound of the intersection of the environments (implicitly) represented by the justification's label and the guard set are propagated to the justification's consequent. Thus, using our previous example, label(z) becomes $\{\langle a\ b\ c\ d \rangle\}$, and only the interesting environments are propagated to z's children.

It is crucial to note that the guard set must only be used for control. It must not be misused for specifying logical dependencies. The guard set must not be used to restrict the validity of a justification, just its interestingness. It should always be the case that if the guard were removed, a program would still be logically correct, though perhaps infinitely inefficient.

5.2 Global Control of Label Propagation

It is worth considering whether the technique of delaying propagation from justification labels can be applied to the focus, too. Can label propagation for *all* justifications be limited by the global focus? The answer is yes. First, we can limit label propagation by the upper bound of the focus. Any environment above the upper bound that appears in some antecedent will result in an environment for the consequent that is at least as large. The resulting environment will thus be out of the focus. If it becomes inconsistent the focus will not be affected. Second, we use the lower bound of the focus to decide which environments we propagate from a node. For example, if a node's label is $\{\langle a \rangle \langle b \rangle\}$ and the lower bound is given by $\{\{c\} \{b\ d\}\}$ then we propagate the environments $\langle a\ c \rangle$, $\langle b\ c \rangle$ and $\langle b\ d \rangle$. The lower bound has the same effect as adding a virtual node to the antecedents of a justification. Now, if e.g. $\langle a \rangle$ without restricting label propagation would become a nogood, then we will detect the nogood $\langle a\ c \rangle$ when applying the lower bound. This is exactly what we want: we detect those nogoods that effect the focus.

By limiting label propagation we loose label completeness as far as the whole context lattice is concerned. We retain soundness and minimality. We give up label completeness and consistency only for those contexts that are out of the focus, as is desired. But label completeness and consistency is guaranteed for the focus.

5.3   Changing the focus

It is natural that the problem solver will want to modify its focus as the current task changes. This is supported in a straight forward and efficient way. If the new focus is more restrictive than the old one, then no additional work need be done. E.g. suppose that $label(x) = \{\langle a\ b\ c \rangle, \langle d \rangle\}$, and there is no focus — all environments are propagated without control. If the focus is now changed to be $\{E | E \supseteq \{a\ d\}\}$, we can leave the label of x as it is. It is still correct, but some part is just uninteresting. Any new propagation from x will be done using the interesting part of the label, $\{\langle a\ d \rangle\}$.

If the focus is relaxed, then we need to propagate the environments which were outside of the old focus, but are within the new one. The overhead is quite small, linear in the number of environments which were not wholly within the old focus. In the worst case of focus change, every environment is initially outside of the focus and after the change is within the new focus. All of the environments must then be propagated, which is just what the ATMS would have done without the focus. Thus, relaxing the focus just forces us to do some of the work which we avoided by using the focus to start with.

The only complication involves deciding when the environments should be propagated, and how to order their propagation. Propagation starts from a node, but a node's label might contain several effected environments. Thus, it is clear that we want to check all of the environments first, so that we do not have to propagate from a node once for each of its effected environments. The second issue is choosing an order in which to propagate from the effected nodes. In order to do a minimum amount of work, we can compute an ordered set of strongly connected components starting with the assumptions and compute new node labels in this order. This is an adaptation of the technique from [7] used there for a justification-based truth maintenance system. A standard algorithm is

$O(max(|nodes|, |justifications|))$, so this requires little additional work, and is well worth the effort.

6   Empirical Results

In this section we provide four examples to illustrate scope of application, conceptual clarity, and pragmatic efficiency gains which can be achieved with COCO. First, we show its effectiveness in *controlling* the multiple model prediction problem. Second, we show how it can be used to suppress uninteresting consumer execution that arises in constraint satisfaction. Third, we show how it can be used to implement flexible and tightly controlled hierarchical modeling. All three of these methods are in daily use as parts of the GDE$^+$ diagnostic system. The first and third examples make use of the global focus to control both consumer execution and label propagation. The second example highlights the use of guarded consumers and guarded justifications. Fourth, we show an implementation of GDE using a nogood consumer.

6.1   Model-based prediction

We look at a model-based predictive problem in which we have a device composed of several components. Each component is described by an OK model describing its behavior when it functions correctly, and several fault models. The task is to compute predictions for the various parameters of the device given these models and observed values for some of the parameters. A combinatoric problem results because combinations of the predictions from different models need to be considered. With the standard ATMS, all (minimal) combinations of all of the models will be computed. This will include what the problem solver might consider to be extremely unlikely combinations involving many fault models. If the problem solver is willing to focus on an interesting subset of the possible combinations, however, COCO provides a means of dramatically reducing the work done by the ATMS.

In the example, we will use an *N-fault* focus which states that a derivation requiring more than N fault models is uninteresting. This is less restrictive than what most authors mean by an *N-fault assumption*. The N-fault assumption is a global statement about the whole device – no more than N of the components are faulty. Our N-fault focus says that no more than N fault models should be used to make any single derivation. Thus, independent failures, each of which require no more than N fault models, will be predicted. This definition fits well with the use of local propagation techniques to determine predicted values.

Two key advantages of using this sort of focus are (1) that derivations made within the focus are sound — they will not be contradicted by a change in the focus; and (2) that the focus can be easily changed by the problem solver and any new interesting deductions will be efficiently computed by COCO. This allows the problem solver to start with a very tight focus, and then gradually relax it until a satisfactory solution is found.

We have used the standard example with 3 multipliers and 2 adders (Figure 2). Each component is described by seven models:

1. OK. The component functions as expected.
2. Unknown. The component may exhibit arbitrary behavior.
3. Zero. The output is 0.
4. One. The output is 1.
5. Left. The component outputs its "left" input.
6. Right. The component outputs its "right" input.
7. Left-Shift. The output is shifted left one bit.

The input values A=3, B=2, C=2, D=3, and E=3 are asserted in succession. From this information, the OK models would predict a value of 12 for both F and G. We then assert the observations F=2 and G=8. These observations cannot be explained by a single fault, but two independent faults are adequate. A reasonable diagnosis might be {zero(M1), left(M2)} or {left(M2), right(A1)}.

Table 1 summarizes the results of using a single-fault focus. There is a dramatic 40-fold speedup in execution time when using the focus! There are several interrelated reasons for this tremendous reduction. Many rules are not fired because there antecedents do not hold in any *interesting* environments. If these rules had fired, they would have introduced justifications, sometimes for previously unpredicted values. These new values then enable additional rule firings, and the effect cascades. Furthermore, the effect of adding a single justification may result in large amounts of work, as the new environments in the label of its consequent must be propagated throughout the justification network.

It is worth noting that using a consumer focus without the environment focus results in almost no improvement in this example. For a more complete discussion see [5].

6.2 Suppressing Spurious Constraint Execution

A notorious problem in ATMS based constraint languages is avoiding needless computations due to retriggering of constraints on their own outputs. For example, consider the component M1 in Figure 2. The model of such a multiplier constraint can be implemented with three consumers: $(a, c \Rightarrow [x := a * c])$, $(a, x \Rightarrow [c := x/a])$, and $(c, x \Rightarrow [a := x/c])$. As in the previous example, let A=3 and C=2 be provided as inputs. The first consumer will fire, introducing the justification [A=3,C=2,ok(M1)] $\rightarrow$ X=6.

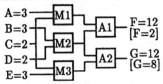

Figure 2: A standard diagnostic problem.

Experiment	Time	Rules fired	Justs	Nodes	Labels Max	Avg	Nogoods Ct	Max	Avg
Focused	40	359	1875	128	28	4	203	10	4
Unfocused	1600	1096	4233	214	186	32	409	10	5

Improvement: 40* 3.05* 2.26* 1.7* |

Table 1: A single-fault focus provides a 40-fold speedup when using seven models per component. The Labels column gives the maximum and average number of environments in a label; Nogoods gives the count of the minimal nogoods, as well as the maximum and average number of assumptions in a nogood.

	Time	Rules fired	Justs	Nodes	Labels Max	Avg	Nogoods Cnt	Max	Avg
Focused	1	424	666	217	9	1.2	36	4	1.7
Unfocused	43.5	4912	5298	2353	19	2.3	197	427	415.4

Improvement: 43.5* 11.6* 7.9* 10.8* |

Table 2: Using hierarchical models, two faults in a circuit of 845 gates provides a 43-fold speedup by limiting prediction to the relevant parts of the circuit.

X=6 may now be used as one of the inputs for the second and third consumers. This will result in two additional justifications being introduced, but no new node is derived nor is any label changed. The execution of the last two consumers could have been suppressed without any loss of information. To accomplish this [1] proposes to *type* consumers and give the same type to every consumer that implements a specific constraint. When a consumer fires it records its type in the (informant of the) justifications it produces. A consumer is only executed when for all its antecedents there exists a valid justification with a type different from the consumer's. In this example, the execution of the second consumer is suppressed because X=6 has only one valid justification, and this justification has the same type as the consumer.

This strategy ignores the contextual information in the node labels. If X=6 receives a second justification that does not change its label, the suppressed consumers are executed but have no effects with respects to new nodes or new labels. This happens for instance in systems with instantaneous feedback, e.g. the system in Figure 1 (adder-multiplier). Given the correct output values F=12 and G=12, the predicted value X=6 will get a second justification by propagating values from C=2 and E=3 along the chain of components M3, A2, A1. Now, the values at M1 all have justifications which do not have the type of the consumers. Hence, all of them are fired although no new node or new label is derived. But even worse, it turns out that in a chain reaction all constraints along the loop fire their consumers in every direction.

Thus, typing of consumers avoids spurious consumer triggering only when no feedback is involved.

A more general solution is the following. The constraint for a component C is implemented as a set of guarded consumers. They all have the same guard set, the set of environments that do not contain the correctness assumption about C, ok(C). Whenever one of the consumers is fired and justifies its result, the assumption ok(C) is one of the antecedents. If an input value of the constraint has no supporting environment other than ones that contain ok(C), then the constraint triggered on its own output. In exactly this case the guarded consumer will not fire.

6.3   Implementing Hierarchical Models

Another interesting application of global focusing is the use of hierarchies in model-based diagnosis. Consider again the device in Figure 1 (adder multiplier), but let each of the components be hierarchically defined in by subcomponents. Let the adder be a ripple-carry adder composed of half– and full-adders. The full-adders are composed of half-adders and gates; the half-adders are composed of gates. This model consists of four levels. Further, suppose that a diagnostic engine has concluded failure in the components M1 and A1 would account for the observations. In order to further localize the malfunction, the diagnostic engine needs to focus on the subcomponents of M1 and A1. Of course, it wants to do this refinement of the model without executing consumers which are associated with components other than M1 and A1 or which are associated with other levels of these two components.

We can easily implement this sort of control by associating an assumption with each component level, e.g. A1-gate-level, M1-adder-level. Let L be the set of these component-level assumptions. Every consumer that implements a predictive piece of knowledge for this component-level has the associated assumption as an additional antecedent. When we want to focus on a specific set of component-levels, *focused-levels*, use the following focus $\{E \mid (E \cap L) \subset focused\text{-}levels\}$. E.g. if we want to focus on the gate level M1 and the adder level of A1 we would use the focus: $\{E \mid (E \cap L) \subset \{a1\text{-}adder\text{-}level \; m1\text{-}gate\text{-}level\}\}$. This focus guarantees that consumers are only fired when their antecedents hold in an environment that depends only on the focused component-levels. Table 2 presents the empirical results. Using hierarchical models, two faults on the gate-level, a faulted AND and OR gate, are identified requiring the resources reported in the first line. Without focusing, the entire device must be simulated on the gate level which consumes the resources reported in the second line, which does not include the time for the diagnosis algorithm, but summarizes only prediction.

6.4 Implementing GDE

The General Diagnostic Engine,GDE, reported in [3] has been one of the most exciting applications of the ATMS. As described, however, GDE itself is not implemented using the ATMS, but uses consumers to implement its constraint system, and then queries the ATMS database to do diagnosis. COCO provides a very simple and elegant means of formulating GDE using a single nogood consumer.

```
(defparameter *last-candidate* nil)
(def-trace gde t "Trace gde")

(defun init-gde ()
  (setq *last-candidate* truth)
  (add-nogood-consumer 'conflicts))

(defun conflicts (nogood)
  (let ((new-candidate (gensym "CANDIDATE-")))
    (trace-gde "Working on nogood ~a" nogood)
    (dolist (a (environment-assumptions nogood))
      (when (correctness-assumption-p a)
        (trace-gde "Adding conflict node ~a to ~a"
                   a new-candidate)
        (justify new-candidate
                 (list '(:not ,a) *last-candidate*))))
    (setq *last-candidate* new-candidate)))

(defun correctness-assumption-p (assumption)
  (eq :correct (car (node-datum assumption))))
```

Figure 3: Complete code to implement conflict recognition and candidate generation.

Figure 3 contains the *complete* code to implement the conflict recognition and candidate generation aspects of GDE .

GDE has two phases: conflict recognition and candidate generation. A conflict is a set of correctness assumptions about components which cannot all be true at the same time. A candidate is a minimal set of correctness assumptions which covers all of the known conflicts. We are interested in collecting all of the candidates which cover the current conflicts.

We can implement this very simply, in an incremental manner. A conflict can be recognized by the nogood consumer `conflicts`. When `conflicts` finds a conflict, it creates a new candidate node. It then loops through each of the correctness assumptions in the conflict, and justifies the new candidate with the negated correctness assumption and the last candidate. The last candidate covered all of the old conflicts, so the new candidate will cover all of the old ones and each element of the new one.

7 Conclusion

We have presented an approach that allows ATMS–based problem solvers to reduce the complexity of their tasks by exploiting additional control knowledge. As the notion of context often has an application dependent meaning, this control knowledge is naturally expressed in terms of contexts. Therefore, we have provided ways for the problem solver to express itself in terms of contexts in addition to the conventional ways in terms of nodes. COCO allows the problem solver to specify a global focus and local guards in order to:

- guide consumer execution,
- limit label propagation.

Furthermore, the problem solver is immediately informed about changes in the search space by:

- nogood consumers

and can take appropriate action.

This new architecture has proven to be both efficient and expressive. We have presented four applications: controlling feedback in a constraint system, providing hierarchical modeling, controlling multiple model prediction, and implementing GDE. Furthermore, we have presented empirical evidence supporting the claim that the gains are real and dramatic.

7.1 Acknowledgments

We would especially like to thank our colleagues Michael Montag for suggesting the feedback technique, and Hartmut Freitag for his invaluable help with the hierarchical model example. We would also like to thank our colleagues Michael Reinfrank, and Peter Struß, as well as the mutual misunderstandings which resulted in the ideas presented here.

References

[1] Johan de Kleer. An assumption-based truth maintenance system, Extending the ATMS, Problem solving with the ATMS. *Artificial Intelligence*, 28(2):127–224, 1986.

[2] Johan de Kleer and Brian Williams. Back to backtracking: Controlling the ATMS. In *AAAI-86 Proceedings of the Fourth National Conference on Artificial Intelligence*, pages 910–917, August 1986.

[3] Johan de Kleer and Brian Williams. Diagnosing multiple faults. *Artificial Intelligence*, 32(1):97–130, April 1987.

[4] Johan de Kleer and Brian Williams. Diagnosis as identifying consistent modes of behavior. In *IJCAI-89 Proceedings of the Eleventh International Joint Conference on Artificial Intelligence*, 1989.

[5] Adam Farquhar. Focusing ATMS-based diagnosis and prediction. In *Proceedings of the Model-Based Reasoning Workshop at IJCAI-89*, 1989.

[6] Kenneth D. Forbus and Johan de Kleer. Focusing the ATMS. In *AAAI-88 Proceedings of the Sixth National Conference on Artificial Intelligence*, pages 193–198, August 1988.

[7] James W. Goodwin. An improved algorithm for non-monotonic dependency net update. Technical Report LITH-MAT-R-82-83, Linkoeping University, 1982.

[8] Paul Morris and Robert Nado. Representing actions with an assumption-based truth maintenance system. In *AAAI-86 Proceedings of the Fourth National Conference on Artificial Intelligence*, pages 13–20, 1986.

[9] Gregory Provan. Efficiency analysis of multiple-context TMSs in scene representation. In *AAAI-87 Proceedings of the Fifth National Conference on Artificial Intelligence*, pages 173–177, 1987.

[10] Peter Struß. Multiple representation of structure and function. In *J. Gero (Ed.) Expert Systems in Computer Aided Design*, Amsterdam, 1987.

Variations on Backtracking for TMS

Ulrich Junker

GMD

P O Box 1240

5205 St. Augustin 1

Fed. Rep. of Germany

Abstract

We review the backtracking technique of Doyle's Truth Maintenance System (TMS). Backtracking in principle is to recover from a failure state by retracting some assumptions. We discuss three possible applications for the TMS: (1) Transforming a contradiction proof into a direct proof if a false-node is labelled with IN. (2) Selecting another extension if an odd loop failure arises. (3) Doing theory revision if no extension exists. In this paper, we elaborate the first and the second alternative. If the TMS is used in an autoepistemic or default prover (as in [15]) it needs sufficient justifications for first-order proofs. We show how backtracking allows to complete this set incrementally by applying a special case of the deduction theorem. For finding extensions, we describe Doyle's label methods as meta rules deriving statements of the form $IN(p)$ and $\neg IN(q)$. If a node q of an odd loop is labelled with IN and OUT we obtain a contradiction in this meta reasoning system. Hence, we can again apply backtracking to identify and retract the label assumptions being responsible for the failure. Thus, we obtain an efficient TMS that detects an extension whenever one exists.

1   Introduction

Reason maintenance systems may be used to record proofs, to support efficient search, and to do non-monotonic reasoning. We are mainly interested in using such a system as a basis for non-monotonic theorem provers. This facility has at best been elaborated in Doyle's TMS [8] because it provides non-monotonic justifications as a basic constituent. Other systems such as the multiple belief reasoner (MBR) of Martins and Shapiro [17], or de Kleer's ATMS [4] must be extended to get a restricted form of non-monotonic reasoning ([3], [11], [14], [12]). Very often, an extra search procedure is needed to find extensions which is itself similar to the TMS. The TMS also seems to be interesting because it can be used to find extensions of autoepistemic and default theories. This has been elaborated in a joint work with Kurt Konolige [15].

However, the TMS suffers from some problems. Most label algorithms are incomplete in the sense that they do not find an existing extension if a so called 'odd loop error' arises: In this case, Doyle's TMS does not terminate [8], whereas Goodwin's system stops without definite result [13]. Chronological backtracking helps, but decreases efficiency. It has been implicitly used by Russinoff [21] and is also considered in [15]. Doyle also implemented a technique called dependency-directed backtracking which misses a clear theoretical analysis and foundation. Our goal is to clarify backtracking and to elaborate well-founded applications in the context of the TMS. Thus, we will get rid of some obstacles towards an efficient non-monotonic theorem prover.

Backtracking in general is to recover from a failure state by retracting some assumptions. We distinguish three possibilities to make this more precise.

1. **Deductive Backtracking:** If the TMS is used in an autoepistemic or default prover it needs sufficient justifications for first-order proofs. We show how backtracking allows to complete this set incrementally by transforming a contradiction proof into a justification. Thus, we can use the monotonic part of the TMS as an efficient propositional prover which is similar to a tableau prover.

2. **Label-Backtracking:** For finding extensions, we describe Doyle's label methods as meta rules deriving statements of the form $\text{IN}(p)$ and $\neg\text{IN}(q)$. If a node q of an odd loop is labelled with IN and OUT we obtain a contradiction in this meta reasoning system. Hence, we can again apply backtracking to identify and retract the label assumptions being responsible for the failure.

3. **Theory Revision:** In Doyle's latter paper on the TMS (cf. [9], [10]), he gives a precise motivation for backtracking: Doing a minimal change if the current belief state becomes inconsistent because of new information. However, the implemented backtracking has not been changed to achieve this requirement. Brewka discusses some problems of minimal changes and backtracking [1]. We do not further pursue this topic because it is beyond the scope of this paper.

2 Doyle's TMS

Doyle's TMS maintains a set of nodes and a set of justifications. Justifications can be applied to nodes and thus derive further nodes. In [15] we have introduced a special notation for this purpose which is based on operators and their closures. This section cites the basic notions of this paper.

Let U be an arbitrary domain and $apply : 2^U \to 2^U$ be a monotonic and compact operator. Hence, it satisfies

$$\text{if } X \subseteq Y \text{ then } apply(X) \subseteq apply(Y) \tag{1}$$

$$\text{if } q \in apply(Y) \text{ then } \exists X \subseteq Y : X \text{ is finite and } q \in apply(X) \tag{2}$$

Usually, we repeat application of such an operator. This motivates the following definition of a closure operation:

Definition 2.1 *(cited from [15]) Let U be a domain and $apply : 2^U \to 2^U$ be a monotonic and compact operator. The closure $apply^*(X)$ is the minimal set that contains X and is closed w.r.t. apply, i.e.*

1. $X \subseteq apply^*(X)$

2. $apply(apply^*(X)) \subseteq apply^*(X)$.

It is easy to show that closedness and minimality are equivalent to closedness and groundedness which are used to define TMS-extensions (cf. [9] and [19]). In the latter approach, finite derivation chains are used to avoid circular arguments:

Lemma 2.1 *(cited from [15]) Let $apply : 2^U \to 2^U$ be a monotonic, and compact operator. Let T be a subset of U. The following conditions are equivalent:*

1. $T = apply^*(\emptyset)$

2. $apply(T) = T \subseteq apply^*(\emptyset)$

3. $apply(T) \subseteq T$ and $\forall q \in T \; \exists q_1, \ldots, q_k : q_i \in apply(\{q_1, \ldots, q_{i-1}\})$ for $i = 1, \cdots, k$ and $q = q_k$.

Now, we can turn our attention to Doyle's TMS. This system is supplied with a justification network $\nu := (N, J)$. N is a set of nodes which are justified by justifications in J. A justification j consists of an in-list I, an out-list O, and a consequent c. Since we miss a unique notation in the literature we write $\langle in(I), out(O) \to c \rangle$ for j which is similar as in [19]. Informally, a justification can be applied if every element of its in-list is valid, but no element of its out-list. In [15], we have used monotonic and compact operators $apply_{J,Y} : 2^N \mapsto 2^N$ for applying justifications. For this purpose, we must handle in-list and out-list separately by using an extra index Y. Otherwise, we would not get monotonicity:

$$apply_{J,Y}(X) := \{c \mid \langle in(I), out(O) \to c \rangle \in J, I \subseteq X \text{ and } O \cap Y = \emptyset\} \tag{3}$$

This operator satisfies some interesting monotonicity properties:

1. if $X_1 \subseteq X_2$ then $apply_{J,Y}(X_1) \subseteq apply_{J,Y}(X_2)$

2. if $Y_1 \subseteq Y_2$ then $apply_{J,Y_1}(X) \supseteq apply_{J,Y_2}(X)$

3. if $J_1 \subseteq J_2$ then $apply_{J_1,Y}(X) \subseteq apply_{J_2,Y}(X)$

A justification network can have extensions (or admissible labellings). As discussed in [15], an extension T can be characterized as the minimal set which is closed w.r.t. $apply_{J,T}$. According to lemma 2.1 this is equivalent to usual definitions in terms of groundedness and closedness (cf. [9], [19]):

Definition 2.2 (*cited from [15]*) *Let* $\nu = (N, J)$ *be a justification network. A subset* T *of* N *is an extension of* ν *iff* $T = apply^*_{J,T}(\emptyset)$.

If a network has no extension then it is called incoherent.

3   Deductive Backtracking

In [15], we showed that the TMS can be used to find extensions of autoepistemic and default theories[1]. For this purpose, we supplied sufficient monotonic justifications for first-order derivations (in addition to non-monotonic justifications for defaults). Thus, we splitted J into a set M of monotonic justifications and a set NM of non-monotonic justifications. In this section, we provide a better encoding of the monotonic part for a special kind of theories, namely propositional horn theories. We consider default theories $\Delta = (D, W)$ where W consists of horn clauses $a_1 \wedge \ldots \wedge a_k \supset c$ and D of defaults $(a : \neg b_1; \ldots; b_k; c/c)$ s.t. a, a_i, and b_j are propositional constants and c is a propositional constant or the unsatisfiable constant $\perp$.

Consider a simple example $\Delta = (\{\frac{:a}{a}, \frac{:b}{b}, \frac{:c}{c}\}, \{a \wedge b \supset d, c \wedge d \supset \perp\})$. According to [15], we get the following justifications:

$$NM = \{\langle out(\neg a) \rightarrow a \rangle, \langle out(\neg b) \rightarrow b \rangle, \langle out(\neg c) \rightarrow c \rangle\}$$

$$M = \{\langle in(b, c) \rightarrow \neg a \rangle, \langle in(a, c) \rightarrow \neg b \rangle, \langle in(a, b) \rightarrow \neg c \rangle\}$$

The three normal defaults are translated into three non-monotonic justifications in a modular way. To retract such a justification we need an argument for a negative formula. For this purpose, we determine all proofs of $\neg a$, $\neg b$, and $\neg c$, thus obtaining three monotonic justifications. This translation step is not modular. However, we want a more modular translation for horn theories and translate every horn clause into a justification:

$$M_W := \{\langle in(a_1, \ldots, a_k) \rightarrow c \rangle \mid a_1 \wedge \ldots \wedge a_k \supset c \in W\} \tag{4}$$

---

[1]Indeed, the same network can be used for both logic due to Konolige's work on their relation [16]. For weakly grounded extensions, a slight revision of a TMS-extension has been introduced in [15]. The results of this paper can easily be adapted to these +-extensions

This set is complete w.r.t. the derivation of contradictions and propositional constants. Let $\mathcal{C}_W$ be the set of all propositional constants occurring in W. If $X \subseteq \mathcal{C}_W$ and $X \cup W \not\models \bot$ then

$$apply^*_{M_W}(X) = \{q \in \mathcal{C}_W \mid X \cup W \models q\} \tag{5}$$

We can also detect inconsistencies:

$$\bot \in apply^*_{M_W}(X) \text{ iff } X \cup W \models \bot \tag{6}$$

Applied to our example, we get $\langle in(a, b) \rightarrow d \rangle$ and $\langle in(c, d) \rightarrow \bot \rangle$. This network is complete for positive queries, but not for negative ones. E.g. we cannot infer $\neg a$ from b and c. However, for TMS we need direct arguments, whereas classical theorem provers mainly perform refutation proofs. However, the deduction theorem can be used to transform results of refutation proofs into direct arguments:

$$\text{if } W \cup X \cup \{q\} \models \bot \text{ then } W \cup X \models \{\neg q\} \tag{7}$$

In the sequel, we adapt this special case of the deduction theorem to the TMS getting deductive backtracking. In the TMS-network $(\ldots, M_W)$ we miss justifications for negated consequents $\neg c$ of defaults $(a : b_1; \ldots; b_k; c/c) \in D$. In order to detect them, we just add c to a global assumption set $A \subseteq \mathcal{C}_W$. If TMS detects an inconsistency it invokes a backtracking procedure to detect the involved assumption set $N \subseteq A$ by tracing back the applied justifications. Then backtracking selects an assumption c in N and creates a new justification $\langle in(N - \{c\}) \rightarrow \neg c \rangle$ which is justified by 7. In our example, $\langle in(b, c) \rightarrow \neg a \rangle$ may be added after $\bot \in apply^*_{M_W}(\{a, b, c\})$ has been detected. Now, we get a missing justification for a negated consequent. Thus, the set of first-order justifications can dynamically be completed by backtracking.

For this application, it is easy to characterize the needed backtracking justifications. Let C_D be the set of consequents of the defaults in D.

$$B_{(D,W)} := \{\langle in(C) \rightarrow \neg c \rangle \mid C \text{ is minimal subset of } C_D \text{ s.t.} \atop \bot \in apply^*_{M_W}(C \cup \{c\}), c \in C_D\} \tag{8}$$

Then $M_W \cup B_\Delta$ is complete w.r.t. the relevant negative queries.

Thus, we use dependency-directed backtracking to get justifications for negative literals. Hence, backtracking dynamically completes the set of classical justifications of a network by exploiting the deduction theorem. It is important that it is only applied to the monotonic justifications of the TMS. Thus, contraposition concerning defaults is avoided.

4 TMS as a Propositional Prover

In addition to prove negative literals, we use deductive backtracking to do reasoning by cases and to use TMS as a propositional prover. Since the monotonic part of TMS is similar to the propositional horn clause prover of Dowling and Gallier it is not astonishing that TMS can be viewed as a propositional prover [7]. We especially need this view in section 6 to realize label-backtracking.

Let P be a set of propositional implications of the form $a_1 \wedge \ldots \wedge a_k \supset c$ where the a_i's are literals and c is a literal or $\bot$. We translate them directly into justifications

$$J'_P := \{\langle in(a_1, \ldots, a_k) \to c \mid a_1 \wedge \ldots \wedge a_k \supset c \in P\} \tag{9}$$

Furthermore, we add some justifications to detect inconsistent cases:

$$J_P := J'_P \cup \{\langle in(q, \neg q) \to \bot\rangle \mid q \text{ is a constant occurring in } P\} \tag{10}$$

These justifications constitute a network ν_P. Finally, we consider all atoms whose negation occurs as a precondition:

$$Q_P := \{a \mid a_1 \wedge \ldots \wedge \neg a \wedge \ldots \wedge a_k \supset c \in P\} \tag{11}$$

Now, we develop an algorithm that checks consistency of the premise set P. In some aspects, it is similar to a tableau prover because it starts refutation proofs for negative preconditions. However, it records a refutation proof by a new justification for the negation of an involved assumption. The algorithm is supplied with a set J of monotonic justifications and an assumption set A. Both sets characterize the current state and can be changed. The justifications have to be correct w.r.t. the premise set P (i.e. $apply^*_J(X) \subseteq \{q \mid P \cup X \models q\}$). In contrast to tableau provers, we allow a liberal strategy for introducing and eliminating assumptions. Justifications generated by backtracking help to avoid earlier states. We distinguish three cases:

- The current state is incomplete w.r.t. Q_P, i.e. we can neither derive q, nor $\neg q$ for some $q \in Q_P$. Then we start a refutation proof for $\neg q$ by adding q to the current assumption set.

- The current state is consistent and complete. Then we can define a model $\mathcal{M}$ for P by taking $\mathcal{M} \models q$ iff $q \in apply^*_J(A)$ for every propositional constant q. Hence, P is satisfiable.

- The current state is inconsistent since we can derive $\bot$ using its assumptions and justifications. Then dependency-directed backtracking is invoked as in [8] to find a conflict set N by tracing back applied justifications. This set contains all assumptions which are responsible for the inconsistency. If it is empty then P is inconsistent because the set of justifications is correct. Otherwise, dependency-directed backtracking selects an element q of the conflict set N and creates a justifcation $\langle in(N - \{q\}) \to \neg q\rangle$. Hence, q cannot be chosen again if $N - \{q\}$ has already been selected. However, we can again encounter this contradiction if we choose the assumptions in another ordering. Then a second justification is generated. This time, another assumption will be selected. Hence, termination is guaranteed since after some time all elements of the conflict set are exhausted.

Thus, we use TMS and dependency-directed backtracking to get a sound and complete propositional prover. Below, we list the precise algorithm. It returns *false* if and only if $P \cup A$ is inconsistent. Otherwise, it returns the final set of justifications and the final assumption set:

Algorithm 1 $DDB(J, A) \equiv$

1. *if* $\perp \in apply_J^*(A)$ *then*
   let N *be a conflict set (s.t.* $N \subseteq A$, $\perp \in apply_J^*(N)$)
   if $N = \emptyset$ *then* false *else*
   select q *from* N *s.t.* $\langle in(N - \{q\}) \rightarrow \neg q \rangle \notin J$;
   $DDB(J \cup \{\langle in(N - \{q\}) \rightarrow \neg q \rangle\}, A - \{q\})$ *else*

2. *if* $\forall q \in Q_P$: q *or* $\neg q$ *is in* $apply_J^*(A)$ *then* (J, A) *else*

3. *select* $q \in Q_P$ *s.t.* $q, \neg q \notin apply_J^*(A)$
   $DDB(J, A \cup \{q\})$

We presume that the algorithm is only supplied with justifications which are in J_P or are obtained by backtracking.

Theorem 4.1 *Let* P *be a finite set of propositional implications. Let* A *be a set of propositional constants and* J *be a set of monotonic justifications that includes* J_P *and is correct w.r.t.* P *(i.e.* $apply_J^*(X) \subseteq \{q \mid P \cup X \models q\}$ *for all sets* X *of propositional formulas). Then*

1. $DDB(J, A)$ *terminates*

2. $DDB(J, A)$ *returns* false *iff* $P \cup A$ *is inconsistent*

5   Labelling = Meta Reasoning

As pointed out in section 1, we also want to use backtracking for finding extensions. To enable this we review existing methods for this task. Usually, an extension of a justification network is computed by propagating labels. If a node is IN then it is contained in an extension T, if it is OUT then it is not in T. Propagation rules can complete this partial information about an extension. In this section, we investigate these rules on different levels: (1) We explore the corresponding properties of extensions enabling the labelling steps. (2) We map the labelling problem to a propositional theory stating the dependencies between labels. (3) In the next section, we encode this meta theory into justifications for labels. Such a label-justification corresponds to Doyle's *supporting nodes*. They enable us to identify the sources of an odd loop error and to retract an assumed-label (i.e. to do label-backtracking).

In contrast to Doyle, we use three labels DERIVED, IN, and ¬IN (or OUT). Thus, we can distinguish between deriving a node and specifying that it must be derived. Below, we list the meaning of our labels:

$$
\begin{aligned}
\text{DERIVED}(q) &\leftrightarrow q \in apply^*_{J,T}(\emptyset) \\
\text{IN}(q) &\leftrightarrow q \in T \\
\neg\text{IN}(q) &\leftrightarrow q \notin T
\end{aligned}
\tag{12}
$$

These labels express partial information about an extension which can be completed. The simplest step is applying a justification to a set of derived nodes. However, we must ensure that all elements of its out-list are not contained in T:

Lemma 5.1 *Let $\nu = (N, J)$ be a justification network and T a subset of N. If $D \subseteq apply^*_{J,T}(\emptyset)$, $O \subseteq N - T$, and $q \in apply_{J,N-O}(D)$ then $q \in apply^*_{J,T}(\emptyset)$*

Proof: $apply_{J,T}(D)$ is an upper bound of $apply_{J,N-O}(D)$ since T is a subset of $N - O$. Hence, $q \in apply_{J,T}(apply^*_{J,T}(\emptyset))$, which is a subset of $apply^*_{J,T}(\emptyset)$. □

If T is an extension it contains derived nodes:

Lemma 5.2 *Let $\nu = (N, J)$ be a justification network and T an extension of ν. If $q \in apply^*_{J,T}(\emptyset)$ then $q \in T$.*

Proof: Since T is an extension $q \in apply^*_{J,T}(\emptyset) = T$. □

Unlike these two properties, the next one is very involved: We want to know when a node is not contained in an extension using the partial information. A first solution is to check whether a node cannot be derived even if all unlabelled nodes are added to T. However, this is not sufficient as the following example demonstrates:

$$\langle \rightarrow a \rangle$$
$$\langle in(a, b) \rightarrow c \rangle \quad \langle in(c), out(d) \rightarrow b \rangle$$
$$\langle out(b) \rightarrow e \rangle$$

Assume that we already know that $a \in T$ and $d \notin T$. Then we cannot proceed with labelling because of the monotonic loop containing b and c. We cannot get a valid justification for one of these nodes even if all unlabelled nodes except the elements of the loops are added to T. Now, we formulate this precisely:

Lemma 5.3 *Let $\nu = (N, J)$ be a justification network and T an extension of ν. If $I \subseteq T$, $O \subseteq N - T$, and there exists a $Q \subseteq N$ s.t. $Q \cap apply_{J,I}((N - O) - Q) = \emptyset$ then $Q \cap T = \emptyset$.*

Proof: We immediately obtain $Q \cap apply_{J,T}(T - Q) = \emptyset$ by putting in a lower bound. $apply_{J,T}(T - Q)$ is a subset of $apply_{J,T}(T)$, which is equal to T since T is an extension. Both results lead to $apply_{J,T}(T - Q) \subseteq T - Q$. Hence, $T - Q$ is closed w.r.t. $apply_{J,T}$. Therefore, $T - Q$ is a superset of $apply^*_{J,T}(\emptyset)$, which is equal to T. Thus, we have shown that Q is disjoint to T. $\square$

Later we use two special cases which are easier to handle:

Lemma 5.4 *Let $\nu = (N, J)$ be a justification network and T an extension of ν. If $I \subseteq T$, $O \subseteq N - T$, and there exists a $q \notin apply_{J,I}(N - O)$ then $q \notin T$.*

Lemma 5.5 *Let $\nu = (N, J)$ be a justification network and T an extension of ν. If $I \subseteq T$, $D \subseteq N$, and $apply_{J,I}(D) \subseteq D$ then $(N - D) \cap T = \emptyset$.*

Proof: Choose $Q := N - D$ and $O = \emptyset$. If the condition-part of the lemma is satisfied then $apply_{J,I}(N - Q) \cap Q = \emptyset$. Hence, $(N - D) \cap T = \emptyset$ according to lemma 5.3. $\square$

Above, we showed how partial information about T can be completed if T is an extension. Using the methods above, we can also detect extensions. Let I be a set of IN-labelled nodes that is closed w.r.t. $apply_{J,I}$. After applying the rule in lemma 5.5 to $D := apply^*_{J,I}(\emptyset)$ all remaining elements in $N - D$ are labelled with OUT. Thus, we either obtain a contradiction since some elements of I are labelled OUT or I is an extension.

Now, we are ready to encode the dependencies between labels into first-order logic. Since we obtain only ground formulas it is easy to obtain an equivalent propositional theory. We use some abbreviations to handle sets of nodes: We write DERIVED*$(\{q_1, \ldots, q_k\})$ for the conjunction DERIVED$(q_1) \wedge \ldots \wedge$ DERIVED(q_k). Similarly, we take IN*$(\{q_1, \ldots, q_k\})$ for IN$(q_1) \wedge \ldots \wedge$ IN(q_k) and OUT*$(\{q_1, \ldots, q_k\})$ for $\neg$IN$(q_1) \wedge \ldots \wedge \neg$IN$(q_k)$. Since we can represent only finite sets the translation works only for finite networks.

Definition 5.1 *Let $\nu = (N, J)$ be a finite justification network. The label-theory P_ν of ν consists of propositional implications which are obtained from the following ground instances by uniquely replacing ground atoms by constants:*

1. for all $I \subseteq N, O \subseteq N, q \in N$ s.t. $q \in apply_{J,N-O}(I)$:

$$\text{DERIVED}^*(I) \wedge \text{OUT}^*(O) \supset \text{DERIVED}(q) \tag{13}$$

2. for all $q \in N$:

$$\text{DERIVED}(q) \supset \text{IN}(q) \tag{14}$$

3. *for all $I \subseteq N, O \subseteq N, q \in N$ s.t. $q \notin apply_{J,I}(N - O)$:*

$$\text{IN}^*(I) \wedge \text{OUT}^*(O) \supset \neg\text{IN}(q) \tag{15}$$

4. *for all $I \subseteq N$:*

$$\text{IN}^*(I) \supset \text{OUT}^*(N - apply_{J,I}^*(\emptyset)) \tag{16}$$

P_ν *contains no other formulas.*

It does not matter that the size of P_ν is large compared with the size of ν. For two reasons, we will not explicitly generate and represent all formulas in P_ν. First, we only use this theory to describe and understand an existing labelling algorithm (e.g. Goodwin's system). Second, we can ignore subsumed formulas:

- If $\text{DERIVED}^*(I) \wedge \text{OUT}^*(O) \supset \text{DERIVED}(q)$ is in the label-theory then q is an element of $apply_{J,N-O}(I)$. Hence there exists an applicable justification $\langle in(I'), out(O') \rightarrow q \rangle \in J$ s.t. $I' \subseteq I$ and $O' \subseteq O$. Hence, $\text{DERIVED}^*(I') \wedge \text{OUT}^*(O') \supset \text{DERIVED}(q)$ is included in our label-theory and subsumes the first formula.

- Now, consider elements $\text{IN}^*(I) \wedge \text{OUT}^*(O) \supset \neg\text{IN}(q)$ of the label-theory, which are instances of 15. Then q is not in $apply_{J,I}(N - O)$. Hence, every justification for q is blocked. A justification is blocked if one of its in-list elements is in O or one of its out-list elements is in I. If we collect these elements in two subsets $I' \subseteq I$ and $O' \subseteq O$ we obtain a formula $\text{IN}^*(I') \wedge \text{OUT}^*(O') \supset \neg\text{IN}(q)$ of our label-theory which subsumes the first formula.

- Finally, consider rule 16. If $I_1 \subseteq I_2$ then $N - apply_{J,I_1}^*(\emptyset) \subseteq N - apply_{J,I_2}^*(\emptyset)$. Hence, if we find a set I satisfying $\text{IN}^*(I)$ and apply the terminate-rule 16 to I then we need not apply it to subsets of I because we have already derived their consequents.

Below, we list the main theorem of this section. A network has an extension if and only if its label-theory is consistent.

Theorem 5.6 *Let $\nu = (N, J)$ be a finite justification network. P_ν is consistent iff ν is coherent.*

Proof: We use models to establish a connection between the label-theory and conditions expressed in terms of *apply*.

($\Rightarrow$): Suppose that P_ν is consistent. Then there exists a model $\mathcal{M}$ of P_ν. Let T be the extension of the predicate IN in $\mathcal{M}$, and D be the extension of DERIVED in $\mathcal{M}$. Hence, $\mathcal{M}$ satisfies $\text{DERIVED}^*(D)$, $\text{IN}^*(T)$, and $\text{OUT}^*(N - T)$. Since $\mathcal{M}$ is a model of P_ν we recognize that the following properties are satisfied:

1. $apply_{J,N-(N-T)}(D) \subseteq D$

2. $D \subseteq T$

3. $N - apply^{*}_{J,T}(\emptyset) \subseteq N - T$

Then D and T are supersets of $apply^{*}_{J,T}(\emptyset)$. Due to the third property, T is also a subset of $apply^{*}_{J,T}(\emptyset)$ and therefore is an extension.

($\Leftarrow$): Suppose that ν has an extension T. Let $\mathcal{M}$ be an interpretation s.t.

- $\mathcal{M} \models \text{DERIVED}(q)$ iff $q \in apply^{*}_{J,T}(\emptyset)$

- $\mathcal{M} \models \text{IN}(q)$ iff $q \in T$

We immediately observe that

- $\mathcal{M} \models \text{DERIVED}^{*}(I)$ iff $I \subseteq apply^{*}_{J,T}(\emptyset)$

- $\mathcal{M} \models \text{IN}^{*}(I)$ iff $I \subseteq T$

- $\mathcal{M} \models \text{OUT}^{*}(O)$ iff $T \subseteq N - O$

We want to show that $\mathcal{M}$ is a model of P_ν. For this purpose, we consider the lemmas 5.1, 5.2, 5.4, 5.5. Assume that $\mathcal{M}$ satisfies the precondition of an implication of the form 13, 14, 15, or 16. Then $\mathcal{M}$ satisfies also the conclusion of the implication according to these lemmas. Hence, $\mathcal{M}$ is a model of P_ν. $\square$

From this proof, we obtain an immediate corollary: Extensions of a network correspond to models of the label-theory of the network.

Theorem 5.7 *Let $\nu = (N, J)$ be a justification network. There exists an injective mapping of the set of extensions of ν to the set of models of P_ν.*

6   Label-Backtracking

In the last section, we described dependencies between labels by propositional formulas. In section 4, we translated a propositional theory into justifications and we used backtracking to add missing justification. Hence, we could compute labellings in the same fashion: Translate the *label-theory* P_ν of a justification network $\nu = (N, J)$ into justifications for labels and apply backtracking to complete this set. Such a *label-justification* is an element of J_{P_ν} and therefore monotonic. As an example consider $\langle in(\{\text{IN}(a), \neg\text{IN}(b), \neg\text{IN}(c)\}) \rightarrow \text{OUT}(d)\rangle$. However, it is expensive to generate all elements of P_ν. This theory has only been needed to describe a labelling algorithm. It is easy to generate justifications for labels by such an algorithm. Moreover, TMS already records such meta justifications: If a node is labelled *supporting nodes* for this label are determined and stored.

In the sequel, we refine the algorithm *DDB* of section 4 in order to compute labellings. We get the following peculiarities:

- The label-justifications in J_{P_ν} are implicitly defined by the standard justifications in J.

- Subsumed elements of P_ν can be ignored. It is sufficient to consider examples of formulas DERIVED$^*(I) \wedge$ OUT$^*(O) \supset$ DERIVED(q) where I and O are the in-list and out-list of a justification of q. For formulas of the form 15, we take into account instances IN$^*(I) \wedge$ OUT$^*(O) \supset \neg$IN(q) where for every justification of q either I contains an out-list element or O contains an in-list element. Other elements are not in I and O.

- Additional label-justifications can be generated by backtracking and are collected in a set B.

- We use the usual TMS-forward-propagator to compute $apply^*_{J_{P_\nu} \cup B}(A)$, and to record the elements of this closure, as well as a set $L \subseteq J_{P_\nu} \cup B$ of the *applied label justifications*. Thus, we get a current state L which is updated in every step. Before the consequents of new label assumptions or justifications are determined an unlabel procedure retracts the consequents of retracted assumptions. The derived labels can be extracted from the label-justifications in L:

$$Cons(L) := \{l \mid \langle in(C) \to l \rangle \in L\}$$

- The set L of applied label-justifications is used to find the conflict set in presence of a label failure. This is easy because every label has at most one justification in L.

- The set Q_{P_ν} of choice points consists of all labels of the form IN(q) where $q \in N$. Thus, it is supplied implicitly.

Thus, the main work consists in developing a suitable forward-propagator *Label* which is supplied with a set $L \subseteq J_{P_\nu} \cup B$ of applied label justifications and computes the closure $apply^*_{J_{P_\nu} \cup B}(A)$. Since elements of L have been applied earlier we require that $Cons(L) \subseteq apply^*_{J_{P_\nu} \cup B}(A))$. To get such a propagator, we modify usual systems as in [8] or [13] as follows:

- An applied label-justification for DERIVED(q), IN(q) or $\neg$IN(q) in L is attached to the corresponding node q. For this purpose, we need three properties DERIVED, IN and OUT per node whose values are a label-justification, an indication *assumed* for a label-assumption, or an indication *unknown*. A single justification per label is sufficient. The justification for a label-contradiction is stored separately.

- Following sets are extracted from the current state L:

$$I_L := \{q \mid \text{IN}(q) \in Cons(L)\}$$
$$O_L := \{q \mid \neg\text{IN}(q) \in Cons(L)\} \tag{17}$$
$$D_L := \{q \mid \text{DERIVED}(q) \in Cons(L)\}$$

Since L consists of applied elements of $J_{P_\nu} \cup B$ we get

$$I_L \subseteq \{q \mid \text{IN}(q) \in apply^*_{J_{P_\nu} \cup B}(A)\}$$
$$O_L \subseteq \{q \mid \neg\text{IN}(q) \in apply^*_{J_{P_\nu} \cup B}(A)\} =: O \tag{18}$$
$$D_L \subseteq \{q \mid \text{DERIVED}(q) \in apply^*_{J_{P_\nu} \cup B}(A)\}$$

Since A contains no assumption of the form DERIVED(q) a DERIVED-label is only obtained by applying a justification from J to other nodes having a DERIVED-label. All out-list elements of such a justification must have a $\neg$IN-label. Therefore, we obtain $D_L \subseteq apply^*_{J,N-O}(\emptyset)$ which is needed below.

- The relabel procedure works as usual. If some label assumptions D are retracted from A then the set L is updated. Every justification for an element of $apply^*_L(A) - apply^*_L(A - D)$ is removed from L (i.e. the corresponding property of the TMS-node is replaced by *unknown*).

- Applicable label-justifications are detected by looking for nodes q satisfying a corresponding condition (e.g. $q \in apply_{J,N-O_L}(I_L)$). If such a test is satisfied it is easy to generate the corresponding label-justification.

- A condition $q \in apply_{J,Y}(X)$ is transferred in a more operational form. According to definition 3 it is equivalent to $\exists \langle in(I), out(O) \rightarrow q \rangle \in J : \forall i \in I : i \in X$ and $\forall o \in O : o \notin Y$.

- If a label error is detected the process of computing the closure of $apply_{J_{P_\nu}}$ is stopped. In this case, the supervising algorithm DDB finds $\bot$ in the result and needs no other elements of the closure.

- Handling the termination rule is more difficult since we need $apply^*_{J,I_L}(\emptyset)$. For this purpose, we consider the set D_L of nodes having a DERIVED-label. If D_L is closed w.r.t. $apply_{J,I_L}$ it is a superset of $apply^*_{J,I_L}(\emptyset)$. As mentioned above it is a subset of $apply^*_{J,N-O}(\emptyset)$. If no label failure occurs then $I_L \subseteq N - O$. In this case D_L is equal to $apply^*_{J,I_L}(\emptyset)$. Hence, if D_L is closed w.r.t. $apply_{J,I_L}$ we can label every node q not in D with OUT. Some of these nodes may already have an IN-label.

In this case, we get a contradiction because the current labelling does not satisfy the groundedness condition. However, since the newly labelled nodes q get a large label justification $\langle in(I_L) \rightarrow \neg\text{IN}(q)\rangle$ there are a lot of sources of the contradiction and dependency-directed backtracking is here not very helpful in contrast to errors which are caused by odd loops. Nevertheless, we need these large label-justifications in order to realize our label-theory properly. Technically, we could avoid the generation of these justifications and just look for IN-labelled elements which got an $\neg$IN-label after application of the termination rule.

Thus, we obtain the following forward propagator:

Algorithm 2 Label(L) $\equiv$

1. **if** $\exists q \in N : \text{IN}(q), \neg\text{IN}(q) \in Cons(L)$
   then *return* $L \cup \{\langle in(\{\text{IN}(q), \neg\text{IN}(q)\}) \rightarrow \bot\rangle\}$ **else**

2. **if** $\exists \langle in(C) \rightarrow l\rangle \in B : C \subseteq Cons(L)$ *and* $l \notin Cons(L)$
   then Label($L \cup \{\langle in(C) \rightarrow l\rangle\}$)

3. **if** $\exists q \in N : \text{DERIVED}(q) \notin Cons(L)$ *and* $\exists\langle in(I), out(O) \rightarrow q\rangle \in J :$
   $\qquad\qquad \forall i \in I : \text{DERIVED}(i) \in Cons(L)$ *and*
   $\qquad\qquad \forall o \in O : \neg\text{IN}(o) \in Cons(L)$
   then *let C be a subset of $Cons(L)$ needed to satisfy the condition above;*
   $\qquad\qquad$ Label($L \cup \{\langle in(C) \rightarrow \text{DERIVED}(q)\rangle\}$)

4. **if** $\exists q \in N : \text{DERIVED}(q) \in Cons(L)$ *and* $\text{IN}(q) \notin Cons(L)$
   then Label($L \cup \{\langle in(\text{DERIVED}(q)) \rightarrow \text{IN}(q)\rangle\}$)

5. **if** $\exists q \in N : \neg\text{IN}(q) \notin Cons(L)$ *and* $\forall\langle in(I), out(O) \rightarrow q\rangle \in J :$
   $\qquad\qquad \exists i \in I : \neg\text{IN}(i) \in Cons(L)$ *or*
   $\qquad\qquad \exists o \in O : \text{IN}(o) \in Cons(L)$
   then *let C be a subset of $Cons(L)$ needed to satisfy the condition above;*
   $\qquad\qquad$ Label($L \cup \{\langle in(C) \rightarrow \neg\text{IN}(q)\rangle\}$)

6. **if** $\exists q \in N : \text{DERIVED}(q) \notin Cons(L)$ *and* $\exists\langle in(I), out(O) \rightarrow q\rangle \in J :$
   $\qquad\qquad \forall i \in I : \text{DERIVED}(i) \in Cons(L)$ *and*
   $\qquad\qquad \forall o \in O : \text{IN}(o) \notin Cons(L)$
   then *return* L

7. **else** Label($L \cup \{\langle in(I_L) \rightarrow \neg\text{IN}(q)\rangle \mid \text{DERIVED}(q) \notin Cons(L)\}$

Finally, we consider an example for label-backtracking. Let's take a network $\nu = (N, J)$ consisting of two even loops, and one odd loop, which depends on the first even loop. Hence, J consists of

$$\langle out(a) \rightarrow b \rangle \qquad \langle out(b) \rightarrow a \rangle$$
$$\langle out(c) \rightarrow d \rangle \qquad \langle out(d) \rightarrow c \rangle$$
$$\langle in(b), out(e) \rightarrow f \rangle \quad \langle out(f) \rightarrow g \rangle \quad \langle out(g) \rightarrow e \rangle$$

We assume that our labelling algorithm introduces the following assumptions during labelling: (1) $\neg\text{IN}(a)$, (2) $\neg\text{IN}(c)$, (3) $\neg\text{IN}(e)$. After that, it detects an odd loop error since it also derives $\text{IN}(e)$. Hence, $\perp \in apply^*_{J_{P_\nu}}(\{\neg\text{IN}(a), \neg\text{IN}(e)\})$. Backtracking generates a new justification for the negation of the latest assumption in this nogood, namely $j_1 \equiv \langle in(\neg\text{IN}(a)) \rightarrow in(e) \rangle$. The last assumption is retracted. Now, we get again a contradiction: $\perp \in apply^*_{J_{P_\nu} \cup \{j_1\}}(\{\neg\text{IN}(a)\})$. Now, backtracking retracts $\neg\text{IN}(a)$, thus skipping the second assumption. The new backtracking justification is $j_2 \equiv \langle \rightarrow \text{IN}(a) \rangle$.

7 Conclusion

In this paper, we elaborated two precise applications of dependency-directed backtracking for Doyle's TMS. Deductive backtracking dynamically completes the set of justifications needed for first-order proofs. Thus, the monotonic part of the TMS becomes an efficient propositional prover. Label-backtracking detects the sources of an odd loop error and retracts an assumed label. Thus, we get an improved TMS that determines an extension whenever one exists. However, some work is still needed to integrate deductive and label backtracking. We also have to elaborate how to achieve incrementality when new justifications are added to the network. In this case, elements of its label-theory are replaced.

As an important prerequisite for label-backtracking, we developed a propositional theory describing the labelling steps and the precise dependencies between labels. In some sense, this theory can be viewed as a semantics for labelling algorithms. In contrast to Brown et. al. [2], we solved the groundedness problem and obtained that coherence is equivalent to consistency of the label-theory. Label-backtracking generates only justifications for labels, not for nodes. Thus, we have a clear distinction between normal and backtracking-justifications as required by Brewka in [1].

As a final remark, we can state that Doyle's TMS already contains the basic ideas and concepts for the work presented in this paper. However, it has not been clear how to combine these techniques appropriately. The main obstacle to more progress has been the lack of the right mathematical formulation, namely the *apply*-operator. This operator simplified a lot of properties and proofs very strikingly.

Acknowledgements

I would like to thank Gerd Brewka, Joachim Hertzberg, and Kurt Konolige for fruitful discussions.

References

[1] Brewka, G., On Minimal Change: A Critique of the Architecture of Nonmonotonic TMS, in: Brewka, G. and Junker, U., Aspects of Non-Monotonic Reasoning, *TASSO Report No 1*, GMD, St. Augustin, Fed. Rep. of Germany, March 1990.

[2] Brown, A., Gaucas, D. and Benanav, D., An Algebraic Foundation for Truth Maintenance, in: *Proceedings of the Tenth International Joint Conference on Artificial Intelligence*, Milano, Italy, 1987, p. 973–980.

[3] Cravo, M.R., Martins, J.P., A Syntactic Approach to Defaults and Belief Revision, in: *DRUMS: Report of the RP1 First Workshop*, Marseille, France, February 1990.

[4] de Kleer, J., An Assumption-based TMS, *Artificial Intelligence* 28 (1986), p. 127–162.

[5] de Kleer, J., Extending the ATMS, *Artificial Intelligence* 28 (1986), p. 163-196.

[6] de Kleer, J., A General Labelling Algorithm for Assumption-based Truth Maintenance, in: *Proceedings of the Seventh National Conference on Artificial Intelligence*, 1988.

[7] Dowling, W.F. and Gallier, J.H., Linear-Time Algorithms for Testing the Satisfiability of Propositional Horn Formulae, *Journal of Logic Programming* 3 (1984), p. 267–284.

[8] Doyle, J., A Truth Maintenance System, *Artificial Intelligence* 12 (1979), p. 231–272.

[9] Doyle, J., Some Theories of Reasoned Assumptions: An Essay in Rational Psychology, Carnegie Mellon University, CMU CS-83-125, 1983.

[10] Doyle, J., The Ins and Outs of Reason Maintenance, in: *Proceedings of the Eighth International Joint Conference on Artificial Intelligence*, Karlsruhe, F.R.G., 1983, p. 349–351.

[11] Dressler, O., An Extended Basic ATMS, in: Reinfrank, M., de Kleer, J., Ginsberg, M.L., Sandewell, E. (Eds.), Non-Monotonic Reasoning, 2nd International Workshop, Springer LNCS 346, 1989, p. 143–163.

[12] Dressler, O., Problem Solving with the NM-ATMS, in: *Proceedings of the Ninth European Conference on Artificial Intelligence*, Stockholm, Sweden, 1990, p. 253–258.

[13] Goodwin, J.W., A Theory and System for Non-Monotonic Reasoning, *Ph.D. Dissertation*, University of Linköping, Linköping, Sweden, 1987.

[14] Junker, U., A Correct Non-Monotonic ATMS, in: *Proceedings of the Eleventh International Joint Conference on Artificial Intelligence*, Detroit, MI, 1989, p. 1049–1054.

[15] Junker, U. and Konolige, K., Computing the Extensions of Autoepistemic and Default Logics with a Truth Maintenance System, in: *Proceedings of the Eighth National Conference on Artificial Intelligence*, Boston, MA, 1988, p. 278–283.

[16] Konolige, K., On the Relation between Default and Autoepistemic Logic, *Artificial Intelligence* **35** (1988), p. 343–382.

[17] Martins, J.P and Shapiro, S.C., A Model for Belief Revision, *Artificial Intelligence* **35** (1988), p. 25–80.

[18] Moore, R.C., Semantical Considerations on Nonmonotonic Logic, *Artificial Intelligence* **25** (1985), p. 75–94.

[19] Reinfrank, M., Dressler, O. and Brewka, G., On the Relation between Truth Maintenance and Autoepistemic Logic, in: *Proceedings of the Eleventh International Joint Conference on Artificial Intelligence*, Detroit, MI, 1989, p. 1206–1212.

[20] Reiter, R., A Logic for Default Reasoning, *Artificial Intelligence* **13** (1980), p. 81–132.

[21] Russinoff, D.M., An Algorithm for Truth Maintenance, *MCC Technical Report No. AI-062-85*, MCC, Austin, Texas, 1985.

An Abductive Procedure for the CMS/ATMS

Katsumi Inoue

ICOT Research Center
Institute for New Generation Computer Technology
1-4-28 Mita, Minato-ku, Tokyo 108, Japan
inoue@icot.or.jp

Abstract

This paper concerns procedural semantics for a variety of ATMSs. Reiter & de Kleer view an ATMS as a kind of abduction in which the best explanation of a formula is defined as a minimal conjunction of hypotheses that explain the formula. However, they do not give any algorithm to compute such minimal explanations of a formula in their CMS that is a generalization of de Kleer's basic ATMS. In this paper, we use the notion of characteristic clauses to make precise definitions of the CMS and the ATMS and to produce a sound and complete abductive procedure based on an extension of linear resolution. By means of this abductive procedure, we give the CMS algorithms for computing minimal explanations in the interpreted approach and for updating them in the compiled approach. We then present algorithms for generating and updating labels of nodes in an extended ATMS that accepts non-Horn justifications and literal assumptions. Finally, how a variation of the abductive procedure can be used to answer queries for circumscription of ground theories is presented.

1   Introduction

An assumption-based truth maintenance system (ATMS) [4] has been widely used when problems require reasoning in multiple contexts. However, this basic ATMS can only handle the restricted form of formulas, and is described algorithmically rather than declaratively or model-theoretically, and no proof of its correctness is given, so it is not obvious how to generalize or refine it. The motivation for this research was the desire to formalize generalizations of the ATMS within simple model and proof theories.

Recent investigations such as those of Reiter & de Kleer [22] and Levesque [16] show that there are strong connections between an ATMS and a logical account of *abduction* or *hypothesis generation* [20, 3, 9, 19]. An ATMS can be characterized by the following type of abduction:

Definition 1.1   Let W be a set of formulas, A a set of ground literals (called the *assumptions*), and G a closed formula. A conjunction H of elements of A is an *explanation* of G from (W, A) if (i) $W \cup \{H\} \models G$ and (ii) $W \cup \{H\}$ is satisfiable.

An explanation H of G from (W, A) is *minimal* if no proper sub-conjunct of H is an explanation of G from (W, A), that is, if no sub-conjunct H' of H satisfies $W \cup \{H'\} \models G$.

The ATMS is precisely intended to generate *all and only* minimal explanations [11]. In the ATMS terminology, the set of minimal explanations of a *node G* from the *justifications W* and the *assumptions A* is called the *label* of G, which is *consistent, sound, complete* and *minimal*. The *basic* ATMS [4] is restricted to accepting only Horn clause justifications and atomic assumptions. In the above declarative conditions for an ATMS, justifications can contain non-Horn clauses, and assumptions are allowed to be literals, so that this generalization covers de Kleer's various extended versions of the ATMS [5, 6, 7], Dressler's extended basic ATMS [8], and Reiter & de Kleer's clause management system (CMS) [22].

In spite of its usefulness in a wide range of applications, the algorithms for the ATMS in [4, 5, 6] have not yet been proved to be correct with respect to the declarative semantics. Although the CMS is well defined and the basic connection between resolution and the CMS processing is given in [22], there has not yet been any complete algorithm for computing labels of a formula for non-Horn theories in terms of popular and useful resolution methods. One of the problems is that although linear resolution is widely used and contains several restriction strategies, it is incomplete for consequence-finding [18] so that it cannot be directly used as an ATMS procedure.

The goal of this paper is to provide a sound and complete abductive procedure which solves the above problems for the CMS and ATMSs. In the remaining sections, we describe abduction as the problem of finding the *characteristic clauses* [1, 24] that are theorems of a given set of clauses and that belong to a distinguished sub-vocabulary of the language. We will give an extension of propositional linear resolution procedures which is complete for characteristic-clause-finding, then show ways in which to implement the CMS and the extended ATMS described above for both label generating (the interpreted approach) and label updating (the compiled approach). Since this extended ATMS can accept literal assumptions and non-Horn clauses, the methods described in this paper can also be applied to better implementations of theorem provers for closed world assumptions [1] and circumscription [21, 10] of ground theories, based on abductive procedures [13]. Unless otherwise specified, proofs for theorems and propositions are shown in Appendix.

2. Characteristic Clauses

We begin with some definitions and notations that will be used throughout this paper. We shall assume a propositional language with finitely many propositional symbols A and with logical connectives. The set of *literals* is defined as: $A^{\pm} = A \cup \neg \cdot A$, where $\neg \cdot S$ means the set formed by taking the negation of each element in S. A *clause* is a finite set of literals, understood disjunctively; the empty clause is denoted by $\square$. A *conjunctive normal form (CNF) formula* is a conjunction of clauses. Let C and C' be two clauses. $C - C'$ denotes a clause whose literals are those in the difference of C and C'. C is said to *subsume* C' if every literal in C occurs in C' ($C \subseteq C'$). In logical notation, C subsumes C' if $\models C \supset C'$. For a set of clauses Σ, by $\mu \Sigma$ or $\mu[\Sigma]$ we mean the set of clauses of Σ not subsumed by any other clause of Σ.

Definition 2.1 Let Σ be a set of clauses.
(1) A clause C is an *implicate* of Σ if $\Sigma \models C$. The set of implicates of Σ is denoted by $Th(\Sigma)$.
(2) The *prime implicates* of Σ are: $PI(\Sigma) = \mu Th(\Sigma)$.

We use the notion of *characteristic clauses*, which helps to analyze the computational aspect of ATMSs. While the idea of characteristic clauses was introduced by Bossu & Siegel [1] to evaluate a form of closed-world reasoning and was later generalized by Siegel [24], neither research focused on abductive reasoning or the ATMS. Informally speaking, characteristic clauses are intended to represent "interesting" clauses to solve a certain problem, and are constructed over a sub-vocabulary of the representation language called a *production field*.

Definition 2.2 (1) A *production field* $\mathcal{P}$ is a pair, $\langle L_{\mathcal{P}}, Cond \rangle$, where $L_{\mathcal{P}}$ (called the *characteristic literals*) is a subset of $\mathcal{A}^{\pm}$, and $Cond$ is a condition to be satisfied. When $Cond$ is not specified, $\mathcal{P}$ is just denoted as $\langle L_{\mathcal{P}} \rangle$. A production field $\langle \mathcal{A}^{\pm} \rangle$ is denoted $\mathcal{P}_{\pi}$.

(2) A clause C *belongs to a production field* $\mathcal{P} = \langle L_{\mathcal{P}}, Cond \rangle$ if every literal in C belongs to $L_{\mathcal{P}}$ and C satisfies $Cond$. The set of implicates of Σ belonging to $\mathcal{P}$ is denoted by $Th_{\mathcal{P}}(\Sigma)$.

(3) A production field $\mathcal{P}$ is *stable* if $\mathcal{P}$ satisfies the condition: for two clauses C and C' where C subsumes C', if C' belongs to $\mathcal{P}$, then C also belongs to $\mathcal{P}$.

Example 2.3 The following are examples of implicates belonging to stable production fields.

(1) $\mathcal{P} = \mathcal{P}_{\pi}$: $Th_{\mathcal{P}}(\Sigma)$ is equivalent to $Th(\Sigma)$.

(2) $\mathcal{P} = \langle \mathcal{A} \rangle$: $Th_{\mathcal{P}}(\Sigma)$ is the set of positive clauses implied by Σ.

(3) $\mathcal{P} = \langle \neg \cdot A, \; below \; size \; k \rangle$ where $A \subseteq \mathcal{A}$: $Th_{\mathcal{P}}(\Sigma)$ is the set of negative clauses implied by Σ containing less than k literals all of which belong to $\neg \cdot A$.

Definition 2.4 Let Σ be a set of clauses.
(1) The *characteristic clauses of* Σ *with respect to* $\mathcal{P}$ are:

$$Carc(\Sigma, \mathcal{P}) = \mu Th_{\mathcal{P}}(\Sigma).$$

In other words, a characteristic clause of Σ is a prime implicate of Σ belonging to $\mathcal{P}$.
(2) Let F be a formula. The *new characteristic clauses of* F *with respect to* Σ *and* $\mathcal{P}$ are:

$$Newcarc(\Sigma, F, \mathcal{P}) = Carc(\Sigma \cup \{F\}, \mathcal{P}) - Carc(\Sigma, \mathcal{P}),$$

that is, those characteristic clauses of $\Sigma \cup \{F\}$ that are not characteristic clauses of Σ.

$Carc(\Sigma, \mathcal{P})$ represents *saturation*: all the unsubsumed implicates of Σ that belong to a production field $\mathcal{P}$ must be contained in it. For example, $Carc(\Sigma, \mathcal{P}_{\pi}) = PI(\Sigma)$. Note that the empty clause $\square$ belongs to every stable production field, and that if Σ is unsatisfiable, then $Carc(\Sigma, \mathcal{P})$ contains only $\square$. On the contrary, the next theorem shows that $Newcarc(\Sigma, F, \mathcal{P})$ represents *abduction*, that is, the set of minimal explanations of $\neg F$ from $(\Sigma, \neg \cdot \mathcal{P})$.

Theorem 2.5 Let Σ be a set of clauses, $A \subseteq \mathcal{A}^{\pm}$, G a formula. The set of all minimal explanations of G from $(\Sigma, \overset{\cdot}{A})$ is $\neg \cdot Newcarc(\Sigma, \neg G, \mathcal{P})$, where $\mathcal{P} = \langle \neg \cdot A \rangle$.

3 Linear Abductive Procedure

In this section, given a set of clauses Σ, a stable production field $\mathcal{P}$ and a formula F, we show how the characteristic clauses $Carc(\Sigma, \mathcal{P})$ and the new characteristic clauses $Newcarc(\Sigma, F, \mathcal{P})$ can be computed by extending linear resolution. Before describing this matter in detail, it is worth noting that, the proof procedure has the following difficulties for dealing with abduction:

1. It should be complete for *consequence-finding*, that is, every relevant theorem can be produced, instead of just *refutation-complete* (producing $\Box$ if the theory is unsatisfiable).

2. It should focus on producing only those theorems that belong to $\mathcal{P}$.

3. It should be able to check produced clauses from $\Sigma \cup \{F\}$ and $\mathcal{P}$ with the condition "not belonging to $Th_{\mathcal{P}}(\Sigma)$", which corresponds to consistency checking in abduction.

The completeness for consequence-finding was investigated by Slagle, Chang & Lee [25] and Minicozzi & Reiter [18]. The second property requires that such consequences belong to $\mathcal{P}$. Bossu & Siegel [1] give an *incremental* resolution procedure to overcome the above three difficulties, which should first deduce all the $Carc(\Sigma, \mathcal{P})$ prior to giving $Carc(\Sigma \cup \{F\}, \mathcal{P})$.

A better approach to compute $Newcarc(\Sigma, C, \mathcal{P})$ does not construct the whole of each saturated set. It is possible by using an extension of linear resolution, given Σ, $\mathcal{P}$, and a newly added single clause C as the *top clause* of a deduction. Siegel [24] proposes such a resolution method by extending SL-resolution [15]. In this paper, we use the basic idea of [24] but introduce a more simplified procedure which is enough to explain our goals. The resolution method, which we call *m.c.l.s. resolution*, is based on *m.c.l.* (merge, C-ordered, linear) *resolution* [18] [1], and is augmented by the *skipping* operation. The following procedure is based on the description of OL-deduction in [2], but the result is not restricted to it. An *ordered* clause is a sequence of literals possibly containing *framed literals* which represents literals that have been resolved upon: from a clause C an ordered clause $\vec{C}$ is obtained just by ordering the elements of C; conversely, from an ordered clause $\vec{C}$ a clause C is obtained by removing the framed literals and converting the remainder to the set. A *structured* clause $\langle P, \vec{Q} \rangle$ is a pair of a clause P and an ordered clause $\vec{Q}$, whose clausal meaning is $P \cup Q$.

Definition 3.1 Given a set of clauses Σ, a clause C, and a production field $\mathcal{P} = \langle L_{\mathcal{P}}, Cond \rangle$, an *m.c.l.s. deduction of a clause S from $\Sigma + C$ and $\mathcal{P}$* consists of a sequence of structured clauses $D_0, D_1, \ldots, D_n$, such that:

1. $D_0 = \langle \Box, \vec{C} \rangle$.

2. $D_n = \langle S, \Box \rangle$.

---

[1] By the term m.c.l. resolution, we mean the family of linear resolution using ordered clauses and the information of literals resolved upon. Examples of m.c.l. resolution are OL-resolution [2], SL-resolution [15], the model elimination procedure [17], and the graph construction procedure [23]. This family is recognized to be one of the most familiar and efficient classes of resolution because of containing several restriction strategies.

3. For each $D_i = \langle P_i, \vec{Q_i} \rangle$, $P_i \cup Q_i$ is not a tautology.

4. For each $D_i = \langle P_i, \vec{Q_i} \rangle$, $P_i \cup Q_i$ is not subsumed by any $P_j \cup Q_j$, where $D_j = \langle P_j, \vec{Q_j} \rangle$ is a previous structured clause, $j < i$.

5. $D_{i+1} = \langle P_{i+1}, \vec{Q_{i+1}} \rangle$ is generated from $D_i = \langle P_i, \vec{Q_i} \rangle$ according to the following steps:

   (a) Let l be the first literal of $\vec{Q_i}$. P_{i+1} and $\vec{R_{i+1}}$ are obtained by applying either of the rules:

      i. **(Skip)** If $l \in L_\mathcal{P}$ and $P_i \cup \{l\}$ satisfies *Cond*, then $P_{i+1} = P_i \cup \{l\}$ and $\vec{R_{i+1}}$ is the ordered clause obtained by removing l from $\vec{Q_i}$.

      ii. **(Resolve)** $P_{i+1} = P_i$ and $\vec{R_{i+1}}$ is an ordered resolvent of $\vec{Q_i}$ with a clause B_i in Σ, where the literal resolved upon in $\vec{Q_i}$ is l.

   (b) $\vec{Q_{i+1}}$ is the reduced ordered clause of the ordered factor of $\vec{R_{i+1}}$.

Remarks. (1) Rules 1, 3, 5(a)ii and 5b form an OL-deduction for the non-production part (the right side) of structured clauses. By the *ordered factor* of $\vec{R_i}$, it implies the ordered clause obtained by merging right for any identical literals in $\vec{R_i}$ and by deleting every framed literal not followed by an unframed literal in the remainder (truncation). The *reduction* (or ancestry) of $\vec{R_i}$ deletes any unframed literal k in $\vec{R_i}$ for which there exists a framed literal $\boxed{\neg k}$ in $\vec{R_i}$.

(2) Rule 4 is included for efficiency. It does not affect the completeness described below [2].

(3) Rules 5(a)i and 5(a)ii are not exclusive; for $l \in L_\mathcal{P}$ either rule may be applied.

The **Skip** rule (5(a)i) reflects the following operational interpretation of a *stable production field* $\mathcal{P}$: by Definition 2.2 (3), if a clause C does not belong to $\mathcal{P}$ and a clause C' is subsumed by C, then C' does not belong to $\mathcal{P}$ either. That is why we can prune a deduction sequence if no rule can be applied for a structured clause D_i; if **Skip** was applied nevertheless, any resultant sequence would not succeed, thus making unnecessary computation.

For m.c.l.s. resolution, the following theorem can be shown to hold.

Theorem 3.2 (1) *Soundness*: If a clause S is derived using an m.c.l.s. deduction from $\Sigma + C$ and $\mathcal{P}$, then S belongs to $Th_\mathcal{P}(\Sigma \cup \{C\})$.

(2) *Completeness*: If a clause T *does not belong to* $Th_\mathcal{P}(\Sigma)$, *but* belongs to $Th_\mathcal{P}(\Sigma \cup \{C\})$, then there is an m.c.l.s. deduction of a clause S from $\Sigma + C$ and $\mathcal{P}$ such that S subsumes T.

Note that m.c.l. resolution is refutation-complete [17, 15, 2], but is incomplete for consequence-finding [18]. Theorem 3.2 (2) says that the procedure of m.c.l.s. resolution is complete for characteristic-clause-finding, and thus complete for consequence-finding if $\mathcal{P} = \mathcal{P}_\pi$, because it includes the additional skipping operation.

---

[2] In fact, in Chang & Lee's version of OL-deduction [2] this rule is overlooked. The deletion rule is clearly present in the model elimination procedure [17]. These two observations were pointed out by Mark Stickel.

Definition 3.3 Given a set of clauses Σ, a clause C, and a stable production field $\mathcal{P}$, the *production from* $\Sigma + C$ *and* $\mathcal{P}$, denoted by $Prod(\Sigma, C, \mathcal{P})$, is defined as:

$$\mu\{S \mid S \text{ is a clause derived using an m.c.l.s. deduction from } \Sigma + C \text{ and } \mathcal{P}\}.$$

In [24], no precise statement about computing $Newcarc(\Sigma, C, \mathcal{P})$ and $Carc(\Sigma, \mathcal{P})$ by using $Prod(\Sigma, C, \mathcal{P})$ can be found. Here we show the connections between them. Firstly, the next theorem shows that we can compute $Newcarc(\Sigma, C, \mathcal{P})$ for a single clause C, without a naive implementation of Definition 2.4 (2) that computes the saturated sets, $Carc(\Sigma, \mathcal{P})$ and $Carc(\Sigma \cup \{C\}, \mathcal{P})$, and that we need check for each clause $S \in Prod(\Sigma, C, \mathcal{P})$, only whether $\Sigma \models S$ or not.

Theorem 3.4 Let C be a clause. $Newcarc(\Sigma, C, \mathcal{P}) = Prod(\Sigma, C, \mathcal{P}) - Th_{\mathcal{P}}(\Sigma)$.

For a CNF formula G, $Newcarc(\Sigma, G, \mathcal{P})$ can be computed incrementally as follows:

Theorem 3.5 Let $G = C_1 \wedge \cdots \wedge C_m$ be a CNF formula. Then

$$
\begin{aligned}
Newcarc(\Sigma, G, \mathcal{P}) &= \mu\left[\bigcup_{i=1}^{m} Newcarc(\Sigma_i, C_i, \mathcal{P})\right] \\
&= \mu\left[\bigcup_{i=1}^{m} Prod(\Sigma_i, C_i, \mathcal{P})\right] - Th_{\mathcal{P}}(\Sigma),
\end{aligned}
$$

where $\Sigma_1 = \Sigma$, and $\Sigma_{i+1} = \Sigma_i \cup \{C_i\}$, for $i = 1, \ldots, m-1$.

Finally, the characteristic clauses $Carc(\Sigma, \mathcal{P})$ can be generated by the following incremental method. This will be used for the compiled approaches to the CMS and an ATMS. Notice that for some propositional symbol p, if $\Sigma \not\models p$, $\Sigma \not\models \neg p$, and $p \vee \neg p$ belongs to some stable production field $\mathcal{P}$, then $p \vee \neg p$ belongs to $Carc(\Sigma, \mathcal{P})$.

Theorem 3.6 The characteristic clauses with respect to $\mathcal{P}$ can be generated incrementally [3]:

$$
\begin{aligned}
Carc(\phi, \mathcal{P}) &= \{p \vee \neg p \mid p \in \mathcal{A} \text{ and } p \vee \neg p \text{ belongs to } \mathcal{P}\}, \text{ and} \\
Carc(\Sigma \cup \{C\}, \mathcal{P}) &= \mu[Carc(\Sigma, \mathcal{P}) \cup Newcarc(\Sigma, C, \mathcal{P})] \\
&= \mu[Carc(\Sigma, \mathcal{P}) \cup Prod(\Sigma, C, \mathcal{P})].
\end{aligned}
$$

4 The CMS

Reiter & de Kleer [22] propose a generalization of the basic ATMS [4] called the *clause management system* (CMS) and show its applications to abductive reasoning. A CMS is intended to work together with a reasoner, which issues queries that take the form of clauses. The CMS is then responsible for finding *minimal supports* for the queries:

Definition 4.1 [22] Let Σ be a set of clauses and C a clause. A clause S is a *support* for C *with respect to* Σ if $\Sigma \models S \cup C$, and $\Sigma \not\models S$.
A support for C with respect to Σ is *minimal* if there is no other support S' for C which subsumes S. The set of minimal supports for C with respect to Σ is written $MS(\Sigma, C)$.

---

[3] In practice, no tautology will take part in any deduction; tautologies decrease monotonically.

Comparing minimal supports with minimal explanations described in Definition 1.1, a minimal support S for C with respect to Σ is exactly a minimal explanation $\neg S$ of C from $(\Sigma, \mathcal{A}^{\pm})$. Therefore, the above definition can be easily extended to handle any formula instead of a clause as a query. Setting the production field to $\mathcal{P}_{\pi} = \langle \mathcal{A}^{\pm} \rangle$, we see that:

Proposition 4.2 Let F be any formula. $MS(\Sigma, F) = Newcarc(\Sigma, \neg F, \mathcal{P}_{\pi})$.

This formulation can solve one of the limitations of the CMS. In [22], the CMS is defined to handle only the queries of the clause form, so that it cannot compute minimal explanations of a conjunctive query. For example, $\mu \{ \neg e \mid \Sigma \models e \supset g_1 \wedge g_2$ and $\Sigma \not\models \neg e \}$ can be computed straightforwardly in our formulation as $Newcarc(\Sigma, \neg g_1 \vee \neg g_2, \mathcal{P}_{\pi})$. And for a disjunctive normal form query F, we can compute $MS(\Sigma, \neg F)$ by using Theorem 3.5.

We thus see that our algorithm can compute minimal supports. However, Reiter & de Kleer [22] consider the two ways the CMS manages the knowledge base: keeping the set of clauses Σ transmitted by the reasoner as it is (the *interpreted* approach), or computing $PI(\Sigma)$ (the *compiled* approach). Theorem 3.4 shows that we can generate the new characteristic clauses $Newcarc(\Sigma, C, \mathcal{P}_{\pi})$ without knowing the saturated sets, $PI(\Sigma)$ and $PI(\Sigma \cup \{C\})$. Therefore, computation using Theorem 3.4 and Proposition 4.2 represents the interpreted approach [4].

When we are faced with a situation where we want to know explanations for many different queries, we must run the algorithm each time a query is issued. Instead of keeping the initial theory Σ as it is and doing the same deductions over and over for different top clauses, some of these inferences can be made once and for all. That is the motivation for the compiled approach: the set Σ is compiled into the saturated set, $PI(\Sigma) = Carc(\Sigma, \mathcal{P}_{\pi})$.

Given $PI(\Sigma)$, to find $MS(\Sigma, G)$ for each query G in the compiled approach, again we do not need to compute the saturated set $PI(\Sigma \cup \{\neg G\})$, as Reiter & de Kleer show some relationships between prime implicates and minimal supports.

Proposition 4.3 [22] Let C be a clause.

$$MS(\Sigma, C) = \mu \{ P - C \mid P \in PI(\Sigma) \text{ and } P \cap C \neq \phi \}.$$

Corollary 4.4 [22] Let $n \in \mathcal{A}^{\pm}$ be a literal.

$$MS(\Sigma, \{n\}) = \{ P - \{n\} \mid P \in PI(\Sigma) \text{ and } n \in P \}.$$

One of the disadvantages of the compiled approach is the high cost of updating the knowledge base. When the reasoner adds a clause C to Σ, we must compute all the $PI(\Sigma \cup \{C\})$. However, for both purposes, that is, constructing the prime implicates and updating them, Theorem 3.6 can be used by setting the production field to $\mathcal{P}_{\pi}$.

Proposition 4.5 Given $PI(\Sigma)$ and a clause C, $PI(\Sigma \cup \{C\})$ can be found incrementally:

$$PI(\phi) = \{ p \vee \neg p \mid p \in \mathcal{A} \}, \text{ and}$$
$$PI(\Sigma \cup \{C\}) = \mu [PI(\Sigma) \cup Prod(PI(\Sigma), C, \mathcal{P}_{\pi})].$$

---

[4] Note that in [22] there is no description of an algorithm for the interpreted approach.

By Proposition 4.5, the prime implicates can be incrementally constructed using every clause as a top clause. Thus the transmitted clauses Σ can be substituted for $PI(\Sigma)$. When a clause C is newly added, we just need to add the theorems deduced from $PI(\Sigma)$ with top clause C and to remove the subsumed clauses. The computation of all prime implicates of Σ by Proposition 4.5 is much more efficient than the brute-force way of resolution proposed briefly by Reiter & de Kleer [22], which makes every possible resolution until no more unsubsumed clauses are produced.

Note that either computing supports with an uncompiled theory or compiling a theory is an enumeration problem of prime implicates and each computational complexity is exponential [5]. The computational superiority of the proposed technique as compared with a brute-force algorithm comes from the restriction of resolution, as the key problem here is to generate as few as possible subsumed clauses together with making as few as possible subsumption tests.

5 An ATMS

In de Kleer's versions of ATMSs [4, 5, 6, 7], there is a distinguished set of assumptions $A \subseteq \mathcal{A}^{\pm}$. One of the most generalized versions of the ATMS can be considered as a CMS with assumptions as described in Definition 1.1. Therefore, based on Theorem 2.5, an ATMS can be defined as a system responsible for finding all the minimal explanations (called the labels) for the queries:

Definition 5.1 An *ATMS* is a triple $\langle N, A, \Sigma \rangle$, where $N \subseteq \mathcal{A}^{\pm}$ is a set of literals, *nodes*; $A \subseteq N$ is a set of literals, *assumptions*; and Σ is a set of clauses all of whose literals belong to $N \cup \neg \cdot N$, *justifications*. The *label of* $n \in N$ *with respect to* $\langle N, A, \Sigma \rangle$ is defined as:

$$L(n, A, \Sigma) = \neg \cdot Newcarc(\Sigma, \neg n, \mathcal{P}), \quad \text{where } \mathcal{P} = \langle \neg \cdot A \rangle.$$

The following properties [4, 6] hold for the label of each node $n \in N$ with respect to an ATMS $\langle N, A, \Sigma \rangle$ given by Definition 5.1:

Proposition 5.2 Let $\langle N, A, \Sigma \rangle$ be an ATMS, $n \in N$ a literal, and $\mathcal{P} = \langle \neg \cdot A \rangle$.
  (1) *Label consistency*: for each $E_i \in L(n, A, \Sigma)$, $\Sigma \cup \{E_i\}$ is satisfiable.
  (2) *Label soundness*: for each $E_i \in L(n, A, \Sigma)$, $\Sigma \cup \{E_i\} \models n$.
  (3) *Label completeness*: for every conjunct E of assumptions in A, if $\Sigma \cup \{E\} \models n$, then there exists $E_i \in L(n, A, \Sigma)$ such that E_i is a sub-conjunct of E.
  (4) *Label minimality*: every $E_i \in L(n, A, \Sigma)$ is not a super-conjunct of any other element.

In the same way as the CMS, we will consider the following two problems, that is, abduction and saturation, concerning the computation of the labels of the nodes with respect to an ATMS:

1. *Generating labels*. Given an ATMS $\langle N, A, \Sigma \rangle$, compute $L(n, A, \Sigma)$ for some node $n \in N$ from the original set Σ. This corresponds to the interpreted approach of the CMS.

---

[5] In [12], another interesting and empirically efficient way to manage the knowledge base that offers an intermediate alternative to the compiled and interpreted disjunctive is shown.

2. *Updating labels.* Given an ATMS $\langle N, A, \Sigma \rangle$, the current label $L(n, A, \Sigma)$ of each $n \in N$, and a newly added clause C, compute the new label $L(n, A, \Sigma \cup \{C\})$ of every $n \in N$ with respect to $\langle N, A, \Sigma \cup \{C\} \rangle$. This corresponds to the compiled approach of the CMS.

Generating the label $L(n, A, \Sigma)$ of a node n is straightforward by Theorem 3.4 and Definition 5.1. Moreover, a query is not restricted to being a literal of N in this case: for a general formula, Theorem 3.5 can be applied by converting it to CNF.

Example 5.3 Let an ATMS be $\langle \{a, b, c, x, \neg y\}, \{x, \neg y\}, \Sigma \rangle$ where

$$\Sigma = \{ \quad \begin{aligned} &\neg a \vee \neg b \vee c && (1)\,, \\ &\neg x \vee \neg b \vee a && (2)\,, \\ &y \vee b \vee c && (3) \quad \}\,. \end{aligned}$$

The following deduction finds c's label $\{x \wedge \neg y\}$:

$$\langle \Box, \quad \underline{\neg c} \rangle\,, \qquad\qquad\qquad\qquad\qquad \text{top clause}$$
$$\langle \Box, \quad \neg \underline{a} \vee \neg b \vee \boxed{\neg c} \rangle\,, \qquad\qquad\qquad \text{resolution with (1)}$$
$$\langle \Box, \quad \neg \underline{x} \vee \neg\!\!\!\not b \vee \boxed{\neg a} \vee \neg b \vee \boxed{\neg c} \rangle\,, \qquad \text{resolution with (2) and factoring}$$
$$\langle \neg x, \quad \boxed{\not\!\neg\!a} \vee \neg\underline{b} \vee \boxed{\neg c} \rangle\,, \qquad\qquad\quad \text{skip and truncation}$$
$$\langle \neg x, \quad y \vee\!\!\not\!b \vee \boxed{\neg b} \vee \boxed{\neg c} \rangle\,, \qquad\qquad \text{resolution with (3) and reduction}$$
$$\langle \neg x \vee y, \quad \boxed{\not\!\neg\!b} \vee \boxed{\not\!\neg\!a} \rangle\,. \qquad\qquad\qquad \text{skip and truncation}$$

The question is how effectively consistency can be checked by testing whether a clause S, produced from $\Sigma + \neg n$ and $\mathcal{P} = \langle \neg \cdot A \rangle$, belongs to $Th_{\mathcal{P}}(\Sigma)$ or not. A direct implementation is to use a theorem prover, as we already know that S belongs to $\mathcal{P}$, but theorem proving is also possible in m.c.l.s. resolution: $\Sigma \models S$ iff $Prod(\Sigma, \neg S, \mathcal{P}) = \{\Box\}$. In this case, since we are not interested in any produced clause from $\Sigma + \neg S$ other than $\Box$, the production field $\mathcal{P}$ can be replaced with $\langle \phi \rangle$ and **Skip** (Rule 5(a)i) will never be applied. Thus, there is an m.c.l. refutation from $\Sigma \cup \{\neg S\}$ iff there is an m.c.l.s. deduction from $\Sigma + \neg S$ and $\langle \phi \rangle$.

However, there is another way for consistency checking that offers an intermediate approach between the interpreted and compiled approaches. Unlike with the CMS, the computation of $Carc(\Sigma, \mathcal{P})$ can be performed better as the search focuses on the restricted vocabulary $\mathcal{P}$ if it is small compared with the whole literals $A^{\pm}$. Having $Carc(\Sigma, \mathcal{P})$, consistency checking is much easier; $S \in Th_{\mathcal{P}}(\Sigma)$ iff there is a clause $T \in Carc(\Sigma, \mathcal{P})$ such that T subsumes S. The characteristic clauses $Carc(\Sigma, \langle \neg \cdot A \rangle)$ are called unsubsumed *nogoods* in the ATMS terminology. This checking can be embedded into an m.c.l.s. deduction: **Skip** (Rule 5(a)i) of Definition 3.1 can be replaced with the following rule:

5(a)i'. **(Skip & Check)** If $P_i \cup \{l\}$ belongs to $\mathcal{P}$ <u>and is not subsumed by any</u> <u>clause of $Carc(\Sigma, \mathcal{P})$</u>, then $P_{i+1} = P_i \cup \{l\}$ and $\vec{R_{i+1}}$ is the ordered clause obtained by removing l from $\vec{Q_i}$.

Proposition 5.4 If **Skip & Check** is used as Rule 5(a)i of an m.c.l.s. deduction instead of the original **Skip** rule, then $Prod(\Sigma, C, \mathcal{P}) = Newcarc(\Sigma, C, \mathcal{P})$.

In the compiled approach to an ATMS, the following result corresponding to Corollary 4.4 for the CMS and to a generalization of [22, Theorem 7] holds:

Theorem 5.5 Let $\langle N, A, \Sigma \rangle$ be an ATMS, $n \in N$ a literal, and $\mathcal{P} = \langle \neg \cdot A \rangle$.

$$Newcarc(\Sigma, \neg n, \mathcal{P}) = \{ P - \{n\} \mid P \in PI(\Sigma),\ n \in P \text{ and } P - \{n\} \text{ belongs to } \mathcal{P} \}.$$

Theorem 5.5 shows that we can compute the label of a node from the prime implicates of Σ. Therefore an approach may keep $PI(\Sigma)$ and when a new clause C is added we compute $PI(\Sigma \cup \{C\})$ by Proposition 4.5 for updating labels of nodes. However, compared with the CMS, many of the prime implicates are not significant for the task of an ATMS when the assumptions A are relatively small, although their computation is extremely high. In such a case, we do not want to compute all the prime implicates. Fortunately, we can compute a subset of $PI(\Sigma)$ enough to give labels by using the following stable production field:

Definition 5.6 Given an ATMS $\langle N, A, \Sigma \rangle$ and a production field $\mathcal{P} = \langle \neg \cdot A \rangle$, a production field $\mathcal{P}^*$ is defined as:

$$\mathcal{P}^* = \langle \neg \cdot A \cup N,\ \text{the number of literals in } N - \neg \cdot A \text{ is at most one} \rangle.$$

Since $\mathcal{P}^*$ is stable, $Carc(\Sigma, \mathcal{P}^*)$ can be constructed incrementally by using Theorem 3.6:

$$Carc(\Sigma \cup \{C\}, \mathcal{P}^*) = \mu [\, Carc(\Sigma, \mathcal{P}^*) \cup Prod(\Sigma, C, \mathcal{P}^*)\,].$$

Here we only need to keep Σ and $Carc(\Sigma, \mathcal{P}^*)$. Looking further at Definition 5.6, the relationship between $Carc(\Sigma, \mathcal{P}^*)$ and $Carc(\Sigma, \mathcal{P})$ can be shown exactly in the next lemma:

Lemma 5.7 $Carc(\Sigma, \mathcal{P}^*) = Carc(\Sigma, \mathcal{P})$
$$\cup \{ S \cup \{n\} \mid n \in N - \neg \cdot A \text{ and } S \in Newcarc(\Sigma, \neg n, \mathcal{P}) \}.$$

Therefore, the knowledge base can consist of the justifications Σ, unsubsumed nogoods $Carc(\Sigma, \mathcal{P})$, and prime implicates mentioning one node with the negation of an element of its label. No other prime implicates are necessary. Having $Carc(\Sigma, \mathcal{P}^*)$, we can find the label of each node easily as follows:

Theorem 5.8 Let $\langle N, A, \Sigma \rangle$ be an ATMS, $n \in N$, $\mathcal{P} = \langle \neg \cdot A \rangle$, and $\mathcal{P}^*$ be the same as in Definition 5.6.

$$Newcarc(\Sigma, \neg n, \mathcal{P}) = \begin{cases} \{ S - \{n\} \mid S \in Carc(\Sigma, \mathcal{P}^*),\ \text{and } n \in S \} & \text{if } n \in N - \neg \cdot A \\ \{ S - \{n\} \mid S \in Carc(\Sigma, \mathcal{P}),\ \text{and } n \in S \} & \text{if } n \in N \cap \neg \cdot A \end{cases}$$

For updating the knowledge base when a new clause C is added, again we just compute $Carc(\Sigma \cup \{C\}, \mathcal{P}^*)$ from the previous $Carc(\Sigma, \mathcal{P}^*)$ incrementally by using Theorem 3.6. Since this computation guarantees the completeness of characteristic-clause-finding, the four properties of the ATMS labels in Proposition 5.2 are also satisfied in this case. Note that the μ operation removes all the previous prime implicates that are subsumed by some newly added prime implicates. This operation is also crucial to guarantee the label consistency because implicates subsumed by some nogood must be removed.

Example 5.9 Suppose that an ATMS is $\langle \{a, b, x, y\}, \{x, y\}, \Sigma \rangle$ where

$$\Sigma = \{a \lor b, \neg y \lor a\}.$$

In this case $Carc(\Sigma, \mathcal{P}^*) = \Sigma \cup \{\neg x \lor x, \neg y \lor y\}$. Now suppose that a new clause $\neg x \lor \neg a$ is added to Σ. Then the updating algorithm will find b's new label x, as well as a new unsubsumed nogood $\neg x \lor \neg y$:

$$\langle \Box, \underline{\neg x} \lor \neg a \rangle, \quad \langle \neg x, \underline{\neg a} \rangle, \quad \langle \neg x, \underline{b} \lor \boxed{\neg a} \rangle, \quad \langle \neg x \lor b, \boxed{\neg q} \rangle .$$
$$\hookrightarrow \quad \langle \neg x, \underline{\neg y} \lor \boxed{\neg a} \rangle, \quad \langle \neg x \lor \neg y, \boxed{\neg q} \rangle .$$

We thus see that $Carc(\Sigma, \mathcal{P}^*)$ can be used for giving labels for nodes. To maximize efficiency, however, it can also be used for caching the result of the production as lemmas; it can be utilized later as the bypass of steps of resolution in the previous computation. In [12], we describe how the updating algorithm can be modified for this purpose and still establish the label completeness for various ATMSs [4, 5, 6, 8], and the correspondence of the modified algorithm with de Kleer's label updating algorithms [4, 6].

6 Related Works

In this section, we compare our characteristic-clause-finding procedure to proof procedures of various abductive and nonmonotonic reasoning systems. The notions of production fields and (new) characteristic clauses are very helpful in understanding the relationships between them and in reconstructing them in our simple and general formalism.

6.1 Saturation and Abduction

Bossu & Siegel [1] define a closed-world reasoning called sub-implication, in which all ground atoms are to be minimized. Their saturation procedure finds $Carc(\Sigma, \mathcal{P})$ where the characteristic literals $L_{\mathcal{P}}$ are fixed to positive ground literals (see Example 2.3 (2)). However, it does not use C-ordering, and their method to compute $Newcarc(\Sigma, C, \mathcal{P})$ is a naive implementation of Definition 2.4. Those versions of closed-world assumptions can be generalized to allow for variable and fixed predicates as well as minimized predicates, that is, circumscription of ground theories (see Section 6.2).

Kean & Tsiknis [14] extend Tison's [26] consensus method of producing prime implicates to generate them incrementally. In our framework, the corresponding result is illustrated in Proposition 4.5. The difference is that their method is based on a set-of-support strategy, where subsumption checking is performed at each resolution step, while ours uses linear resolution and thus naturally has more restriction strategies.

De Kleer [7] introduces hyperresolution rules to pre-compile a set of clauses Σ, all of which are either positive or negative. This technique is also given in [5] in more general form. An interesting approach in [7] is to use a rule limiting the inference only to negative clauses below a size k. The resulting set of negative clauses closed under these rules and subsumption are the characteristic clauses $Carc(\Sigma, \mathcal{P})$ where $\mathcal{P} = \langle \neg \cdot A, \text{ below size } k \rangle$ (see Example 2.3 (3)). In our formulation, instead of using hyperresolution, linear resolution can be used to produce such characteristic clauses for any clause set Σ and any characteristic literals $L_\mathcal{P} \subseteq \mathcal{A}^\pm$. In practice, this size-restriction is very useful for minimizing the computational effort, because it causes earlier pruning in m.c.l.s. deduction sequences.

There are many systems for logic-based abductive reasoning. However, many systems [19, 9, 21] other than [20] do not require minimality of explanation. Pople [20] proposed the mechanization of abduction via deduction based on SL-resolution [15], with "synthesis" operation which corresponds to our skipping operation. However, his system does not distinguish literals, that is, the production field is fixed to $\mathcal{P}_\pi$, and "hypothesizes whatever cannot be proven". This criterion is also used by Cox & Pietrzykowski [3]. It can be implemented if **Skip** (Rule 5(a)i) is preceded by **Resolve** (Rule 5(a)ii) and is applied only if **Resolve** cannot be applied in Step 5a of an m.c.l.s. deduction (Definition 3.1).

Finger [9] gives residue procedures for abductive reasoning where assumptions are restricted to only atoms, but his "resolution residue" uses set-of-support resolution.

6.2 Query Answering for Circumscription

Let $\langle N, A_1 \cup \neg \cdot A_2, \Sigma \rangle$ be an ATMS such that $A_1 \subseteq \mathcal{A}$ and $A_2 \subseteq \mathcal{A}$. We wish to know whether or not a formula is satisfied by every preferred model of Σ. This problem is equivalent to *circumscription* of propositional theories: A_2 is to be *minimized* and A_1 is to be maximized (that is, for each $a \in A_1$, $\neg a$ is to be minimized); $A_1 \cap A_2$ represents the *fixed* propositional symbols and $N - (A_1 \cup A_2)$ represents *variables*. In this case, the production field is $\langle \neg \cdot A_1 \cup A_2 \rangle$.

Przymusinski [21] defines MILO-resolution, a variant of OL-resolution [2], which is used in his circumscriptive theorem prover. Inoue & Helft [13] characterize MILO-resolution as m.c.l.s. resolution where the characteristic literals $L_\mathcal{P}$ are set to the positive occurrence of minimized predicates and any occurrence of fixed predicates in the circumscription policy.

Proposition 6.1 [21, 10, 13] Suppose that $L_\mathcal{P}$ is the same as in the above description and that $\mathcal{P} = \langle L_\mathcal{P} \rangle$. Every circumscriptive minimal model satisfies a formula F if and only if there is a conjunct G of clauses of $[Th_\mathcal{P}(\Sigma \cup \{\neg F\}) - Th_\mathcal{P}(\Sigma)]$ such that $[Th_\mathcal{P}(\Sigma \cup \{\neg G\}) - Th_\mathcal{P}(\Sigma)] = \phi$.

There is a big difference between MILO-resolution and the ATMS [13]. In Proposition 6.1, to get theorems in $[Th_\mathcal{P}(\Sigma \cup \{C\}) - Th_\mathcal{P}(\Sigma)]$ for some clause C, MILO-resolution does not actually compute $Newcarc(\Sigma, C, \mathcal{P})$, while the ATMS does. Let us divide the produced clauses from $\Sigma + C$ and $\mathcal{P}$ possibly containing subsumed clauses into two sets, say $S1$ and $S2$, such that $\Sigma \cup S1 \models S2$. Then adding $S2$ to $S1$ does not change the models of the production. Thus only $S1$ needs to be computed model-theoretically [6]. We call a set $S1$ verifying this condition a *precursor* of the production. Note that a clause in a precursor is not always a prime implicate of Σ. MILO-resolution computes such a precursor, because when the first literal belongs to $L_\mathcal{P}$ in Step 5a of an m.c.l.s. deduction (Definition 3.1), only **Skip** (Rule 5(a)i) is applied. On the contrary, since the CMS and the ATMS are used for computing *all and only minimal* supports for a query,

---

[6]Note that a clause in $S1$ is the weakest in the sense that for any clause $A_2 \in S2$ there exists a clause $A_1 \in S1$ such that $\Sigma \cup \{\neg A_2\} \models \neg A_1$ holds (recall that for $A \in S1 \cup S2$, $\neg A$ is an explanation of $\neg C$ from $(\Sigma, \neg \cdot \mathcal{P})$ if $\Sigma \not\models A$).

if the literal resolved upon belongs to L_P, they apply either **Skip** or **Resolve**. Thus a precursor-finding algorithm [13] can be written by ordering two rules as:

5(a)i'. (**Skip & Cut**) If $P_i \cup \{l\}$ belongs to $\mathcal{P}$, then then $P_{i+1} = P_i \cup \{l\}$ and $\vec{R}_{i+1}$ is the ordered clause obtained by removing l from $\vec{Q}_i$.

5(a)ii'. (**Resolve'**) Otherwise, $P_{i+1} = P_i$ and $\vec{R}_{i+1}$ is an ordered resolvent of $\vec{Q}_i$ with a clause B_i in Σ, where the literal resolved upon in $\vec{Q}_i$ is l.

Theorem 6.2 If a clause T is derived by an m.c.l.s. deduction from $\Sigma + C$ and $\mathcal{P}$, then there is a deduction of a clause S with the **Skip & Cut** rule from $\Sigma + C$ and $\mathcal{P}$ such that $\Sigma \cup \{S\} \models T$.

7   Conclusion

We have shown a procedural interpretation of the CMS and the ATMS based on an extension of linear resolution. The **Skip** rule can be safely embedded in linear resolution strategies making characteristic-clause-finding complete, due to the stability of production fields. While we used the description of OL-resolution as the definition of our linear resolution procedure, **Skip** can be applied to other, superior versions of propositional linear resolution, such as Shostak's graph construction procedure [23], and further improvements on these methods can be used to improve efficiency still more. We should also note that the control of inference can be made to the production in various ways as breadth-first or best-first search [2], integration of top-down and bottom-up strategies [9], reordering subgoal trees [24], and others.

Using the methods described in this paper, many AI techniques such as preferential-models approaches to nonmonotonic reasoning and constraint satisfaction problems, as well as direct applications of abduction or the ATMS, may be helped on the way to better implementation.

Acknowledgment

I would like to thank Koichi Furukawa, Nicolas Helft, Ken Satoh, Yoshihiko Ohta, David Poole and Wolfgang Bibel for helpful discussions on this work.

References

[1] Bossu, G. and Siegel, P., "Saturation, Nonmonotonic Reasoning, and the Closed-World Assumption", *Artificial Intelligence* **25** (1985), pp.23–67.

[2] Chang, C. L., and Lee, R. C. T., *Symbolic Logic and Mechanical Theorem Proving* (Academic Press, 1973).

[3] Cox, P. T. and Pietrzykowski, T., "Causes for Events: Their Computation and Applications", *Proc. 8th Conf. on Automated Deduction*, Lecture Notes in Computer Science 230, Springer-Verlag (1986), pp.608–621.

[4] de Kleer, J., "An Assumption-based TMS", *Artificial Intelligence* **28** (1986), pp.127–162.

[5] de Kleer, J., "Extending the ATMS", *Artificial Intelligence* **28** (1986), pp.163–196.

[6] de Kleer, J., "A General Labeling Algorithm for Assumption-based Truth Maintenance", *Proc. AAAI-88* (1988), pp.188–192.

[7] de Kleer, J., *Propositional Inference in CSP and ATMS Techniques*, SSL Paper P89-00023, Xerox Palo Alto Research Center, 1989.

[8] Dressler, O., "An Extended Basic ATMS", *Proc. 2nd Int'l Workshop on Non-Monotonic Reasoning*, Lecture Notes in Artificial Intelligence 346, Springer-Verlag (1989), pp.143–163.

[9] Finger, J. J., *Exploiting Constraints in Design Synthesis*, Department of Computer Science, STAN-CS-88-1204, Stanford University, 1987.

[10] Ginsberg, M. L., "A Circumscriptive Theorem Prover", *Artificial Intelligence* **39** (1989), pp.209–230.

[11] Inoue, K., "Generalizing the ATMS: A Model-based Approach (Preliminary Report)", *IPSJ SIG Reports*, SIG AI 63-3, pp.21–28, Information Processing Society of Japan, March 1989.

[12] Inoue, K., *Procedural Interpretation for an Extended ATMS*, ICOT Technical Report TR-547, ICOT, March 1990.

[13] Inoue, K. and Helft, N., "On Theorem Provers for Circumscription", *Proc. CSCSI-90*, Ottawa (May 1990), pp.212–219.

[14] Kean, A. and Tsiknis, G., *An Incremental Method for Generating Prime Implicants/Implicates*, Technical Report 88-16, Department of Computer Science, The University of British Columbia, 1988.

[15] Kowalski, R. A. and Kuhner, D. G., "Linear Resolution with Selection Function", *Artificial Intelligence* **2** (1971), pp.227–260.

[16] Levesque, H. J., "A Knowledge-level Account of Abduction (preliminary version)", *Proc. IJCAI-89* (1989), pp.1061–1067.

[17] Loveland, D., *Automated Theorem Proving: A Logical Basis*, (North-Holland, 1978).

[18] Minicozzi, E. and Reiter, R., "A Note on Linear Resolution Strategies in Consequence-Finding", *Artificial Intelligence* **3** (1972), pp.175–180.

[19] Poole, D., "A Logical Framework for Default Reasoning", *Artificial Intelligence* **36** (1988), pp.27–47.

[20] Pople, H. E., "On the Mechanization of Abductive Logic", *Proc. IJCAI-73* (1973), pp.147–152.

[21] Przymusinski, T. C., "An Algorithm to Compute Circumscription", *Artificial Intelligence* **38** (1989), pp.49–73.

[22] Reiter, R. and de Kleer, J., "Foundations of Assumption-based Truth Maintenance Systems: Preliminary Report", *Proc. AAAI-87* (1987), pp.183–188.

[23] Shostak, R., "Refutation Graphs", *Artificial Intelligence* **7** (1976), pp.51–64.

[24] Siegel, P., *Représentation et Utilisation de la Connaissance en Calcul Propositionnel*, PhD thesis, University of Aix-Marseille II, 1987.

[25] Slagle, J. R., Chang, C. L., and Lee, R. C. T., "Completeness Theorems for Semantic Resolution in Consequence Finding", *Proc. IJCAI-69* (1969), pp.281–285.

[26] Tison, P., "Generalized Consensus Theory and Application to the Minimization of Boolean Functions", *IEEE transactions on electronic computers* **16** (1967), pp.446–456.

A   Appendix: Proofs of Theorems

The next proposition is used to prove Theorem 2.5.

Proposition A.1 $Newcarc(\Sigma, F, \mathcal{P}) = \mu[Th_{\mathcal{P}}(\Sigma \cup \{F\}) - Th_{\mathcal{P}}(\Sigma)]$.

Proof: Let $A = Th_{\mathcal{P}}(\Sigma \cup \{F\})$ and $B = Th_{\mathcal{P}}(\Sigma)$. Notice that $B \subseteq A$. We will prove that $\mu[A - B] = \mu A - \mu B$.

Let $c \in \mu[A - B]$. Then obviously $c \in A - B$ and thus $c \in A$. Now assume that $c \notin \mu A$. Then there exists d in μA such that $d \subset c$. By the minimality of $c \in A - B$, $d \in B$. Since $d \subset c$, $c \in B$, contradiction. Therefore $c \in \mu A$. Clearly, by $c \notin B$, $c \notin \mu B$. Hence, $c \in \mu A - \mu B$.

Conversely, assume that $c \in \mu A - \mu B$. Firstly we must prove that $c \in A - B$. Suppose to the contrary that $c \in B$. Since $c \notin \mu B$, there exists d in μB such that $d \subset c$. However, as $B \subseteq A$, $d \in A$, contradicting the minimality of $c \in A$. Therefore, $c \in A - B$. Now assume that c is not minimal in $A - B$. Then, there exists e in $A - B$ such that $e \subset c$, again contradicting the minimality of $c \in A$. Hence, $c \in \mu[A - B]$. $\square$

Theorem 2.5 Let Σ be a set of clauses, $A \subseteq \mathcal{A}^{\pm}$, G a formula. The set of all minimal explanations of G from (Σ, A) is $\neg \cdot Newcarc(\Sigma, \neg G, \mathcal{P})$, where $\mathcal{P} = \langle \neg \cdot A \rangle$.

Proof: Suppose that H is an explanation of G from (Σ, A). By Definition 1.1, it is observed that (1) $\Sigma \cup \{H\} \models G$ can be written as $\Sigma \cup \{\neg G\} \models \neg H$, (2) the fact that $\Sigma \cup \{H\}$ is satisfiable means $\Sigma \not\models \neg H$, and (3) $\neg H$ is a clause all of whose literals belong to $\neg \cdot A$. Thus $\neg H \in [Th_{\mathcal{P}}(\Sigma \cup \{\neg G\}) - Th_{\mathcal{P}}(\Sigma)]$. Conversely, it can be easily shown that if $F \in [Th_{\mathcal{P}}(\Sigma \cup \{\neg G\}) - Th_{\mathcal{P}}(\Sigma)]$, then $\neg F$ is an explanation of G from (Σ, A). By Proposition A.1, H is a minimal explanation of G from (Σ, A) if and only if $\neg H \in Newcarc(\Sigma, \neg G, \mathcal{P})$. $\square$

Theorem 3.2 (1) *Soundness*: If a clause S is derived using an m.c.l.s. deduction from $\Sigma + C$ and $\mathcal{P}$, then S belongs to $Th_{\mathcal{P}}(\Sigma \cup \{C\})$.
(2) *Completeness*: If a clause T does not belong to $Th_{\mathcal{P}}(\Sigma)$, but belongs to $Th_{\mathcal{P}}(\Sigma \cup \{C\})$, then there is an m.c.l.s. deduction of a clause S from $\Sigma + C$ and $\mathcal{P}$ such that S subsumes T.

Proof: The proof for the completeness can be seen as an extension of the result for linear resolution by Minicozzi & Reiter [18]. And these results follow easily using the same method as in the proofs for Siegel's procedure described in [24]. $\square$

The next lemma is a direct consequence of Theorem 3.2, and is used for the proof of Theorem 3.4.

Lemma A.2 Let C be a clause. $Newcarc(\Sigma, C, \mathcal{P}) \subseteq Prod(\Sigma, C, \mathcal{P}) \subseteq Th_\mathcal{P}(\Sigma \cup \{C\})$.

Proof: Let $T \in Newcarc(\Sigma, C, \mathcal{P})$. By Proposition A.1, $T \in \mu[Th_\mathcal{P}(\Sigma \cup \{C\}) - Th_\mathcal{P}(\Sigma)]$. By Theorem 3.2 (2), there is a clause S in $Prod(\Sigma, C, \mathcal{P})$ such that $S \subseteq T$. By the minimality of T, $T = S$. Hence, $Newcarc(\Sigma, C, \mathcal{P}) \subseteq Prod(\Sigma, C, \mathcal{P})$. By Theorem 3.2 (1), the second set-inclusion relationship easily follows. $\square$

Theorem 3.4 Let C be a clause. $Newcarc(\Sigma, C, \mathcal{P}) = Prod(\Sigma, C, \mathcal{P}) - Th_\mathcal{P}(\Sigma)$.

Proof: By Lemma A.2, $Newcarc(\Sigma, C, \mathcal{P}) \subseteq Prod(\Sigma, C, \mathcal{P})$. It remains to show that $Prod(\Sigma, C, \mathcal{P}) - Newcarc(\Sigma, C, \mathcal{P}) \subseteq Th_\mathcal{P}(\Sigma)$. Suppose to the contrary, for $S \in Prod(\Sigma, C, \mathcal{P}) - Th_\mathcal{P}(\Sigma)$, that $S \notin Newcarc(\Sigma, C, \mathcal{P})$. As $S \notin Th_\mathcal{P}(\Sigma)$, $S \notin Carc(\Sigma, \mathcal{P})$. Because $S \in Prod(\Sigma, C, \mathcal{P})$, $S \in Th_\mathcal{P}(\Sigma \cup \{C\})$ by Lemma A.2. Since S is not minimal by the supposition, there is a clause S' in $Carc(\Sigma \cup \{C\}, \mathcal{P})$ such that $S' \subset S$. Then, clearly $S' \notin Th_\mathcal{P}(\Sigma)$ as $S' \subset S$. Thus, $S' \in Th_\mathcal{P}(\Sigma \cup \{C\}) - Th_\mathcal{P}(\Sigma)$. By Theorem 3.2 (2), there must be a clause S'' in $Prod(\Sigma, C, \mathcal{P})$ such that $S'' \subseteq S' \subset S$. However, by Definition 3.3, $Prod(\Sigma, C, \mathcal{P})$ is μ-closed, that is, does not contain any redundant clauses, contradiction. Hence, $S \in Newcarc(\Sigma, C, \mathcal{P})$. $\square$

Theorem 3.5 Let $G = C_1 \wedge \cdots \wedge C_m$ be a CNF formula. Then

$$
Newcarc(\Sigma, G, \mathcal{P}) \quad = \quad \mu\left[\bigcup_{i=1}^{m} Newcarc(\Sigma_i, C_i, \mathcal{P})\right]
$$

$$
= \quad \mu\left[\bigcup_{i=1}^{m} Prod(\Sigma_i, C_i, \mathcal{P})\right] - Th_\mathcal{P}(\Sigma),
$$

where $\Sigma_1 = \Sigma$, and $\Sigma_{i+1} = \Sigma_i \cup \{C_i\}$, for $i = 1, \ldots, m - 1$.

Proof: Notice that in the following proof, for sets, A, B, and C, such that $C \subseteq B \subseteq A$, $A - C = (A - B) \cup (B - C)$ holds.

$$
Newcarc(\Sigma, G, \mathcal{P})
$$
$$
= \quad \mu[Th_\mathcal{P}(\Sigma \cup \{C_1, \cdots, C_m\}) - Th_\mathcal{P}(\Sigma)] \text{ (by Proposition A.1)}
$$
$$
= \quad \mu[(Th_\mathcal{P}(\Sigma_m \cup \{C_m\}) - Th_\mathcal{P}(\Sigma_m)) \cup \cdots \cup (Th_\mathcal{P}(\Sigma \cup \{C_1\}) - Th_\mathcal{P}(\Sigma))]
$$
$$
= \quad \mu[\mu[Th_\mathcal{P}(\Sigma_m \cup \{C_m\}) - Th_\mathcal{P}(\Sigma_m)] \cup \cdots \cup \mu[Th_\mathcal{P}(\Sigma_2) - Th_\mathcal{P}(\Sigma_1)]]
$$
$$
= \quad \mu[Newcarc(\Sigma_m, C_m, \mathcal{P}) \cup \cdots \cup Newcarc(\Sigma_1, C_1, \mathcal{P})]
$$
$$
= \quad \mu\left[\bigcup_{i=1}^{m} Newcarc(\Sigma_i, C_i, \mathcal{P})\right].
$$

Now, by applying Theorem 3.4, we get the following equation, which can be used successively to prove the last equality:

$$
Newcarc(\Sigma_{k+1}, C_{k+1}, \mathcal{P}) \cup Newcarc(\Sigma_k, C_k, \mathcal{P})
$$
$$
= \quad (Prod(\Sigma_k \cup \{C_k\}, C_{k+1}, \mathcal{P}) - Th_\mathcal{P}(\Sigma_k \cup \{C_k\})) \cup (Prod(\Sigma_k, C_k, \mathcal{P}) - Th_\mathcal{P}(\Sigma_k))
$$

$$
\begin{aligned}
= \quad & (\, Prod(\Sigma_k \cup \{C_k\}, C_{k+1}, \mathcal{P}) \cup Prod(\Sigma_k, C_k, \mathcal{P}) \,) \\
& - (\, Th_{\mathcal{P}}(\Sigma_k \cup \{C_k\}) - Prod(\Sigma_k, C_k, \mathcal{P}) \,) \\
& - (\, Th_{\mathcal{P}}(\Sigma_k) - Prod(\Sigma_k \cup \{C_k\}, C_{k+1}, \mathcal{P}) \,) - (\, Th_{\mathcal{P}}(\Sigma_k \cup \{C_k\}) \cap Th_{\mathcal{P}}(\Sigma_k) \,) \\
= \quad & (\, Prod(\Sigma_{k+1}, C_{k+1}, \mathcal{P}) \cup Prod(\Sigma_k, C_k, \mathcal{P}) \,) - \phi \\
& - (\, Th_{\mathcal{P}}(\Sigma_k) - Prod(\Sigma_k \cup \{C_k\}, C_{k+1}, \mathcal{P}) \,) - Th_{\mathcal{P}}(\Sigma_k) \\
= \quad & (\, Prod(\Sigma_{k+1}, C_{k+1}, \mathcal{P}) \cup Prod(\Sigma_k, C_k, \mathcal{P}) \,) - Th_{\mathcal{P}}(\Sigma_k) \, .
\end{aligned}
$$

Hence, $Newcarc(\Sigma, G, \mathcal{P}) = \mu \, [\, \bigcup_{i=1}^{m} Prod(\Sigma_i, C_i, \mathcal{P}) \,] - Th_{\mathcal{P}}(\Sigma)$. $\square$

Theorem 3.6 The characteristic clauses with respect to $\mathcal{P}$ can be generated incrementally:

$$
\begin{aligned}
Carc(\phi, \mathcal{P}) \quad &= \quad \{ \, p \vee \neg p \mid p \in \mathcal{A} \text{ and } p \vee \neg p \text{ belongs to } \mathcal{P} \, \}, \quad \text{and} \\
Carc(\Sigma \cup \{C\}, \mathcal{P}) \quad &= \quad \mu \, [\, Carc(\Sigma, \mathcal{P}) \cup Newcarc(\Sigma, C, \mathcal{P}) \,] \\
&= \quad \mu \, [\, Carc(\Sigma, \mathcal{P}) \cup Prod(\Sigma, C, \mathcal{P}) \,] \, .
\end{aligned}
$$

Proof: The first equation follows immediately from Definition 2.4 (1). Now,

$$
\begin{aligned}
Carc(\Sigma \cup \{C\}, \mathcal{P}) \quad &= \quad \mu \, Th_{\mathcal{P}}(\Sigma \cup \{C\}) \\
&= \quad \mu \, [\, Th_{\mathcal{P}}(\Sigma \cup \{C\}) \cup Th_{\mathcal{P}}(\Sigma) \,] \\
&= \quad \mu \, [\, \mu Th_{\mathcal{P}}(\Sigma \cup \{C\}) \cup \mu Th_{\mathcal{P}}(\Sigma) \,] \quad (*) \\
&= \quad \mu \, [\, Carc(\Sigma, \mathcal{P}) \cup Carc(\Sigma \cup \{C\}, \mathcal{P}) \,] \\
&= \quad \mu \, [\, Carc(\Sigma, \mathcal{P}) \cup (\, Carc(\Sigma \cup \{C\}, \mathcal{P}) - Carc(\Sigma, \mathcal{P})) \,] \\
&= \quad \mu \, [\, Carc(\Sigma, \mathcal{P}) \cup Newcarc(\Sigma, C, \mathcal{P}) \,] \\
&= \quad \mu \, [\, Carc(\Sigma, \mathcal{P}) \cup (Prod(\Sigma, C, \mathcal{P}) - Th_{\mathcal{P}}(\Sigma)) \,] \quad \text{(by Theorem 3.4)} \\
&= \quad \mu \, [\, Carc(\Sigma, \mathcal{P}) \cup Prod(\Sigma, C, \mathcal{P}) \,] \, .
\end{aligned}
$$

Notice that at $(*)$, for two sets, A and B, $\mu [A \cup B] = \mu [\mu A \cup \mu B]$ holds. $\square$

Proposition 4.2 Let F be any formula. $MS(\Sigma, F) = Newcarc(\Sigma, \neg F, \mathcal{P}_{\pi})$.

Proof: A clause S is a support for F with respect to Σ
$\Leftrightarrow \Sigma \models S \cup F$, and $\Sigma \not\models S$
$\Leftrightarrow \Sigma \cup \{\neg F\} \models S$, and $\Sigma \not\models S$
$\Leftrightarrow S \in [Th(\Sigma \cup \{\neg F\}) - Th(\Sigma)]$.
Therefore, $S \in MS(\Sigma, F) \Leftrightarrow S \in Newcarc(\Sigma, \neg F, \mathcal{P}_{\pi})$ (by Proposition A.1). $\square$

The next lemma says that the set Σ of clauses is logically equivalent to $PI(\Sigma)$ in the sense that both sets can produce the same (new) characteristic clauses with respect to a production field $\mathcal{P}$.

Lemma A.3 For any stable production field $\mathcal{P}$,

$$
Newcarc(\Sigma, C, \mathcal{P}) = Newcarc(PI(\Sigma), C, \mathcal{P}) \, .
$$

Proof: Firstly, $Carc(PI(\Sigma), \mathcal{P}) = Carc(Carc(\Sigma, \mathcal{P}_\pi), \langle L_\mathcal{P} \rangle) = Carc(\Sigma, \langle \mathcal{L}^\pm \cap L_\mathcal{P} \rangle) = Carc(\Sigma, \mathcal{P})$.

Now, $Carc(PI(\Sigma) \cup \{C\}, \mathcal{P}) = \mu Th_\mathcal{P}(\mu Th_{\mathcal{P}_\pi}(\Sigma) \cup \{C\}) = \mu Th_\mathcal{P}(Th(\Sigma) \cup \{C\}) = Carc(\Sigma \cup \{C\}, \mathcal{P})$.

The lemma follows immediately by Definition 2.4 (1). $\square$

Proposition 4.5 Given $PI(\Sigma)$ and a clause C, $PI(\Sigma \cup \{C\})$ can be found incrementally:

$$PI(\phi) = \{ p \vee \neg p \mid p \in \mathcal{A} \}, \text{ and}$$
$$PI(\Sigma \cup \{C\}) = \mu [PI(\Sigma) \cup Prod(PI(\Sigma), C, \mathcal{P}_\pi)].$$

Proof: The proposition follows by setting $\mathcal{P}$ to $\mathcal{P}_\pi$ in Theorem 3.6 and by using Theorem 3.4 and Lemma A.3. $\square$

Proposition 5.2 Let $\langle N, A, \Sigma \rangle$ be an ATMS, $n \in N$ a literal, and $\mathcal{P} = \langle \neg \cdot A \rangle$.

(1) *Label consistency*: for each $E_i \in L(n, A, \Sigma)$, $\Sigma \cup \{E_i\}$ is satisfiable.

(2) *Label soundness*: for each $E_i \in L(n, A, \Sigma)$, $\Sigma \cup \{E_i\} \models n$.

(3) *Label completeness*: for every conjunct E of assumptions in A, if $\Sigma \cup \{E\} \models n$, then there exists $E_i \in L(n, A, \Sigma)$ such that E_i is a sub-conjunct of E.

(4) *Label minimality*: every $E_i \in L(n, A, \Sigma)$ is not a super-conjunct of any other element.

Proof: By Definition 5.1 and Theorem 2.5, $E_i \in L(n, A, \Sigma)$ is a minimal explanation of n from (Σ, A). Therefore, these four properties obviously hold by Definition 1.1. $\square$

Proposition 5.4 If **Skip & Check** is used as Rule 5(a)i of an m.c.l.s. deduction instead of the original **Skip** rule, then $Prod(\Sigma, C, \mathcal{P}) = Newcarc(\Sigma, C, \mathcal{P})$.

Proof: Because every clause belonging to $Th_\mathcal{P}(\Sigma \cup \{C\})$ that is subsumed by some clause in $Carc(\Sigma, \mathcal{P})$ must be pruned in a deduction sequence, every clause produced from $\Sigma + C$ is not a super-clause of any clause in $Carc(\Sigma, \mathcal{P})$ and thus does not belong to $Th_\mathcal{P}(\Sigma)$. Hence, by Theorem 3.4, the proposition follows. $\square$

Theorem 5.5 Let $\langle N, A, \Sigma \rangle$ be an ATMS, $n \in N$ a literal, and $\mathcal{P} = \langle \neg \cdot A \rangle$.

$$Newcarc(\Sigma, \neg n, \mathcal{P}) = \{ P - \{n\} \mid P \in PI(\Sigma), n \in P \text{ and } P - \{n\} \text{ belongs to } \mathcal{P} \}.$$

Proof: ($\supseteq$) Let $P \in PI(\Sigma)$ such that $n \in P$ and $P - \{n\}$ belongs to $\mathcal{P}$. Then, since $P - \{n\} \subset P$, $\Sigma \not\models P - \{n\}$. Since $n \in P$ and $\Sigma \models P$, $\Sigma \cup \{\neg n\} \models P - \{n\}$. Therefore, $P - \{n\} \in Th_\mathcal{P}(\Sigma \cup \{\neg n\}) - Th_\mathcal{P}(\Sigma)$. As $P \in PI(\Sigma)$ and $n \in P$, for any clause $S \subset P - \{n\}$, $\Sigma \not\models S \cup \{n\}$, and thus $\Sigma \cup \{\neg n\} \not\models S$ holds. This implies that $P - \{n\} \in Carc(\Sigma \cup \{\neg n\}, \mathcal{P})$, and thus $P - \{n\} \in Newcarc(\Sigma, \neg n, \mathcal{P})$ (by Proposition A.1)[7].

($\subseteq$) Let $S \in Newcarc(\Sigma, \neg n, \mathcal{P})$. As $\Sigma \cup \{\neg n\} \models S$, $\Sigma \models S \cup \{n\}$ holds. Suppose that there is a clause T in $Th(\Sigma)$ such that $T \subset S \cup \{n\}$ and that $T - \{n\}$ belongs to $\mathcal{P}$. Clearly, $\Sigma \models T \cup \{n\}$. Now for any clause S' such that $S' \subset S$, since $\Sigma \cup \{\neg n\} \not\models S'$,

---

[7] Note that in this direction n need not be a literal in N; the relation holds for a clause C: if $P \in PI(\Sigma)$, $C \subseteq P$, and $P - C$ belongs to $\mathcal{P}$, then $\neg \cdot (P - C)$ is a minimal explanation of C from (Σ, A). This result corresponds to a generalization of [22, Theorem 3] for a general $\mathcal{P}$.

$\Sigma \not\models S' \cup \{n\}$ holds. Therefore, $S \subseteq T \subset S \cup \{n\}$. As n is a literal, $T = S$. However, $S \notin Carc(\Sigma, \mathcal{P})$, contradiction. Hence, $S \cup \{n\} \in PI(\Sigma)$. Replacing $S \cup \{n\}$ with P, we get the theorem. $\square$

Lemma 5.7 $Carc(\Sigma, \mathcal{P}^*) = Carc(\Sigma, \mathcal{P})$
$$\cup \{ S \cup \{n\} \mid n \in N - \neg \cdot A \text{ and } S \in Newcarc(\Sigma, \neg n, \mathcal{P}) \}.$$

Proof: $Carc(\Sigma, \mathcal{P}^*)$ can be divided into two disjoint sets of clauses: (1) containing no literal in $N - \neg \cdot A$, and (2) containing exactly one literal in $N - \neg \cdot A$. The former is exactly $Carc(\Sigma, \mathcal{P})$. Assume that C belongs to the latter set, and that $n \in C$ is a literal in $N - \neg \cdot A$. Then, $C - \{n\}$ contains only literals in $\neg \cdot A$ and thus belongs to $\mathcal{P}$. We must show that $C - \{n\} \in Carc(\Sigma \cup \{\neg n\}, \mathcal{P})$. Since $C \in Carc(\Sigma, \mathcal{P}^*)$, $\Sigma \models C$ and thus $\Sigma \cup \{\neg n\} \models C - \{n\}$. Suppose to the contrary that $Th_{\mathcal{P}}(\Sigma \cup \{\neg n\})$ contains a clause S such that $S \subset C - \{n\}$. Then, $S \cup \{n\} \subset C$ and $S \cup \{n\} \notin Th_{\mathcal{P}^*}(\Sigma)$ by the minimality of $C \in Th_{\mathcal{P}^*}(\Sigma)$. Since $\Sigma \not\models S \cup \{n\}$, $\Sigma \cup \{\neg n\} \not\models S$, contradiction. Therefore, $C - \{n\} \in Carc(\Sigma \cup \{\neg n\}, \mathcal{P})$. Since $C \in Carc(\Sigma, \mathcal{P}^*)$, obviously $C - \{n\} \notin Carc(\Sigma, \mathcal{P})$ holds. Hence, the lemma. $\square$

Theorem 5.8 Let $\langle N, A, \Sigma \rangle$ be an ATMS, $n \in N$, $\mathcal{P} = \langle \neg \cdot A \rangle$, and $\mathcal{P}^*$ be the same as in Definition 5.6.

$$Newcarc(\Sigma, \neg n, \mathcal{P}) = \begin{cases} \{ S - \{n\} \mid S \in Carc(\Sigma, \mathcal{P}^*), \text{ and } n \in S \} & \text{if } n \in N - \neg \cdot A \\ \{ S - \{n\} \mid S \in Carc(\Sigma, \mathcal{P}), \text{ and } n \in S \} & \text{if } n \in N \cap \neg \cdot A \end{cases}$$

Proof: ($\supseteq$) Obvious from Theorem 5.5 and Lemma 5.7.
($\subseteq$) Let $T \in Newcarc(\Sigma, \neg n, \mathcal{P})$. By Theorem 5.5, $T \cup \{n\} \in PI(\Sigma)$.
(1) If $n \in N - \neg \cdot A$, then $T \cup \{n\}$ belongs to $\mathcal{P}^*$ because T belongs to $\mathcal{P}$. Therefore, $T \cup \{n\} \in Carc(\Sigma, \mathcal{P}^*)$.
(2) If $n \in N \cap \neg \cdot A$, then $T \cup \{n\}$ belongs to $\mathcal{P}$. Therefore, $T \cup \{n\} \in Carc(\Sigma, \mathcal{P})$. $\square$

Theorem 6.2 is in essence the same as [13, Theorem 4.2].

Theorem 6.2 If a clause T is derived by an m.c.l.s. deduction from $\Sigma + C$ and $\mathcal{P}$, then there is a deduction of a clause S with the **Skip & Cut** rule from $\Sigma + C$ and $\mathcal{P}$ such that $\Sigma \cup \{S\} \models T$.

Proof: Let $D_0, D_1, \cdots, D_n$ be an m.c.l.s. deduction of T from $\Sigma + C$ and $\mathcal{P}$. Let l_i be the first literal of $\vec{Q}_i$, where $D_i = \langle P_i, \vec{Q}_i \rangle$ and $0 \leq i \leq n - 1$.

Firstly, if **Skip** is applied for every l_j ($0 \leq j \leq n - 1$) such that $l_j \in L_{\mathcal{P}}$, then T is actually derived from $\Sigma + C$ and $\mathcal{P}$ by using the **Skip & Cut** rule, and of course $\Sigma \cup \{T\} \models T$ holds.

Next, suppose that there exists a structured clause D_j in the m.c.l.s. deduction such that $l_j \in L_{\mathcal{P}}$ but that **Resolve** is applied upon l_j in $\vec{Q}_j$ with a clause $B_j \in \Sigma$. Let m ($1 \leq m \leq n$) be the number of such clauses, and D_k be such a clause where k ($0 \leq k \leq n - 1$) is the largest number. In this case, $D_{k+1} = \langle P_{k+1}, \vec{Q}_{k+1} \rangle$, where

$$\begin{aligned} P_{k+1} &= P_k, \quad \text{and} \\ R_{k+1} &= (B_k - \{\neg l_k\}) \cup (Q_k - \{l_k\}). \end{aligned}$$

In the following proof, to simplify the discussion, we assume that there are no identical, truncated, or reduced literals in R_{k+1}; if they exist, then we can modify the proof appropriately. Now, let U be a clause m.c.l.s. derived from $\Sigma + (B_k - \{\neg l_k\})$ and $\mathcal{P}$, V a clause m.c.l.s. derived from $\Sigma + (Q_k - \{l_k\})$ and $\mathcal{P}$. Here, we can choose such U and V to satisfy

$$T = P_k \cup U \cup V,$$

because T is m.c.l.s. derived from $\Sigma + (P_{k+1} \cup R_{k+1})$ and $\mathcal{P}$.

Now assume that instead of applying **Resolve**, **Skip & Cut** is applied to D_k, deducing $D'_{k+1} = \langle P'_{k+1}, \overrightarrow{Q'_{k+1}} \rangle$, where

$$P'_{k+1} = P_k \cup \{l_k\}, \quad \text{and}$$
$$R'_{k+1} = Q_k - \{l_k\}.$$

Then, $P_k \cup \{l_k\} \cup V$ is m.c.l.s. derived from $\Sigma + (P'_{k+1} \cup R'_{k+1})$ and $\mathcal{P}$, and thus from $\Sigma + C$ and $\mathcal{P}$. Since $\Sigma \cup \{l_k\} \models B_k - \{\neg l_k\}$, $\Sigma \cup \{l_k\} \models U$ holds, and therefore it holds that

$$\Sigma \cup \{(P_k \cup \{l_k\} \cup V)\} \models T.$$

Now let $T_0 = T$ and $T_1 = (P_k \cup \{l_k\} \cup V)$. In the similar way, we can find an m.c.l.s. deduction of T_2 from $\Sigma + C$ and $\mathcal{P}$ such that $\Sigma \cup \{T_2\} \models T_1$, by resetting k to the second largest number. By using the bottom-up manner, we can successively find clauses T_j $(1 \leq j \leq m)$ m.c.l.s. derived from $\Sigma + C$ and $\mathcal{P}$ such that $\Sigma \cup \{T_j\} \models T_{j-1}$. Therefore,

$$\Sigma \cup \{T_m\} \models T_{m-1}, \ \Sigma \cup \{T_{m-1}\} \models T_{m-2}, \ \cdots, \ \Sigma \cup \{T_1\} \models T_0.$$

Hence, $\Sigma \cup \{T_m\} \models T_0$, and we get the theorem. $\square$

KNOWLEDGE ASSIMILATION
and
ABDUCTION

A.C. Kakas[*] and P. Mancarella[**]

[*]Department of Computing, Imperial College,180 Queen's Gate, London SW7 2BZ, UK.
[**]Dipartimento di Informatica, Università di Pisa, Corso Italia, 40, I-56125 Pisa, Italy.

Abstract

We argue that Abduction is useful for the problem of Knowledge Assimilation and use it to study the problems of Belief Revision and Truth Maintenance (TM) associated with the task of assimilating a series of observations $Q_1,...Q_n$. The close connection between Abduction and TM shown in [Reiter&de Kleer87] is explored further to provide a non-monotonic extension of ATMS that incorporates a dependency-directed backtracking mechanism thus combining the capabilities of ATMS and Doyle's TMS. This TM system has a well-defined semantics inherited from the semantics for abduction which is defined through a generalization of stable models based on autoepistemic logic.

1. Introduction

This paper is concerned with the problem of evolution of knowledge and its relation to abductive (hypothetical) reasoning. Abduction has recently received much attention in Artificial Intelligence and has been recognized as an appropriate form of non-monotonic reasoning with incomplete knowledge(see e.g. [Finger&Genesereth85, Cox&Pietrzykoski86, Reiter&de Kleer87 Eshghi88, Poole88, Eshghi&Kowalski89, Kakas&Mancarella89a, Levesque89, Sattar&Goebel89, Shanahan89]). Incomplete knowledge is handled by adopting a knowledge representation framework <T,Ab> where those relations, Ab, which are not defined by the theory T are designated as *abducibles*. Abduction can then be viewed as the process of generating sets of hypotheses (or beliefs) from the abducibles which need to be added to the theory for a given observation to hold. Such a set is referred to as an abductive explanation for the observation.

Abduction can play an important role in the task of Knowledge Assimilation. In many cases, a newly acquired piece of information (observation), Q, should not necessarily be assimilated into the theory by the explicit addition of this information. Instead, it may be useful to use abduction and add an explanation (cause) for Q ie. a set of consistent hypotheses that together with the current theory is sufficient to prove the new information. In other words, the new information is assimilated implicitly by the explicit addition of the hypotheses. Such situations are common eg. in fault diagnosis where assimilating a fault or a symptom naturally demands an explanation. Furthermore, when the new information (observation) conflicts with what is already "known" in the theory an abductive explanation can be used to resolve the potential inconsistency. Consider for example a variant of Kautz's "stolen car " problem [Kautz87] where a theory for natural language contains the fact that "Mary has Book1 at time t_0 " and which uses default persistence to predict that Mary has Book1 at any time after t_0. Then a new piece of information such as "Bob has Book1 at t_1" where $t_1>t_0$ conflicts with the previous default predictions of the theory. One way to handle this is to assimilate the new observation by abducing that some event of transfer of Book1 from Mary to Bob has happened between t_0 and t_1 eg. Mary gave Book1 to Bob or someone stole Book1 from Mary(see [Shanahan89, Kakas&Mancarella89a]).

The particular way in which the knowledge is represented and organized in the theory is another pragmatic reason that makes the implicit assimilation of some information through abductive explanations desirable. Often relevant new information may not always be acquired in terms directly related to the way the theory (or knowledge base) is itself organized. Furthermore, in some cases a new piece of information may carry with it other information that would be lost if this is just added explicitly to the knowledge base only because of the way the knowledge is organized. Such new pieces of information need first to be "translated" into a form that reflects the organization of the knowledge within the theory (knowledge base) if this is to maintain its original structure and no information is lost. This process of translation is an abductive task. An important example of these ideas is the problem of updating deductive databases. Consider for example a deductive database about families organized primarily in terms of the "parent" relation. The database has a relational part containing facts about the Parent relation which is shared by many "Views", (the deductive part of the database), each one consisting of a set of rule definitions of other relations such as "sister", "brother" etc in terms of the parent relation. Then a new piece of information such as sister(Mary,Ann) at one particular view if added explicitly would be contrary to the organization of the database and would not capture related information carried with it such as the fact that Mary and Ann have the same grandparents. Moreover this will not be communicated to the other Views of the database. On the other hand, when this is assimilated, according to the way the database is organized , by adding a common parent for Mary and Ann the new state of the database does not suffer from these problems (see eg. [Kakas&Mancarella90a] and references therein).

The process of KA within a theory with incomplete information is generally faced with the problem of the existence of multiple possible states (models) that can support a new piece of information. This results in the need of a TM component for KA to manage these multiple extensions and to provide a mechanism for revising them whenever an inconsistency occurs. In this paper we will consider the problem of assimilating a series of new pieces of information (observations) $Q_1, ..., Q_n$ and identify this task of TM with that of abduction for these observations. Reiter and de Kleer in [Reiter&de Kleer87] have pointed out a close connection between abduction and the task of Truth Maintenance (TM). We will explore further this connection by developing a TM system based on the abductive framework and procedures of [Eshghi&Kowalski89, Kakas&Mancarella90a, Kakas&Mancarella90b]. This will result in a non-monotonic extension of ATMS [de Kleer86] that incorporates a dependency-directed backtracking mechanism for revision of beliefs with a well defined semantics inherited from an appropriate semantics of abduction which in turn is based on autoepistemic logic [Moore85, Konolige88].

In abductive reasoning within a framework <T,Ab> the problem of multiple states (models), that results in the need of TM, manifests itself in the existence of multiple possible explanations(causes) for any given observation. The introduction of integrity constraints, IC, that the theory together with any required set of abducibles must satisfy, helps to reduce the number of possible explanations by rendering some of these inconsistent. Despite this reduction it is not always true that only a single explanation exists within <T,Ab,IC> but many, possibly incompatible, explanations can still exist. Also at each stage, Q_i, of the process of assimilating Q_1, ..., Q_n it is possible for this new knowledge Q_i to invalidate some of the explanations used to assimilate the previous observations Q_1, ..., Q_{i-1}. Thus the truth maintenance task of abduction is to generate explanations for Q_i and to ensure that these are consistent with those for the previous observations.

There are two main ways for handling the problem of multiple abductive explanations which in turn give rise to different features of any TM system based on abduction. One way is to generate *all* consistent explanations for a given observation and work with all of them simultaneously. This results in a TM system with multiple contexts as in ATMS [de Kleer86]. On the other hand, in some cases it may not be feasible to generate all explanations as there could be a large number of them (possibly infinite [Kakas&Mancarella89a]) and it is more appropriate to handle the problem of multiple explanations by generating only *one* "preferred" explanation at a time. This may be chosen according to some priority or probability assignment on the abducibles([Goebel&Goodwin87, Charniak&Goldman89, Hobbs etal88, Brewka89, Kakas&Mancarella89a]). The choice of explanation could be wrong in the light of subsequent observations and should be retracted. This requires a revision of beliefs mechanism as in Doyle's TMS [Doyle79]. Both these features will be accommodated within our abductive approach resulting in a TM system that combines the capabilities of ATMS and Doyle's TMS.

The rest of the paper is organized as follows. In section 2, we define an appropriate semantics for abduction and develop an abductive proof procedure for a class of frameworks <T,Ab,IC> emphasizing the properties of the explanations generated by this procedure relevant for TM. In section 3 the notion of a consistency environment for an assumption is introduced and the TM system for KA associated to abduction is studied. The generation of tests within the TM whose results can discriminate between incompatible explanations is also discussed in section 3. A comparison with other related work is drawn in section 4.

2. Abduction

We refer to an *abductive framework* as a triple <P, Ab, IC> where[1]

    1) P is a theory comprising of a set of clauses of the form

$$H \leftarrow L_1, \dots , L_k \qquad k \geq 0$$

---

[1] In this paper we will use logic programming terminology found for example in [Lloyd87].

where H is an atom with predicate symbol not in Ab and L_i is a literal. Hence P is a general logic program (with negation) with the only restriction that predicates in Ab have no definition in P^2.

2) Ab is a set of predicate symbols, called *abducible predicates*. The *abducibles* are then all ground atoms with predicate symbol in A.

3) IC is a consistent set of closed formulae.

The semantics of abduction within a framework <P,Ab,IC> depends on the particular way in which the negation and the integrity constraints are treated. In this paper, the negation appearing in P will be given a meaning different from classical negation relying on the stable model semantics [Gelfond&Lifschitz88] and the form of closed world assumption embodied by this semantics. This is a generalization of negation as failure. Let us briefly recall the notion of stable models:

Let P be a logic program and I a Herbrand interpretation. We denote by Π^I the following (possibly infinite) set of ground definite Horn clauses:

$$\Pi^I \quad = \quad \{H \leftarrow B_1,...,B_k \mid H \leftarrow B_1,...,B_k, \neg L_1, ... , \neg L_m \text{ is a clause in}$$
$$\text{in ground(P) and } L_i \notin I \text{ for each } i=1,...,m\}^3.$$

Definition 1([Gelfond&Lifschitz88])
Let P be a logic program and M a Herbrand interpretation. M is a *stable model* of P iff M is equal to the minimal Herbrand model of Π^M.

Abductive explanations within <P,Ab,IC> are then defined as:

Definition 2 ([Kakas&Mancarella90b])
Let <P,Ab,IC> be an abductive framework and Q, a first order closed formula, an observation. Then Q has an *abductive explanation* with set of hypotheses (abducibles) Δ iff there exists a stable model M of $P \cup \Delta$ such that

$$M \models Q \text{ and } M \models IC$$

where $\models$ denotes truth in a ground atomic model.

Stable models find their roots in Moore's Autoepistemic logic [Moore85] for beliefs. A stable model M of P is a closed rational set of beliefs that can be drawn from the theory P and these beliefs. The above definition of abduction is motivated from the fact that abducibles can be viewed as representing *basic* possible beliefs and that the integrity constraints IC express necessary relations on the various beliefs held by an agent (cf. [Reiter88]). Based on this motivation, the notion of stable models for a logic program P can be generalized appropriately for abductive frameworks <P,Ab,IC> as:

Definition 3 ([Kakas&Mancarella90b])
Let <P,Ab,IC> be an abductive framework . Then a *generalized stable model (GSM)*, M, of this framework is any stable model of $P \cup \Delta$ where Δ is any subset of abducibles such that $M \models IC$.

---

2 The assumption that abducibles have no definition in P is not restrictive since any framework in which this is not true can be transformed by introducing new abducibles to an equivalent framework that satisfies this condition.

3 Given a program P, we denote by ground(P) the set of all ground instances of formulae in P over its Herbrand universe.

It can be shown ([Kakas&Mancarella90b]) that the GSMs of <P,Ab,IC> are in one to one correspondence with the stable expansions of an autoepistemic theory obtained from <P,Ab,IC>[4]. Consequently, autoepistemic logic (AEL) will underlie our semantics of abduction and associated TM system. This relation between AEL and TM has recently been studied by many authors (see section 4).

With this definition a framework <P,Ab,IC> can be regarded as representing the collection of its generalized stable models where each such model corresponds to a possible allowed state of the world that the framework describes and an observation has an abductive explanation iff there exists a GSM of <P,Ab,IC> in which the observation is true. In assimilating a new observation Q the collection of models (states) that the framework represents changes allowing only those in which Q is true or in other words those whose defining abducibles (beliefs) can consistently support (explain) Q. The task of TM, provided by abduction, is then to manage the GSMs of the framework as new information is acquired.

In order to simplify the presentation and facilitate a closer comparison with existing TM systems we will make some further restrictions on the abductive frameworks. Firstly, we will consider the case where P is propositional. Then P will correspond directly to the *justifications* of TM [Doyle79] where positive literals correspond to IN justifications and negative literals to OUT justifications. We will assume that the integrity constraints in IC have been transformed into denials (here read "$\leftarrow$" as "$\neg$")

$$\leftarrow L_1, \ldots, L_m$$

where each L_j is a positive or negative literal of an abducible[5], $a^\dagger$ ie $L_j = a^\dagger$ or $L_j = \neg a^\dagger$. These integrity constraints are to be compared with the "nogoods" of ATMS [de Kleer86] where abducibles correspond to the assumables of ATMS. They generalize the "nogoods" by allowing negative literals, ie. OUT assumptions, to be present in these sets of incompatible assumptions. Note that integrity constraints which are not in the form of a denial can be easily accommodated since these can be equivalently transformed to a denial eg. $a^\dagger \lor b^\dagger$ is transformed to $\leftarrow \neg a^\dagger, \neg b^\dagger$.

In [Kakas&Mancarella90b] following the work of [Eshghi&Kowalski89] it is shown that an alternative equivalent way for treating the negation in <P,Ab,IC> is to consider the negations to be part of the abducibles. This treatment of negation is motivated from the fact that in general a logic program P is incomplete in its representation of knowledge about the negations of its predicates and hence, as mentioned in the introduction this incompleteness can be handled by designating the negations as abducibles. This treatment of negation through abduction will enable us to develop in a natural way *non-monotonic* TM systems through abduction.

For this treatment of negation the original abductive framework <P,Ab,IC> is transformed to <P*,Ab$\cup$A*,IC*$\cup$I*> where

     1) P* is the definite Horn clause program obtained from P by replacing each negative literal, $\neg p$ say, by a positive literal, p*, where p* is a new predicate symbol.

---

4 Lack of space does not allow us to describe this transformation into an autoepistemic theory. For further discussion on the relation with autoepistemic logic see [Gelfond&Lifschitz88, Kakas&Mancarella90b].

5 Henceforth abducibles in Ab will be denoted by "$\dagger$".

2) A* is a set of new abducible predicates p*,q*, ... one for each predicate symbol p,q,... in P including the abducible ones in Ab. For an abducible, $a^\dagger$, we will denote its "negative" abducible in A* by a*.

3) IC* is obtained from IC in the same way as P* from P. The new integrity theory I* is defined by $\leftarrow \alpha \wedge \alpha^*$ and $\alpha \vee \alpha^*$ for every predicate symbol α^* in A*.

The integrity theory I* will allow us to assume a negation ,¬q, corresponding to an OUT justification by assuming the abducible q* provided that this is consistent (cf, [Morris88]). Abductive explanations generated in this transformed framework are in 1-1 correspondence with those generated in the original framework:

Theorem 1 ([Kakas&Mancarella90b])
Let <P,Ab,IC> be an abductive framework and <P*,Ab∪A*,IC*∪I*> its transformed framework. Let also an observation Q be a conjunction of literals and Q* its transformation obtained by replacing each negative literal, ¬H by H*. Then Q has an abductive explanation Δ in <P,Ab,IC> iff Q* has an abductive explanation $\Delta^*=\Delta\cup\Delta'$ within <P*,Ab∪A*,IC*∪I*> where Δ' contains abducibles in A* only. Equivalently Q has an abductive explanation Δ iff there exists a set $\Delta^*=\Delta\cup\Delta'$ such that

$$P^*\cup\Delta^* \text{ entails } Q^* \text{ and } M (P^*\cup\Delta^*) \vDash IC^*\cup I^*$$

where M denotes the minimal Herbrand model.

Theorem 1 enables us to define an abductive proof procedure for generating explanations in <P,Ab,IC> by working in the transformed framework. This procedure with its GSM semantics will constitute the basis of · our TM system. Before defining the abductive procedure formally let us illustrate its basic features through an example:

example 1

P: $p \leftarrow \neg q$ IC: $\leftarrow a^\dagger, \neg b^\dagger$
     $q \leftarrow \neg a^\dagger$

The transformed framework is:

P*: $p \leftarrow q^*$ IC*: $\leftarrow a^\dagger, b^*$
     $q \leftarrow a^*$ I*: $\leftarrow q, q^*$ $q \vee q^*$ $\leftarrow p, p^*$ $p \vee p^*$
                                $\leftarrow a^\dagger, a^*$ $a^\dagger \vee a^*$ $\leftarrow b^\dagger, b^*$ $b^\dagger \vee b^*$

Given the observation Q=p to explain the corresponding abductive query $\leftarrow p$ succeeds with the following search space where $\square$ denotes success of a branch and $\blacksquare$ failure:

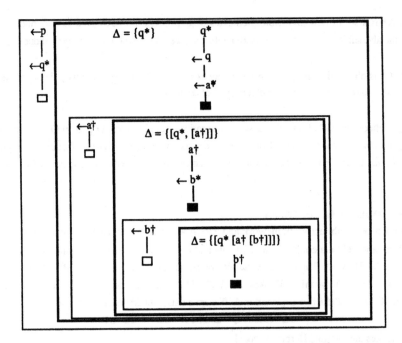

This gives $\Delta^*_p = \{[q^* \, [\, a^\dagger \, [b^\dagger]]]\}$ and subsequently the explanation $\Delta_p = \{a^\dagger, b^\dagger\}$ for Q=p. The structure of Δ^* and its relevance for TM will be explained in the next section. The abductive proof procedure is an interleaving of two activities: (a) searching backwards for a refutation collecting any required abductive assumptions , shown inside an ordinary box, and (b) checking that any required abducible in (a) is consistent, shown in the bold boxes. Note that in a consistency tree success in showing the consistency of the "top" abducible requires that all its branches end up in failure. In the first consistency box of the example the hypothesis q^* is checked against the integrity constraint $\leftarrow q,q^*$. At the tip of the branch the required failure triggers the query $\leftarrow a^\dagger$ due to the integrity constraint $a^\dagger \lor a^*$ which in turn requires $a^\dagger$ to be added to Δ^*_p and checked for consistency as shown in the second bold box.

We will define this procedure by extending the procedures in [Eshghi&Kowalski89, Kakas&Mancarella90a]. In the following definition, given an abducible $L=a^\dagger$ (resp. $L=a^*$) we will denote by L^* the abducible a^* (resp. $a^\dagger$). If $L=q^*$ then L^* will denote q .

Definition (*abductive proof procedure*)
An *abductive derivation* from $(G_1 \, \Delta^*_1)$ to $(G_n \, \Delta^*_n)$ in $<P^*, Ab \cup A^*, IC^* \cup I^*>$ via a selection rule R is a sequence

$$(G_1 \, \Delta^*_1), \; (G_2 \, \Delta^*_2), \; \ldots \; , (G_n \, \Delta^*_n)$$

such that each G_i has the form $\leftarrow L_1, \ldots, L_k$, $R(G_i)=L_j$ and $(G_{i+1} \, \Delta^*_{i+1})$ is obtained according to one of the following rules:

A1)   If L_j is not abducible, then $G_{i+1}=C$ and $\Delta^*_{i+1}=\Delta^*_i$ where C is the   resolvent of   some clause in P^* with G_i on the selected literal L_j;

A2)   If L_j is abducible and $L_j \in \Delta_i$, then $G_{i+1}= \leftarrow L_1, \ldots, L_{j-1}, L_{j+1}, \ldots, L_k$ and $\Delta^*_{i+1}=\Delta^*_i$;

A3)   If L_j is abducible, $L_j \notin \Delta^*_i$ and $L_j^* \notin \Delta^*_i$ and there exists a *consistency*   *derivation* from $(\{L_j\} \Delta^*_i \cup \{L_j\})$ to $(\{\} \Delta')$ then $G_{i+1} = \leftarrow L_1,...,L_{j-1}, L_{j+1},...,L_k$ and $\Delta^*_{i+1} = \Delta'$.

Steps A1) and A2) are SLD-resolution steps with the rules of P^* and abductive hypotheses, respectively. In step A3) a new abductive hypotheses is required and it is added to the current set of hypotheses provided it is consistent.

A *consistency derivation* for an abducible α from (α, Δ^*_1) to $(F_n \Delta^*_n)$ in $<P^*,Ab \cup A^*,IC^* \cup I^*>$ is a sequence

$$(\alpha, \Delta^*_1), (F_1 \Delta^*_1), (F_2 \Delta^*_2) ... (F_n \Delta^*_n)$$

where :

i)F_1 is the union of all goals of the form $\leftarrow L_1,...,L_n$ obtained by resolving the abducible α with the denials in $IC^* \cup I^*$ with no such goal being empty, $\square$;

ii)for each $i>1$ F_i has the form $\{\leftarrow L_1,...,L_k\} \cup F_i'$ and *for some* $j=1,...,k$ $(F_{i+1} \Delta^*_{i+1})$ is obtained according to one of the following rules:

C1)   If L_j is not abducible, then $F_{i+1} = C' \cup F_i'$ where C' is the set of all   resolvents of clauses in P^* with $\leftarrow L_1,...,L_k$ on the literal L_j and $\square \notin C'$,   and $\Delta^*_{i+1}=\Delta^*_i$;

C2)   If L_j is abducible, $L_j \in \Delta^*_i$ and $k>1$, then $F_{i+1}=\{\leftarrow L_1,...,L_{j-1},$ $L_{j+1},...,L_k\} \cup F_i'$ and $\Delta^*_{i+1}=\Delta^*_i$;

C3)   If L_j is abducible, $L_j^* \in \Delta^*_i$, then $F_{i+1}=F_i'$ and $\Delta^*_{i+1}=\Delta^*_i$;

C4)   If L_j is an abducible, $L_j \notin \Delta^*_i$ and $L_j^* \notin \Delta^*_i$, and there exists an *abductive*   *derivation* from $(\leftarrow L_j^* \Delta^*_i)$ to $(\square \Delta')$ then $F_{i+1}=F_i'$ and $\Delta^*_{i+1}=\Delta'$.

The consistency derivations do not rely on a particular selection rule, since in general all the possible ways in which a conjunction $\leftarrow L_1,...,L_k$ can fail should be explored. In case C1) the current branch splits into as many branches as the number of resolvents of $\leftarrow L_1,...,L_k$ with the clauses in P^* on L_j. If the empty clause is one of such resolvents the whole consistency check fails. In case C3) the current branch is already consistent under the assumptions in Δ^*_i, and this branch is dropped from the consistency checking. Case C4) corresponds to the enforcement of the disjunctive integrity constraint $L_j^* \vee L_j$: the current branch of the consistency search space can be dropped provided $\leftarrow L_j^*$ is abductively provable.

Theorem 2 *(soundness)*

Let $<P,Ab,IC>$ be an abductive framework where P is call consistent and a literal Q an observation. If $(\leftarrow Q^* \{\})$ has an adbuctive derivation to $(\square, \Delta^*)$ then the subset Δ of Δ^* of abducibles in Ab is an abductive explanation of Q.

The procedure as defined here is complete when no predicate in P depends on itself ie. P contains no "loops". Also an explanation generated by the procedure is minimal , ie. no proper subset is an explanation, with respect to the particular "path" (ie. the set of cluases of P) from which this is found but it is possible for another solution to be a proper subset of the first. When all solutions are generated it is often useful to consider only the minimal ones. (We will not be concerned further with the minimality requirement.). For simplicity, in the rest of this paper we will restrict ourselves to the case where P is stratified (ie. no proposition depends on its negation , see eg. [Lloyd87]) although the definitions and results can be extended to the non-stratified case.

A property of the procedure which is important for the problem of knowledge assimilation and TM that concern us here is the fact that an inconsistency between any two sets of abducibles is always reduced to a direct clash between some abducible, $a^\dagger$, in Ab and the abducible , a^*, representing its negation.

Theorem 3
Let $<P,Ab,IC>$ be an abductive framework where P is stratified. Let also Δ^*_1, Δ^*_2 be any two explanations, not necessarily for the same observation, generated by the abductive procedure such that not all the integrity constraints IC are true in the stable model of $P \cup \Delta_1 \cup \Delta_2$ where Δ_1, Δ_2 are the subsets of abducibles in Ab of Δ^*_1, Δ^*_2 respectively. Then there exists at least one pair of abducibles $(a^\dagger, a^*)$ such that $a^\dagger \in \Delta^*_1$ and $a^* \in \Delta^*_2$ or vice versa[6].

To illustrate this theorem consider the following example:

example 2
P: $p \leftarrow \neg q$ $q \leftarrow \neg a^\dagger$ $r \leftarrow b^\dagger$;   IC: $\leftarrow a^\dagger, c^\dagger$ $\leftarrow \neg c^\dagger, b^\dagger$

and the two observations $Q_1 = p$, $Q_2 = r$. Possible explanations for these are $\{a^\dagger\}$ and $\{b^\dagger, c^\dagger\}$ respectively which are incompatible with each other. The corresponding explanations that are generated by the abductive proof procedure are $\Delta^*_p = \{[q^* [a^\dagger [c^* [b^*]]]]\}$ and $\Delta^*_r = \{[b^\dagger [c^\dagger [a^*]]]\}$ showing explicitly the incompatibility between these two sets of abducibles. In other words the procedure takes account of the integrity constraints in such a way that all potentially incompatible explanations explicitly display their incompatibility. This will play an important role in TM not only in signalling an inconsistency but also in directing the required revision of beliefs.

3.Truth Maintenance

In order to describe in more detail the TM system associated with our abductive proof procedure let us examine more closely the explanations Δ^* generated by this procedure. As indicate by the examples in the previous section, these are not simply a collection of hypotheses but in fact have a structured form according to the interleaving of abductive and consistency derivations.

Definition 4
Let $(\alpha, \{\alpha\}), ..., (\{\}, \{\alpha\} \cup \Delta^*)$ be a successful consistency derivation for an abducible α. Then the set Δ^* of abducibles is called a *consistency environment* for α, denoted by *con_env(α)*.

---

6   These abducibles can be used to derive discriminating tests for incompatible explanations whose results can decide between them as we shall see below in section 3.2 (cf. with the crucial literals of [Sattar&Goebel89]).

In example 1, $con\_env(q^*) = \{a^\dagger, b^\dagger\}$ and $con\_env(a^\dagger) = \{b^\dagger\}$. In example 2, $con\_env(q^*) = \{a^\dagger, c^*, b^*\}$. Note that an abducible can have many different, possibly incompatible with each other, consistency environments. The logical meaning of the consistency environments is given as follows:

Proposition 1

Let <P,Ab,IC> be a given abductive framework and Δ^* be any consistency environment for an abducible α. Then for any generalized stable model M in which Δ^* is true[7] $M \cup \{\alpha\}$ also satisfies the integrity constraints IC ie. $M \cup \{\alpha\} \models IC$. Conversely, if there exists at least one generalized stable model M of <P,Ab,IC> where α is true then at least one of its consistency environments must also be true in M.

The general form of an explanation Δ^*_Q for an observation Q will be as:
$$\Delta^*_Q = \{ \ (ab_1 [\ (ab_{11} [\ (ab_{111} ...)] \ ]) ... (ab_{1n} [\ (ab_{1n1} ...)] \ )])$$
$$(ab_2 [\ (ab_{21} [\ (...)] \ ) ...])$$
$$...$$
$$(ab_k ...) \ \}.$$

Equivalently, we have the following "labels":

    i) $(ab_1, ... ab_k)$ for Q indicating that Q would follow from the theory if $ab_1, ..., ab_k$ are true.

and

    ii) recursively for each abducible a consistency environment "label" namely $[ab_{11}, ... ab_{1n}]$ for ab_1, $[ab_{111}, ... ab_{11m}]$ for ab_{11} etc.

The consistency environments allow the integrity constraints to play a *dynamical* role in the generation of explanations and in TM. The structured form of the explanations Δ^*_Q together with the result of theorem 3 will enable us to guide the TM by providing a dependency-directed backtracking mechanism in the required revision of beliefs. Another important consequence of these properties of the explanations is that during the consistency checking of an abducible no reasoning forward from it with the rules (justifications) in P is required (see the definition of consistency derivation above).

Let us now return to the problem of assimilation through abduction of a series of observations $Q_1,...,Q_n$ together with its TM problem, as discussed in the introduction, and study the main characteristics of the related TM system. The task of TM is as follows: given the next observation Q_i in the series $Q_1, ..., Q_n$ generate explanations, Δ_{Q_i}, for Q_i and augment the already existing explanations for $Q_1, ..., Q_{i-1}$ to produce compatible sets of hypotheses under which $Q_1, ..., Q_{i-1}, Q_i$ hold true. The explanations Δ_{Q_i} can be viewed as "labels" under which a piece of "data", Q_i, holds. Comparing with ATMS [de Kleer86] the explanation sets correspond to the *environments* sets of assumptions under which *nodes* hold.

The main problem of TM is to handle correctly the integrity constraints so that it avoids generating hypotheses (or environments) which are incompatible with each other. When a new observation Q_i is acquired its explanations $\Delta^*_{Q_i}$, generated by the abductive proof procedure, are such that possible incompatibilities with the explanations for the previous observations can be handled dynamically during the

---

7   Here by abuse of terminology we say that an abducible α^*(resp. q^*) in A^* is true in a model if $\neg a \dagger$(resp. $\neg q$) is true in this model.

generation of $\Delta^*{}_{Qi}$. Incompatible explanations for Q_i and $Q_1,..., Q_{i-1}$ are spotted (see Theorem 3) and rejected as the explanations for Q_i are generated. Depending on the way chosen to handle the problem of multiple explanations either by finding all of them, case1, or finding a "preferred" one, case 2, a different type of TM system is obtained. In the first case where it is possible to generate all explanations this results in maintaining the list of all consistent sets of hypotheses under which all observations $Q_1,..., Q_i$ hold. Some elements of this list may be incompatible with each other. In the second case where only one explanation is generated at a time the new observation Q_i may invalidate some of the chosen explanations for the observations in $Q_1,..., Q_{i-1}$ and a revision of beliefs that may involve backtracking to re-explain one or more of these observations is required.

3.1 Truth Maintenance Systems

Case1: Consider first the case where all explanations are generated for each observation and the problem of assimilation of two observations Q_1, Q_2 . For a set of observations Q_1 , ...,Q_i , i>2, at each stage this can be effectively reduced to two observations, namely $Q \equiv Q_1, ..., Q_{i-1}$ and Q_i. Hence we assume that all the explanations for Q_1 have been generated and we want to consider the generation of explanations for Q_2. During the generation of any specific explanation $\Delta^*{}_2$ for Q_2 by the abductive proof procedure there are two cases of interest:

    a) An abducible $a^\dagger$(resp. a*) is needed for $\Delta^*{}_{Q2}$ where a*(resp. $a^\dagger$) already appears in some explanation of Q_1, $\Delta^*{}_{1(k)}$ say. Then as far as this particular explanation $\Delta^*{}_2$ is concerned the explanation $\Delta^*{}_{1(k)}$ is rejected and is not considered any more. If at any stage all the explanations for Q_1 have been rejected this particular attempt to generate an explanation for Q_2 fails and another one is sought. (See below in case 2 for comments about how we backtrack from this failure.)

    b) An abducible α is needed for $\Delta^*{}_2$ which already appears in one of the currently remaining (from (a)) explanations of Q_1, $\Delta^*{}_{1(k)}$ say. Then this abducible α is included in $\Delta^*{}_2$ together with its consistency environment from $\Delta^*{}_{1(k)}$ without the need for the abductive proof procedure to examine the consistency of α. Accordingly, the abductive proof procedure should be modified (step A2) so that if an abducible is required in more than one consistency environment then this is recorded in each one with its own consistency environment. If the same abducible α appears in more than one explanation for Q_1 then we have a forking in the generation of the explanation for Q_2 which may result in more than one such explanation.

When the generation of an explanation $\Delta^*{}_2$ for Q_2 ends successfully the union of $\Delta^*{}_2$ with each remaining explanation $\Delta^*{}_{1(j)}$ for Q_1 is taken giving a set of explanations $\Delta_{1,2(j)} = \Delta^*{}_{1(j)} \cup \Delta^*{}_2$ for Q_1 and Q_2. Then other explanations for Q_2 are sought in the same way , by backtracking to the choice points of the abductive proof procedure.

Case 2: Let us now consider the case where only one explanation is generated at a time for each observation and assume that explanations $\Delta^*{}_1, ..., \Delta^*{}_{i-1}$ have been generated for $Q_1, ..., Q_{i-1}$ respectively. Again during the generation of the explanation $\Delta^*{}_i$ for Q_i the same two cases of interest can occur. When an abducible $a^\dagger$(resp. a*) is needed for the current state of $\Delta^*{}_i$ where a*(resp. $a^\dagger$) already appears in some explanation Δ^*_j (j <i) we need to revise one of these incompatible explanations Δ^*_i, Δ^*_j. We may try first to continue the currently generated explanation for Q_i in another path from the point at which $a^\dagger$(resp. a^*) was found. If this fails we are directed to backtrack to the observation Q_j and more specifically to the abducible α in Δ^*_j whose consistency environment in Δ^*_j contains a^*(resp. $a^\dagger$) and try to find another consistency environment for α eg. if $\Delta^*_j=\{$ (ab_1 [(ab_{11} [(ab_{111} ...)]) ...(ab_{1n} [(ab_{1n1} ...)])]) } and a^*(resp. $a^\dagger$) is, ab_{423} say, then we backtrack to ab_{42}. This may in turn introduce new incompatibilities with Δ^*_i or Δ^*_k for some k, (k<i), which are resolved in the same way[8]. The result of the TM is the union of Δ^*_1, ..., Δ^*_{i-1} and Δ^*_i.

The soundness of these TMS follows from the soundness of the abductive proof procedure (theorem 3). If Δ^* is a resulting set of hypotheses in either case 1 or 2 as described above then Δ^* corresponds, according to theorem 1, to an explanation for the conjunction of Q_1, ..., Q_n ie. there exists a GSM of <P,Ab,IC>, defined by the subset of Δ^* of abducibles in Ab, in which the conjunction of Q_1, ..., Q_n is true.

3.2 Discriminating Tests

Within abduction and hypothetical reasoning in general, the problem of the existence of multiple different sets of hypotheses can be tackled further by finding and performing tests whose outcome can help to decide which explanations are more appropriate(see eg.[de Kleer&Williams87, Console et al89, Sattar&Goebel89, Evans&Kakas90]) . The general idea is to use these tests to refute some of the explanations .

Definition
An explanation Δ^* is said to be *refuted* if $P^* \cup \Delta^*$ entails some atom t and t has been observed and found false ie. $\neg$t is found to be true.

This is particularly useful when it is known that the different explanations are finite in number and mutually exclusive (incompatible). In this case it may be possible to refute all explanations except one : the "actual" cause of the observation (cf. with competing scientific theories and experimental tests to decide between them (see eg. [Popper59]). Here we will study briefly the problem of generation of discriminating tests within the TM systems developed above based on the result of theorem 3. Since this theorem ensures that the incompatibility between any two sets of hypotheses is always made explicit by the abductive proof procedure such discriminating tests are not considered until this happens eg. at case (a) of the TM above.

When this happens ie. when an abducible a^*(resp. $a^\dagger$) is needed during the generation of some explanation, Δ_2, and $a^\dagger$(resp. a^*) already appears in a completed explanation, Δ_1, we can use this "identification" of the incompatibility of Δ_2 and Δ_1 to suggest a series of tests that can decide which of the two should be rejected. (NB. Such an atom $a^\dagger$ corresponds to a crucial literal in [Sattar&Goebel89].) It may be that $a^\dagger$ itself can be tested (eg. $a^\dagger$ is "askable" in Query-the-User [Sergot83]) and so depending on the outcome of this test one of Δ_2, Δ_1 will be refuted and hence rejected eg. if $a^\dagger$ is found to be true(false) then $\Delta_2(\Delta_1)$ is refuted. When

---

8   If the explanations are chosen according to some priority or probability assignment then this task of choosing which observation of the conflicting ones to re-explain becomes more involved.

$a^\dagger$ can not be tested directly we reason forward from $a^\dagger$ and its consistency environment in Δ_1 with the rules of P* to a find a testable (eg. "askable") conclusion, t say. Then if the result of testing finds t false Δ_1 is refuted. On the other hand, if t is found to be true we continue the process of forward reasoning to testable conclusions. This process can be made more sophisticated eg. by first checking that the conclusion t reached from $a^\dagger$ does not also follow from a* and P* but we will not pursue this further here (see eg. [de Kleer&Williams87]). Also an analogous process can be used to discriminate between two completed incompatible explanations . It is worth noting that the results of the tests can be viewed as "active" information that is assimilated alongside with $Q_1, ..., Q_2$ but this knowledge is of a different nature. Their effect is to "filter out" explanations and hence their status is the same as that of the integrity constraints IC.

4. Related work

It is useful to compare again the TM system defined here directly with ATMS. The program P corresponds to the justifications of ATMS with the important difference that these can contain negation corresponding to OUT justifications. The structured abductive explanations generalize the basic ATMS environments in two ways: (i) the assumptions, through the negations, effectively contain both IN and OUT information and (ii) there is an extra level in the abductive explanations: each assumption in the environment has its own "environment" namely its consistency environment. With these consistency environments all integrity constraints are effectively reduced to the simple form of nogood($a^\dagger$,a*) and this in turn provides the TM system with a dependency-directed mechanism for revision of beliefs. Furthermore the integrity constraints IC generalize the nogoods of ATMS since due to the fact that we allow the presence of negation other forms of integrity constraints can be equivalently transformed to a denial. These generalizations provide a non-monotonic extension to ATMS. In [de Kleer88] the ATMS has been generalized to allow negated assumptions but this has not fully captured non-monotonic justifications.

In [Reiter& de Kleer87] an extension of the ATMS is defined generalizing the Horn clause justifications of ATMS to allow any propositional clause, and its relation to abductive reasoning is studied. In the particular case of Horn clause theories their results show that the ATMS can be used to generate all minimal abductive explanations for any atomic observation. A related abductive characterization of TM is presented in [Giordano&Martelli90] based on a transformation that introduces all the contrapositives of the justifications and integrity constraints and then maps this into an abductive framework. The relation of TM to abduction has also been used in [Inoue90] to develop TM systems based on abductive proof procedures.

Our treatment of negations as abducibles is related to techniques employed in [Dressler88] where OUT-justifiers are replaced by new propositions called out-assumptions. A nogood inference rule is then introduced to deal with inconsistencies. This rule has a similar effect to our integrity constraints $\leftarrow \alpha \wedge \alpha^*$ and $\alpha \vee \alpha^*$ for each negated abducible α^*.

In [Junker89] a non-monotonic extension of ATMS that incorporates the dependency-directed backtracking feature of Doyle's TMS is defined: a hybrid TM system as described by Junker. This is achieved by extending the basic ATMS with an additional test algorithm based on an adaptation of Doyle's TMS rule for labelling a node with OUT, namely "if all justifications of a node are invalid label this node with OUT". This again is directly related to the integrity constraints for the negation abducibles in our system. Furthermore, in view of the close relationship (see [Konolige88]) between default logic [Reiter80], which is used to verify the correctness of the system developed in [Junker89], and autoepistemic logic which underlies our GSM semantics for abduction, the semantic characterizations of our systems are closely related. Similar connections also exist with the work in [Junker&Konolige90] where the relation between autoepistemic and default logics with non-monotonic TM systems is considered. These authors show a one to one correspondence between a subclass of default theories and TMS theories and use this to compute the extensions of such theories.

A semantic formalization of TM systems in the absence of integrity constraints within autoepistemic logic has been recently proposed by various authors [Elkan90, Fujiwara&Honiden89, Pimentel&Cuadrado89, Reinfrank et al89]. Our semantics of GSMs for abduction and TM, with their direct relation to autoepistemic logic [Kakas&Mancarella90b], follows this proposal and extends their formalization to the case where integrity constraints are allowed.

In [Southwick90] a reason maintenance system for backward reasoning systems in a Prolog environment is developed with an effective mechanism for revision of beliefs. This has been successfully applied to the problem of user dialogue maintenance between the user and knowledge-based systems.

Conclusions

We have developed through abduction a non-monotonic TM system and applied it to the problem of Knowledge Assimilation. The TM system has a well-defined semantics inherited from an appropriate semantics for abduction based on autoepistemic logic. This has resulted in a non-monotonic extension of ATMS which incorporates a dependency-directed mechanism as in Doyle's TMS. The abductive proof procedure underlying the TM system can be implemented in Prolog using standard meta-programming techniques to extend SLD resolution.

More general non-monotonic TM systems can be developed in the same way by exploiting further the connection with abduction. For example, we can consider abductive frameworks <P,Ab,IC> where P is non-propositional and hypotheses need not be ground but can involve variables. Also the integrity constraints IC can be generalized to allow any well formed first order formula.

An important area where these ideas can be applied is that of updating Databases where the abductive truth maintenance system can be used to manage the updates and maintain consistency as the database evolves through a series of updates. This application is studied in [Kakas90].

68

Acknowledgements

We wish to thank K. Eshghi, C. Evans, R.A. Kowalski, F. Sadri, M. Sergot and M. Shanahan for many useful discussions. This work has been partly carried out under the COMPULOG ESPRIT Basic Research Project 3012. The second author acknowledges financial support from the Italian National Research Council (CNR).

References

[Brewka89] Brewka G., Preferred Subtheories: An Extended Logical Framework for Default Reasoning, in Proceedings IJCAI-89 (1989) p 1043.

[Cox&Pietrzykowski86] Cox P.T. and Pietrzykowski T., Causes for Events: Their Computation and Applications, in Proceedings CADE-86, p 608.

[Charniak&Goldman89] Charniak E. and Goldman R., A Semantics for Probabilistic Quantifier-Free First-Order Languages, with Particular Application to Story Understanding, in Proceedings IJCAI-89 (1989) p1074.

[Console et al89] Console L., Dupre D.T. and Torasso P., A Theory of Diagnosis for Incomplete Causal Models, in Proceedings IJCAI 89 (1989) p. 1311.

[de Kleer86] de Kleer J., An Assumption-Based TMS, Artificial Intelligence 28 (1986), p 127.

[de Kleer88] de Kleer J., A General Labelling Algorithm for Assumption-Based Truth Maintenance, in Proceedings of AAAI-88 (1988) p. 188.

[Doyle79] Doyle J. , A Truth Maintenance System, Artificial Intelligence 12 (1979), p 231.

[Dressler88] Dressler O., Extending the basic ATMS, in Proceedings of ECAI-88 (1988).

[Eshghi88] Eshghi K., Abductive Planning with Event Calculus, in Proceedings 5th International Conference on Logic Programming (1988), p 562.

[Eshghi&Kowalski89] Eshghi K. and Kowalski R.A., Abduction Compared with Negation by Failure, in Proceedings 6th International Conference on Logic Programming (1989), p 234.

[Evans&Kakas90] Evans C. and Kakas A.C., Hypothetico-Deductive Reasoning, Imperial College preprint, (1990).

[Elkan90] Elkan , A Rational Reconstruction of Non-Monotonic Truth Maintenance Systems, Artificial Intelligence 43 (1990), p 219.

[Finger&Genesereth85] Finger J.J. and Genesereth M.R., RESIDUE: A Deductive Approach to Design Synthesis, Stanford University Report no. CS-85-1035. (1985).

[Fujiwara&Honiden89] Fujiwara Y. and Honiden S., Relating the TMS to Autoepistemic Logic, in Proceedings IJCAI-89 (1989) p 1199.

[Gelfond&Lifschitz88] Gelfond M., and Lifschitz V., The Stable Model Semantics for Logic Programming, in Proceedings 5th International Conference on Logic Programming (1988), p 1070.

[Giordano&Martelli90] Giordano L. and Martelli A., An Abductive Characterization of the TMS, in Proceedings of the nineth European Conference on Artificial Intelligence, ECAI-90, Stockholm, (1990) p 308.

[Goebel& Goodwin87] Goebel R.G., Goodwin S.D>, Applying Theory Formation to the Planning Problem, in The Frame Problem in Arificial Intelligence : Proc. 1987 Workshop, (ed.) F. Brown, Morgan Kaufman, Los Altos, CA, (1987).

[Hobbs et al88] Hobbs J.R., Stickel M., Martin P. and Edwards D., Interpetation as Abduction, in Proceedings of the 26th Annual Meeting of the ACL, (1988), p 95.

[Inoue90] Inoue K., An Abductive Procedure for the CMS/ATMS, this volume.

[Junker89] Junker U., A Correct Non-Monotonic ATMS, in Proceedings IJCAI-89 (1989) p 1049.

[Junker&Konolige90] Junker U. and Konolige K., Computing the Extensions of Autoepistemic and Default Logics with a TMS, in Proceedings of Conference on Theoretical Aspects of Reasoning about Knowledge, Asilomar, CA, (1990).

[Kakas90] Kakas A.C., Belief Revision for Deductive Databases, in Proceedings of the first International Workshop on the Deductive Approach to Information Systems and Databases, Barcelona, Spain, (1990) p 111.

[Kakas&Mancarella89a] Kakas A.C. and Mancarella P., Anomalous models and Abduction, in Proceedings 2nd International Symposium on Artificial Intelligence, Monterrey, Mexico, 23-27 October 1989.

[Kakas&Mancarella90a] Kakas A.C. and Mancarella P., Database Updates through Abduction, in Proceedings of the 16th International Conference on Very Large Databases, VLDB-90, Brisbane, Australia, (1990) p 48.

[Kakas&Mancarella90b] Kakas A.C. and Mancarella P., Generalized Stable Models: a Semantics for Abduction, in Proceedings of the ninth European Conference on Artificial Intelligence, ECAI-90, Stockholm, (1990) p 385.

[Kautz86] Kautz H., The Logic of Persistence, in Proceedings AAAI-86, (1986) p 401.

[Konolige88] Konolige K., On the relation between Default and Autoepistemic Logic, Artificial Intelligence 35 (1988), p 343.

[Levesque89] Levesque H.J., A Knowledge-level Account of Abduction, in Proceedings IJCAI-89 (1989), p 1061.

[Lloyd87] Lloyd J.W., Foundations of Logic Programming, Second Edition, Springer Verlag (1987).

[Moore85] Moore R.C., Semantical Considerations on Nonmonotonic Logic Artificial Intelligence, Artificial Intelligence 25 (1985), p 75.

[Mooris88] Mooris P.H., The Anomalous Extension Problem in Default Reasoning, Artificial Intelligence 35 (1988), p 383.

[Poole88] Poole D.L., A Logical Framework for Default Reasoning, Artificial Intelligence 36 (1988), p 27.

[Popper59] Popper K., The Logic of Scientific Discovery, Basic Books, New York, 1959.

[Pimentel&Cuadrado89] Pimentel S.G. and Cuadrado J.L., A Truth Maintenance System Based on Stable Models, in Proceedings of North American Conference on Logic Programming (1989), p 274.

[Reinfrank et al88] Reinfrank M., Dressler O. and Brewka G., On the Relation between Truth Maintenance and Autoepistemic logic, in Proceedings IJCAI-89 (1989) p1206.

[Reiter80] Reiter R., A Logic for Default Reasoning, Artificial Intelligence 13 (1980), p 81.

[Reiter88] Reiter R., On Integrity Constraints, in Proceedings of 2nd Conference on Theoretical Aspects of Reasoning about Knowledge, Asilomar, CA (1988), p 97.

[Reiter&de Kleer87] Reiter R., J. de Kleer, Foundations of Assumption-Based Truth Manintenance Systems, in Proceedings AAAI-87, Seattle, WA,(1987), p183.

[Sattar&Goebel89] Sattar A. and Goebel R., Using Crucial Literals to Select Better Theories, University of Alberta preprint (1989).

[Sergot83] Sergot M., A Query-the-User Facility for Logic Programming" in Integrated Interractive Computer Systems, (eds.) P. Degano and E. Sandewell North Holland Press (1983).

[Shanahan89] Shanahan M.P., Prediction is Deduction but Explanation is Abduction, in Proceedings IJCAI-89 (1989).

[Southwick90] Southwick R.W., ABRMS: A Reason Maintenance System for Backward Reasoning Systems, Imperial College preprint (1990).

TRUTH MAINTENANCE SYSTEMS
AND BELIEF REVISION

Laura Giordano and Alberto Martelli

Dipartimento di Informatica - Università di Torino
C.so Svizzera 185 - 10149 TORINO (ITALY)
E-mail: mrt@di.unito.it
i2unix!leonardo!mrt

Abstract

In this paper we give some equivalent characterization of the TMS [1] contradiction resolution process, relying mainly on the intuitive idea that a contrapositive use of justifications is needed to resolve inconsistencies. To this purpose, we define a notion of three-valued labelling in which a new label FALSE is introduced with the meaning of "being believed to be false". Moreover, we show that, given a set of justifications, it is possible to translate it into an equivalent set of justifications which can be labelled with the usual two-valued labelling. This translation can be used together with the transformation in [3] to convert a set of non-monotonic justifications to an abduction framework, thus providing the TMS with an abductive characterization. Finally, we propose an equivalent characterization for the TMS which is based on a generalization of stable models.

1 Introduction

Usually, the set J of justifications the TMS is given consists of implications of the form

$$A_1 \wedge ... \wedge A_n \wedge OUT(B_1) \wedge ... \wedge OUT(B_m) \rightarrow C,$$

where each A_i (IN-justifier), each B_j (OUT-justifier or out-assumption) and C are propositions and $n, m \geq 0$. The intended meaning of such a justification is the following: "belief in $A_1, ..., A_n$ and disbelief in $B_1, ..., B_m$ justify the belief in C". A distinguished propositional letter $\perp$ is used to represent contradiction and, when used as consequent of a clause, it allows constraints to be stated.

The purpose of a TMS is to assign all propositions in J a label IN (believed) or OUT (disbelieved) in such a way that all the justifications in J are satisfied by the labelling, the labelling is *consistent* and each proposition labelled IN is justified by a non circular argument (that is, the labelling is *well-founded*). The presence of constraints in the language allows inconsistencies to be generated. A labelling is consistent if it labels the proposition $\perp$ OUT.

Given a set of justifications, the TMS tries to compute a consistent and well-founded labelling. If it is the case that the $\perp$ node is labelled IN, a contradiction has been found and the TMS has to trace back to find the non-monotonic justifications underlying the contradiction, so as to revise the labelling. This process, called *dependency-directed backtracking*, consists in installing a new justification to get rid of the contradiction by putting IN one of the OUT nodes supporting the belief in $\perp$. Therefore, not only does dependency-directed backtracking produce the switching from a belief state to another one for the given set of justifications, but it also modifies the set of justifications itself. We will show that conflict resolution process mainly relies on an *active* use of constraints, which consists in reasoning backward from the contradiction $\perp$ using justifications in their contrapositive directions. In fact, performing several inference steps through the contrapositives of the justifications, starting from $\perp$, allowes belief revision by forcing some OUT-assumptions to be labelled IN. Let us consider the following well-known example.

Example 1:
    (1) REPUBLICAN
    (2) QUAKER
    (3) QUAKER $\wedge$ OUT(AB_QUAKER) $\rightarrow$ DOVE
    (4) REPUBLICAN $\wedge$ OUT(AB_REPUBLICAN) $\rightarrow$ HAWK
    (5) DOVE $\wedge$ HAWK $\rightarrow \perp$
The only well-founded labelling for this set of justifications
    L:
        IN { QUAKER, REPUBLICAN, HAWK, DOVE, $\perp$ }
        OUT { AB_QUAKER, AB_REPUBLICAN }
is inconsistent. On the other hand, the labellings
    L_1:
        IN { QUAKER, REPUBLICAN, AB_QUAKER , HAWK }
        OUT { AB_REPUBLICAN, DOVE, $\perp$ }
and
    L_2:
        IN { QUAKER, REPUBLICAN, AB_REPUBLICAN, DOVE }
        OUT { AB_QUAKER, HAWK, $\perp$ },
that correspond to the two possible intended interpretations, are not well-founded since there is no support for AB_QUAKER being IN in the labelling L_1 and for AB_REPUBLICAN being IN in L_2. However, they can be obtained by the process of dependency-directed backtracking by introducing new justifications. For instance, the labelling L_1 can be computed by the TMS by introducing the new justification HAWK $\wedge$ QUAKER $\rightarrow$ AB_QUAKER. This labelling turns out to be well-founded w.r.t. the new set of justifications. To explain how the new justification is obtained, notice that in labelling L, the contradiction $\perp$ is supported by justification (5), and, in turn, the proposition DOVE is supported by justification (3). Thus $\perp$ is supported by HAWK and QUAKER being labelled IN and AB_QUAKER being labelled OUT. To eliminate the contradiction the TMS adds the above justification which states that if HAWK and QUAKER are believed, then AB_QUAKER must be believed as well.

Recent proposals have provided TMSs with declarative and logic semantics [4, 11-13]. All of them, however, do not capture the idea of dependency-directed backtracking, but they only provide a semantic characterization of TMS well-founded labelling in absence of conflicting informations. In [9] non-normal defaults are recognized as being suitable for characterizing well-founded labellings. However, non-normal defaults, in contrast to TMS, do not allow beliefs to be revised on account for new conflicting informations. In [10] a solution is proposed by defining the notion of *stable closure*, that "appears to capture at least in part the idea of dependency-directed backtracking". It is noted, however, that stable closure semantics give some unexpected results from the TMS viewpoint.

In this paper we aim at giving an alternative characterization of the contradiction resolution process, by relying mainly on the intuitive idea that a contrapositive use of justifications is needed to resolve inconsistencies. To convince of this, let us come back to Example 1. It is easy to see that, as regards the labelling L_1, a justification for AB_QUAKER can be found if we are allowed to use the initial justifications also in their contrapositive direction. In fact, if we assume that AB_REPUBLICAN is OUT, by justification (4) we have a support for HAWK to be IN. Moreover, since $\perp$ has to be false, we can deduce, using constraint (5) in the contrapositive direction, that DOVE has to be false too and, using justification (3) in its contrapositive direction, we can deduce that AB_QUAKER has to be IN, since QUAKER is IN. In this way, making inferences using the contrapositives of the justifications produces the same effect as installing a new justification (as the TMS does), that is, to force an OUT-assumption (AB_QUAKER) to be labelled IN.

It is clear, from the example above, that the notion of well-founded labelling is not able, by itself, to capture the idea of dependency-directed backtracking. We would like to give an alternative definition of well-founded labelling so as to allow also the labelling obtained by the backtracking process to be considered well-founded w.r.t. the initial set of justifications. This doesn't happen, as we have seen, with the usual notion of well-founded labelling, since in the revised labelling some out-assumptions may have an IN label, while lacking a forward non cyclic justification w.r.t the initial set of justifications. The IN status of such out-assumptions is, however, supported by an inference, starting from the $\perp$ and using some contrapositives of the initial justifications.

This suggests an alternative definition of well-founded labelling, that can be obtained by allowing IN propositions to be considered well-justified in case they can be proved by using justifications also in their contrapositive direction.

It must be noticed that, in order to use a justification in its contrapositive direction, it is not sufficient to have its consequent OUT (that is, not being able to prove it); it is needed, instead, that the consequent is FALSE, i.e. that its negation is provable or, in other words, that the consequent cannot be consistently assumed. As an example, let the set of justifications J contain the only justification

$$OUT(B) \rightarrow C$$

If we were allowed, by contraposition, to infer that B is IN when C is OUT, we could assume C OUT and then we would get an unwanted labelling. On the contrary, if J contains the additional justification, $C \rightarrow \perp$, then B can be reasonably derived by contraposition. In this last case, in fact, not only is C not provable, but it is inconsistent, i.e. it is labelled FALSE, and thus contraposition can be performed. This is the reason why the new label FALSE is needed.

While a proposition is labelled OUT when there is no support to believe it, a proposition is labelled FALSE if it is inconsistent to assume it, that is, its assumption produces an inconsistency. Clearly, the notion of being FALSE subsumes that of being OUT, since what cannot be consistently assumed, cannot also be supported to be believed in a consistent theory. However, the vice versa does not hold, since what is not supported to be believed is not necessarily inconsistent with the set of justifications. Obviously, the proposition $\perp$ has to be labelled FALSE in any consistent labelling.

It is worth noticing that the presence of the new label FALSE and the possibility of using justifications in their contrapositive direction allows "classical" negation to be dealt with in addition to the default negation allowed by out-justifiers. Therefore, it is possible to allow for more general justifications with also the negation in the consequent. However, throughout this paper, we will assume for simplicity that justification are the usual ones with a non-negated proposition in their consequent.

2 Three-Valued Labellings

We will now define a consistent and well-founded three-valued labelling for a set J of justifications. A three-valued labelling for J is an assignment of a label IN, OUT or FALSE to each proposition occurring in J. It is said to be *consistent* if the proposition $\perp$ is given the value FALSE. Moreover, we say that the labelling is *valid* for J if each of the justifications in J is satisfied by the labelling. A justification

$$A_1 \wedge ... \wedge A_n \wedge OUT(B_1) \wedge ... \wedge OUT(B_m) \rightarrow C,$$

is *satisfied* by a labelling if the conclusion of the justification is labelled IN or one of the IN-justifiers is labelled OUT or FALSE or one of the OUT-justifiers is labelled IN.

A three-valued labelling is *well-founded* for J if it is valid for J and if any IN or FALSE proposition in the labelling is *well-justified*, in the following sense:
- an IN proposition P is well-justified if it is the consequent of a justification in J whose IN-justifiers are all IN and well-justified and all OUT-justifiers are OUT or FALSE; or, otherwise, if it is an OUT-justifier of a justification with the consequent FALSE and well-justified, whose IN-justifiers are all IN and well-justified and whose other OUT-justifiers are all OUT or FALSE;
- a FALSE proposition P is well-justified if it is an IN-justifier of a justification with the consequent FALSE and well-justified, whose other IN-justifiers are all IN and well-justified and whose OUT-justifiers are all OUT or FALSE;
- if $\perp$ is FALSE, it is well-justified.

In each one of the previous cases, if j is the justification which is used to show that a proposition P is well-justified, we will say that j *justifies* P.

Going back to Example 1, there are two consistent and well-founded three-valued labellings,

M_1: IN { QUAKER, REPUBLICAN, AB_QUAKER , HAWK }
  FALSE { DOVE, $\perp$ }
  OUT { AB_REPUBLICAN }

and

M_2: IN { QUAKER, REPUBLICAN, AB_REPUBLICAN, DOVE }

FALSE { HAWK, $\perp$ },

OUT { AB_QUAKER }

that precisely correspond to the two labellings L_1 and L_2 obtained by dependency-directed backtracking. The only difference is that the propositions previously labelled OUT are now either labelled OUT or FALSE.

It has to be noticed that, when computing a well-founded and consistent three-valued labelling, the labels of the nodes have to be propagated throughout the justifications, either in the direction of the implication (to put IN the consequent of a justification when its IN-justifiers are all IN and its OUT-justifiers are all OUT or FALSE) or in the contrapositive direction (when the consequent of the justification is FALSE). In the latter case, it is possible that some different contrapositive uses of the justification are feasible and one of them has to be chosen.

Well-founded and consistent three-valued labellings are intended to capture the behaviour of the TMS. As noticed before, dependency-directed backtracking, by installing a new justification, produces the same effects as performing an inference (involving the FALSE label) through the contrapositives of the justifications: it forces an OUT-assumption to be labelled IN. As a consequence, it is easy to convince that, if a labelling is incrementally computed by the TMS (propagating forward the values IN and OUT of the nodes and possibly installing new justifications by dependency-directed backtracking) it can also be obtained, apart from the presence of the additional label FALSE, by propagating the labels of the nodes through the justifications both in the direction of the implication and in the contrapositive direction. The contrapositives chosen for propagating the labels through the justifications with the FALSE consequent are precisely those whose unfolding produces the backward justifications installed by the TMS.

It is less obvious to show the converse, i.e. that all well-founded and consistent three-valued labellings are also computed by the TMS. In fact, when computing a well-founded three-valued labelling, we are allowed to employ all justifications in their contrapositive direction, whereas, on the other hand, the TMS only introduces the new justifications on demand, when a contradiction has to be solved (in particular, it introduces the fewest new justifications as possible).

We argue that, given a set J of justifications, there is a one to one correspondence between the labellings computed by the TMS and the consistent and well-founded three-valued labellings for J. The only difference between TMS labellings and the corresponding three-valued labelling is that the nodes labelled OUT by the TMS can either be OUT or FALSE in the three-valued labelling. Let us consider the following example.

Example 2 (taken from [10]):

(1) OUT(ab_Animal) $\rightarrow$ Cannot_Fly

(2) OUT(ab_Bird) $\rightarrow$ Can_Fly

(3) Can_Fly $\wedge$ Cannot_Fly $\rightarrow$ $\perp$

(4) OUT(ab_Bird) $\rightarrow$ ab_Animal

For this set of justifications there are two well-founded and consistent three-valued labellings, precisely:

M_3: IN { ab_Animal,Can_Fly } M_4:   IN { ab_Bird,Cannot_Fly }
        OUT { ab_Bird }   OUT { ab_Animal }
        FALSE { Cannot_Fly,$\perp$ }   FALSE { Can_Fly,$\perp$ }

Essentially the same example was used by Morris [9] to show that a TMS will find only solution M_3, whereas both solutions will be obtained by formulating the problem in a nonmonotonic logic with normal defaults. Morris claims that solution M_3 is the one that corresponds to our intuition and it is to be preferred to the other one which is counter-intuitive (that is, an anomalous extension).

Clearly, the two-valued labelling
        IN { ab_Animal,Can_Fly }   OUT { ab_Bird,Cannot_Fly,$\perp$ },
which corresponds to M_3, is the only one computed when the TMS is considered from a *static* standpoint, i.e. when the problem is to find a correct labelling with respect to a fixed set of justifications. However, the behaviour of the TMS can also be described as being *incremental*: whenever the TMS is given a new justification, a truth maintenance process is started, with the goal of updating the labelling, possibly through dependency-directed backtracking. It is possible to see that the incremental process can obtain more solutions w.r.t. those expected in the static approach. In fact, once the TMS has installed a new justification in order to get rid of a contradiction at an intermediate step, that justification cannot be discharged any more, even if the contradiction is removed by the incoming of new justifications, and thus that justification can be used to compute a labelling which, otherwise, would not have been obtained.

Turning back to Example 2, let us consider the case when the TMS is given the justifications incrementally. After the TMS has been given the first three justifications, it detects a contradiction and, in order to eliminate it, it adds a new backward justification (say Cannot_Fly $\rightarrow$ ab_Bird), thus obtaining the following labelling:
        IN {Cannot_Fly,ab_Bird}   OUT {ab_Animal,Can_Fly,$\perp$}.
When, at the next step, justification (4) is added, the previous labelling will not be changed by the truth maintenance process, because the new justification does not alter any label. Thus the incremental TMS will find a solution which is not considered correct in the static case (the label IN of ab_Bird is not well-founded for the original set of justifications) and which corresponds to the three-valued labelling M_4.

It is possible to prove [8] that, given a set J of justifications, the TMS computes all the solutions corresponding to the well-founded and consistent three-valued labellings for J, provided that it is given the justifications in a suitable order.

3 A fixpoint definition of three-valued well-founded labellings

An alternative definition of well-founded and consistent three-valued labelling can be given by means of a fixpoint construction, which closely resembles that given for default logic [14]. It is not a constructive definition; however, given a labelling, it provides a way to check if it is a well-founded and consistent labelling. A similar fixpoint definition is introduced in [12] to characterize *admissible extensions*, that is, well-founded two-valued labellings for the TMS without contradiction resolution.

Let J be a set of justifications, P the set of premises in J and E a pair <IN,FALSE>, where IN and FALSE are sets of propositions occurring in J. E represents a three-valued labelling which labels IN all propositions in the set IN, FALSE all propositions in the set FALSE and OUT all the remaining propositions of J. Clearly, for E being a labelling, it is needed that no proposition can occur both in the set IN and in the set FALSE.

We define a sequence of sets $E_1, E_2, \ldots$ as follows:

$E_0 = \langle P, \{\bot\} \rangle$

$E_{i+1} = \Gamma(E_i) = \langle IN_{i+1}, FALSE_{i+1} \rangle$, where

$IN_{i+1} = IN_i \cup \{ C : A_1 \wedge \ldots \wedge A_n \wedge OUT(B_1) \wedge \ldots \wedge OUT(B_m) \to C \in J$ and

for all $h=1,\ldots,n$ $A_h \in IN_i$ and for all $j=1,\ldots,m$ $B_j \notin IN \}$

$\cup \{ B_k : A_1 \wedge \ldots \wedge A_n \wedge OUT(B_1) \wedge \ldots \wedge OUT(B_m) \to C \in J$ and for all $h=1,\ldots,n$
$A_h \in IN_i$ and for all $j=1,\ldots,k-1,k+1,\ldots,m$ $B_j \notin IN$ and $C \in FALSE_i \}$

$FALSE_{i+1} = FALSE_i \cup \{ A_k : A_1 \wedge \ldots \wedge A_n \wedge OUT(B_1) \wedge \ldots \wedge OUT(B_m) \to C \in J$ and
for all $h=1,\ldots,k-1,k+1,\ldots,n$ $A_h \in IN_i$ and for all $j=1,\ldots,m$ $B_j \notin IN$ and
$C \in FALSE_i \}$

It is easy to prove that a pair E=<IN, FALSE> such that $IN \cap FALSE = \varnothing$ is a consistent and well-founded three-valued labelling for J if and only if there is a sequence $E_1, E_2, \ldots$ (as defined above) such that $E = \cup_{i=0}^{\infty} E_i$.

This is a quite immediate consequence of the definition of well-founded labelling. The consistency of the labelling is provided by the fact that if $E = \cup_{i=0}^{\infty} E_i$, then $\bot$ is labelled FALSE in E by construction.

4 A characterization of the TMS with two-valued labellings

In this section we are going to define a transformation of a set J of justifications into an equivalent set J^1 of justifications which can be labelled with a usual two-valued labelling, without the need to install backward justifications, as defined in [12]. In fact, since the translation introduces all the contrapositives of the justifications, no dependency-directed backtracking (that is, no new justification) is needed for computing a consistent and well-founded two-valued labelling for J^1. The constraints occurring in J^1 only allow the inconsistent labellings (in which $\bot$ is IN) to be thrown away. By two-valued well-founded labellings, we mean admissible extensions as defined in [12].

The translation is intended to preserve the well-founded consistent labellings. Thus, there is a one to one correspondence between the well-founded and consistent three-valued labellings of a set J of justifications and the well-founded and consistent two-valued labellings for the set of justifications obtained by translating J.

In order to perform the translation of a set of justifications, we have to introduce new propositions associated with the old ones. We will denote with $P^{\smile}$, the new proposition associated with P. The new propositions are needed since we cannot use the logical negation to state the contrapositives. From an intuitive viewpoint, $P^{\smile}$ has the intended meaning "P is believed to be false" (i.e., $P^{\smile}$ represents the negation of P). Given a set J of justifications, we define a new set J^1 of justifications as follows:

- if

$$A_1\wedge...\wedge A_n\wedge OUT(B_1)\wedge...\wedge OUT(B_m) \rightarrow C,$$

is a justification in J, then for all k=1,..,m and for all j=1,..,n

$$A_1\wedge...\wedge A_n\wedge OUT(B_1)\wedge...\wedge OUT(B_m) \rightarrow C,$$
$$A_1\wedge...\wedge A_n\wedge OUT(B_1)\wedge...\wedge OUT(B_{k-1})\wedge OUT(B_{k+1})\wedge...\wedge OUT(B_m)\wedge C^\sim \rightarrow B_k,$$
$$A_1\wedge...\wedge A_{j-1}\wedge A_{j+1}\wedge...\wedge A_n\wedge OUT(B_1)\wedge...\wedge OUT(B_m)\wedge C^\sim \rightarrow A_j^\sim$$

are all justifications in J^1;

- nothing else is contained in J^1.

Moreover, if the consequent C of the clause to be translated is $\perp$, the new propositional symbol True is introduced in place of $\perp^\sim$ in the bodies of the contrapositives in J^1. True is considered as denoting truth.

Example 1(cont.)

By applying the transformation to the set of justifications (1),..,(5), we have to add them the following justifications:

QUAKER $\wedge$ DOVE$^\sim$ $\rightarrow$ AB_QUAKER

OUT(AB_QUAKER) $\wedge$ DOVE$^\sim$ $\rightarrow$ QUAKER$^\sim$

REPUBLICAN $\wedge$ HAWK$^\sim$ $\rightarrow$ AB_REPUBLICAN

OUT(AB_REPUBLICAN) $\wedge$ HAWK$^\sim$ $\rightarrow$ REPUBLICAN$^\sim$

DOVE $\wedge$ True $\rightarrow$ HAWK$^\sim$

HAWK $\wedge$ True $\rightarrow$ DOVE$^\sim$.

We will now define a one to one correspondence between three-valued labelling for J and two-valued labelling for J^1, so as to be able to show that the above translation preserves all the well-founded consistent labellings.

Let J be a set of justifications and let J^1 be its translation as defined above. We denote with L the set of all propositions in J and with L$^\sim$ the set of all new propositions in J^1 (including True). As we have seen in section 3, a three-valued labelling for J can be represented by a pair <IN, FALSE>; likewise, a two-valued labelling for J^1 can be represented by the set T of all IN propositions.

Following [12] we define the notion of well-founded two-valued labelling for a set J^1 of justifications as follows.

Definition. Let T be a subset of $L\cup L^\sim$. T is a well-founded two-valued labelling for J^1 iff there is a sequence $T_0,T_1,T_2,...$ of subsets of $L\cup L^\sim$ such that

$T_0=P\cup\{True\}$ (the set of premises of J^1)

$T_{i+1}=T_i \cup \{ C : A_1\wedge...\wedge A_n\wedge OUT(B_1)\wedge...\wedge OUT(B_m) \rightarrow C \in J^1$ and

for all h=1,..,n $A_h\in T_i$ and for all j=1,..,m $B_j\notin T$ },

and

$$T=\cup_{i=0}^{\infty}T_i.$$

We say that a two-valued labelling $T\subseteq L\cup L^\sim$ is *consistent* if neither $\perp$ is in T nor there is a proposition $p\in L$ such that both p and p$^\sim$ are in T.

Let T be a two-valued labelling for J^1. We define a mapping $M:2^{L\cup L^\sim}\rightarrow 2^L x 2^L$ as follows:

$M[T]=<IN_T, FALSE_T>$, where

$$IN_T = \{ P \in L : P \in T \}$$
$$FALSE_T = \{ P \in L : P^\smile \in T \} \cup \{ \perp \}$$

Notice that True is not an element of IN_T. It has to be noticed that, if T is inconsistent, then $M[T]=<IN,FALSE>$ is not a three-valued labelling, since $IN \cap FALSE \neq \emptyset$. Hence, for $M[T]$ to be a labelling, T is required to be consistent. The mapping M is a bijection and its inverse $N:2^L \times 2^L \to 2^{L \cup L^\smile}$ is defined as follows:

$$N[<IN,FALSE>] = \{ P : P \in L \text{ and } P \in IN \} \cup \{ P^\smile : P \in L \text{ and } P \in FALSE \}.$$

It can be proved that M and N are monotone and continuous mappings.

Theorem 1. If T is a consistent and well-founded two-valued labelling for J^1, then $M[T]$ is a consistent and well-founded three-valued labelling for J. Vice-versa, if $<IN,FALSE>$ is a consistent and well-founded three-valued labelling for J, then $N[<IN,FALSE>]$ is a consistent and well-founded two-valued labelling for J^1.

Proof. We give an outline of the proof of the first half of the theorem; the second half can be proved in the same way. Let us assume that T is a consistent and well-founded two-valued labelling for J^1. Since T is well-founded, then $T=\cup_{i=0}^{\infty}T_i$ for some sequence $T_0,T_1,T_2,...$ of subsets of $L \cup L^\smile$ defined as above. Let $E=M[T]$. We have to prove that E is a well-founded and consistent three-valued labelling for J, that is, there is a sequence $E_0,E_1,E_2,...$ of subsets of $L \times L$, such that $E_{i+1}=\Gamma(E_i)$ and $E=\cup_{i=0}^{\infty}E_i$. To this purpose, we can take $E_i=M[T_i]$. In fact, it is quite straightforward to prove that the following conditions hold:
1) $E_0=M[T_0]=<P,\{\perp\}>$
   $E_{i+1}=M[T_{i+1}]=\Gamma(M[T_i])=\Gamma(E_i)$;
2) $E=\cup_{i=0}^{\infty}E_i$, in fact:
   $E = M[T] =$
   $= M[\cup_{i=0}^{\infty}T_i]$
   $= \cup_{i=0}^{\infty}M[T_i]$ (since M is a continuous mapping on the powerset of $L \cup L^\smile$)
   $= \cup_{i=0}^{\infty}E_i$

For $E=M[T]=<IN,FALSE>$ to be a consistent and well-founded three-valued labelling, we only require, in addition, that for no proposition $p \in L$ both $p \in IN$ and $p \in FALSE$, and this is obviously true, since T is consistent.

$\square$

For instance, the set of justifications previously obtained by the transformation has the following consistent and well-founded two-valued labellings:
   IN { QUAKER, REPUBLICAN, AB_QUAKER, HAWK, DOVE$^\smile$, True }
   OUT { AB_REPUBLICAN, DOVE, QUAKER$^\smile$, REPUBLICAN$^\smile$, HAWK$^\smile$, $\perp$ }
and IN { QUAKER, REPUBLICAN, AB_REPUBLICAN, DOVE, HAWK$^\smile$, True }
   OUT { AB_QUAKER, HAWK, QUAKER$^\smile$, REPUBLICAN$^\smile$, DOVE$^\smile$, $\perp$ }
corresponding to the three-valued labellings M_1 and M_2 above.

The transformation above is defined in such a way that every justification contained in J is also contained in J^1. However it is easy to see that, because of the presence of contrapositives, the "active" constraints that are originally present in J and are still present in J^1 are useless. In fact, it can be proved that, if T is a well-founded two-valued labelling for J^1, then $\perp$ is not labelled IN in T. The only possibility for T to be an inconsistent labelling is that it labels IN both p and p˜, for some proposition p. As a consequence, the constraints that are present in the initial set J of justifications can be eliminated: we can avoid to introduce them in J^1. In this way we can define a transformation from a set of justifications J to a new set J^1 that does not contain any active constraint. Active constraints are discharged, once all their contrapositives have been introduced.

Previously, we have defined a two-valued labelling to be consistent when $\perp$ is not labelled IN and there is no proposition p such that both p and p˜ are labelled IN in the labelling. To enforce this condition, the transformation can be modified by introducing in the set J^1 new constraints of the form $P \wedge P^˜ \rightarrow \perp$ (we will call them *pruning* constraints in analogy with Junker's pruning nogoods). In this way the usual consistency condition, i.e. $\perp$ being OUT, allows to get rid of the labelling in which both P is IN (i.e. P is believed) and P˜ is IN (i.e. P is believed to be false). However, it is possible to see that P and P˜ can both be labelled IN only if the set of justifications J^1 has no consistent and well-founded labellings. Otherwise, the contrapositives of the justifications introduced by the transformation will enforce the fact that if P is IN then P˜ must be OUT, or vice-versa.

It is clear that the new symbol True, which has been introduced by the transformation with the only purpose to allow a more easy proof of the correspondence between two-valued and three-valued labellings, could be omitted from the bodies of the contrapositives, since it is intended to be always true.

To summarize, with these modifications, the transformation modified as defined above produces, given a set J of justifications, a set of justifications J^1 as follows:
- if

$$A_1 \wedge ... \wedge A_n \wedge OUT(B_1) \wedge ... \wedge OUT(B_m) \rightarrow C,$$

is a justification in J, then for all k=1,..,m and for all j=1,..,n

$$A_1 \wedge ... \wedge A_n \wedge OUT(B_1) \wedge ... \wedge OUT(B_m) \rightarrow C,$$
$$A_1 \wedge ... \wedge A_n \wedge OUT(B_1) \wedge ... \wedge OUT(B_{k-1}) \wedge OUT(B_{k+1}) \wedge ... \wedge OUT(B_m) \wedge C^˜ \rightarrow B_k ,$$
$$A_1 \wedge ... \wedge A_{j-1} \wedge A_{j+1} \wedge ... \wedge A_n \wedge OUT(B_1) \wedge ... \wedge OUT(B_m) \wedge C^˜ \rightarrow A_j^˜$$

are all justifications in J^1;
- if

$$A_1 \wedge ... \wedge A_n \wedge OUT(B_1) \wedge ... \wedge OUT(B_m) \rightarrow \perp,$$

is a constraint in J, then for all k=1,..,m and for all j=1,..,n

$$A_1 \wedge ... \wedge A_n \wedge OUT(B_1) \wedge ... \wedge OUT(B_{k-1}) \wedge OUT(B_{k+1}) \wedge ... \wedge OUT(B_m) \rightarrow B_k ,$$
$$A_1 \wedge ... \wedge A_{j-1} \wedge A_{j+1} \wedge ... \wedge A_n \wedge OUT(B_1) \wedge ... \wedge OUT(B_m) \rightarrow A_j^˜$$

are all justifications in J^1;
- for any newly introduced proposition P˜, J^1 contains the constraint $P \wedge P^˜ \rightarrow \perp$;
- nothing else is contained in J^1.

This transformation, which is obviously equivalent to the previous one, is the transformation we will refer to in the following.

5 A Logical Semantics for the TMS

An equivalent characterization of the TMS has been proposed in [6], where a logical semantics for the TMS has been defined by introducing *generalized stable models*. In this section we give a brief account of it.

In [11] the *stable models* of [5] have been shown to be suitable for defining a logical semantics for a TMS without constraints. In this section, we aim at showing that also the process of dependency-directed backtracking can be modelled by suitably extending *stable models*.

Our purpose is that of defining a semantics for the TMS which performs belief revision by an active use of constraints. Therefore, we define a notion of *generalized stable model* for a set of justifications (i.e. general clauses and constraints) taking care of the fact that we need to use justifications also in their contrapositive form.

From a logical perspective, a set of justifications can be considered as a set of propositional general clauses and constraints of the form
$$A_1 \wedge ... \wedge A_n \wedge \neg B_1 \wedge ... \wedge \neg B_m \rightarrow C$$
(where the consequent C is omitted when the justification is a constraint and the negation in the body is regarded as a default negation). Moreover, a TMS labelling can be considered as a propositional model, the true propositions corresponding to the propositions labelled IN. Let J be a set of justifications and M an interpretation for J in the classical propositional calculus. M can be regarded as the set of the propositions of J that are assigned the value true. Let J'_M be the set of justifications obtained from J by deleting from the antecedents of each implication in J all the negative literals $\neg B_i$ such that $B_i \notin M$.

We can now consider each implication clause occurring in J'_M
$$A_1 \wedge ... \wedge A_n \wedge \neg B_1 \wedge ... \wedge \neg B_h \rightarrow C$$
as the disjunction of literals (propositions or negated propositions),
$$\neg A_1 \vee ... \vee \neg A_n \vee B_1 \vee ... \vee B_h \vee C .$$
Let J_M be the set of clauses in J'_M having one and only one literal true in M.

Definition. Let M be a set of propositions occurring in J. M is a *generalized stable model* of J if M is a model of J and if
$$M = \{ A : A \text{ proposition in J and } J_M \models A \}$$

As a difference with stable models [5], where the transformed program Π_M is a set of Horn clauses, J_M is a set of clauses with negation. Moreover, J_M is obtained from J by deleting all the negative literals $\neg B$ such that B is not in the model M, but, differently from stable models, not all implications that have a negative literal $\neg B$ such that B is in the model M are deleted. In fact, the contrapositives of such implications can be possibly needed.

The generalized stable models of a set of justifications are intended to represent its correct labellings. Indeed, it is possible to see that there is a one to one correspondence between the generalized stable models of a set J of justifications and the three-valued labellings for J. Given a generalized stable model M of J, the propositions true in M are those IN in the corresponding labelling, while the propositions whose negation is derivable from J_M are those FALSE in the labelling (the remaining propositions are those labelled OUT).

A way to prove the correspondence between well-founded and consistent three-valued labellings for a set J of justifications and generalized stable models of J is by making use of the transformation defined above. In fact, since, from a logical perspective J^1 is a set of general clauses and (pruning) constraints, its logical semantics can be defined using stable models, (each stable model representing a two-valued labelling). Actually, stable models are defined for sets of general clauses (we mean Horn clauses with negation in the body) without constraints, and, in fact, in [11] they have been used for defining the logical semantics of a TMS without constraints. However, the notion of stable model can be adapted to the case when (pruning) constraints are present, since constraints can be used to get rid of those stable models of the set of general clauses that do not satisfy them (that is, the inconsistent stable models). In this way, the pruning constraints are *passively* used to cut out some inconsistent extensions.

We will call *consistent* stable models for a set of justifications including constraints the stable models of the set of general clauses that satisfy the constraints.

It can be proved that the above transformation preserves the semantics of the set of justifications. In fact, given a set J of justifications, there is a one to one correspondence between the generalized stable models of J and the consistent stable models of J^1. It is possible to prove the following theorems.

Theorem 1. Let M be a subset of L and let M^1 be a subset of $L \cup L^-$ defined as follows

$$M^1 = M \cup \{ A^- \in L^- : J_M \models \neg A \}.$$

If M is a generalized stable model of J, then M^1 is a consistent stable model of J^1.

Theorem 2. Let M^1 be a subset of $L \cup L^-$ and let $M = M^1 \cap L$. If M^1 is a consistent stable model of J^1, then M is a generalized stable model of J.

Now me have the following results:

1) there is a one to one correspondence between the well-founded and consistent three-valued labellings for J and the well-founded and consistent two-valued labellings for J^1;

2) there is a one to one correspondence between the generalized stable models of J and the consistent stable models of J^1.

Moreover, as regards the TMS without constraints, in a paper by Elkan [2] is proved that

a model of a set of justifications is stable if and only if it is grounded (that is, if it is a well-founded two-valued labelling).

By making use of this result, we have immediately, for a set J^1 of justifications including also (pruning) constraints, that

3) there is a one to one correspondence between the consistent stable models of J^1 and the well-founded and consistent two-valued labellings for J^1.

Result 3) together with 1) and 2) proves the following proposition.

Proposition 1. Given a set J of justifications with constraints, there is a one to one correspondence between the generalized stable models of J and the well-founded and consistent three-valued labellings for J.

6 An Abductive Characterization of the TMS

In this section we define a transformation of a set of non-monotonic justifications into an abduction framework, whose abductive solutions correspond to the labellings computed by the TMS for the given set of justifications.

While it is well-known that the (basic) ATMS performs abduction [15], the TMS has not yet been considered from this point of view. The TMS tries to label all propositions by putting OUT all the ones lacking a well-founded proof. In particular, the out-assumptions that are not well-justified are labelled OUT, unless they are forced IN by backtracking to remove a contradiction. In general there are different possibilities in doing this, and then multiple labellings. It can be noticed, however, that once the set of out-assumptions being OUT has been fixed, then the labelling is univocally determined. Thus, abduction can be used in order to characterize exactly those sets of out-assumptions which determine a correct labelling.

As defined in [3] an *abduction framework* is a triple <T,I,A> where T is a set of Horn clauses, I is a set of integrity constraints, being either denials or meta-level integrity constraints, and A is set of *abducible* propositions. Given an abduction framework <T,I,A>, let an *abductive solution* for it be a set of abducible propositions $\Delta \subseteq A$ such that

$T \cup \Delta \cup I$ is consistent (i.e. Δ satisfies the constraints).

Clearly, to turn a set of non-monotonic justifications into an abduction framework the OUT-justifiers in the bodies of the justifications have to be eliminated by converting non-monotonic justifications to monotonic ones. This is done by replacing each OUT(B) in the body of a justification with a new abducible proposition B^*, representing the assumption that B is OUT. Moreover, in accordance with our view of the backtracking process, which relies on an active use of constraints, the transformation has also to introduce all the contrapositives of the justifications. In fact, within an abduction framework integrity constraints are used in a passive way only to verify the consistency of the abductive solutions.

The transformation can be divided in two distinct and rather independent steps. The first step, to introduce the contrapositives, is the one described in section 4. The second one allows a set of non monotonic justifications (possibly containing pruning constraints) to be transformed into a set of monotonic justifications, by introducing new propositional symbols B^* so as to replace each OUT(B) in the bodies of the justifications. Moreover, the set of the justifications is enlarged with new object-level and meta-level constraints. As pointed out in the introduction, this second step is very similar to the transformation used in [3] to convert logic programs with negation (by failure) to abduction frameworks by eliminating negation.

The transformation is defined as follows. Let J be a set of justifications (whose propositions are in L) and let J^1 be the set of justifications obtained by the first step of transformation (whose propositions are in $L \cup L^-$). Then a new set of justifications J^2 is obtained from J^1 by replacing all the occurrences of OUT(B) (with $B \in L$) in the body of each justification with a new proposition B^*. Moreover, for each newly introduced proposition B^*, a pruning (object-level) constraint

$$B \wedge B^* \rightarrow \perp,$$

and a "meta-level" constraint

$$demo(B) \lor demo(B^*) \ ,$$

whose meaning is "either B is believed or B^* is believed", are introduced in J^2. All the propositions occurring in J^2 are contained in $L \cup L^{\tilde{}} \cup L^*$, where L^* is the set of new propositions A^* (with $A \in L$) introduced by the second step of transformation.

Notice that a meta-level constraint expresses a condition on what is entailed by a knowledge base. The new proposition B^* has the intended meaning "B is disbelieved" and represents the assumption that B is OUT. Clearly, B cannot be both believed and disbelieved, and this is the reason why the new pruning constraint is needed. It has to be noticed that, while the proposition $B^{\tilde{}}$ has been introduced in order to represent the classical negation of B, the proposition B^* has been introduced to represent a default negation of B.

An abduction framework $<T,I,L^*>$ can be defined from the set J^2 of monotonic justifications, by taking T as the set of the Horn clauses in J^2 and I as the set of all (both object and meta-level) constraints in J^2. Object-level constraints are regarded as denials of the form

$$A_1 \land ... \land A_n \rightarrow .$$

Notice that the set L^* has been taken as the set of abducible propositions. Each *abductive solution* for $<T,I,L^*>$, that is, each set of abducible propositions $\Delta \subseteq L^*$ satisfying the constraints, is intended to correspond to a possible labelling of the initial set J of justifications. Each abductive solution Δ defines a context consisting of the set of all propositions derivable from $T \cup \Delta$. It can be proved that there is a one to one correspondence between the abductive solutions Δ of the abduction framework defined from J^2 and the well-founded and consistent two-valued labellings of J^1, each proposition $B \in L \cup L^{\tilde{}}$ in the context of Δ being labelled IN in the corresponding labelling and vice-versa. Each abducible proposition B^* in Δ corresponds to an out-assumption B that is labelled OUT in the labelling.

Moreover, it can be proved that there is a one to one correspondence between the stable models of J^1 and the abductive solutions of an abduction framework associated with J^2. Indeed, a theorem in [3] states a one-to-one correspondence between the stable models of a logic program and the abductive solutions Δ satisfying the integrity constraints of the corresponding abduction framework. As an obvious consequence the following proposition holds.

Proposition 2. Let J be a set of non-monotonic justifications, let J^1 and J^2 be defined as above and let $<T,I,L^*>$ be the abduction framework associated with J^2. Then
   (a) if M^1 is a stable model of J^1, then $\Delta=\{ B^* \in L^* : B \notin M^1 \}$ is an abductive solution of $<T,I,L^*>$;
   (b) if Δ is an abductive solution of $<T,I,L^*>$, then the set $\{ A \in L \cup L^{\tilde{}} : T \cup \Delta \models A \}$ is a stable model of J^1.

As a difference with the case of logic programs with negation considered in [3], J^1, along with general clauses with negation, also contains pruning constraints of the form $B \land B^{\tilde{}} \rightarrow \perp$, which have been introduced by the first step of the translation.

Since both steps of transformation preserve the semantics of the set of justifications, the transformation is correct as a whole, i.e. there is a one to one correspondence between each abductive solution of J^2 and each generalized stable model of J (each three-valued labelling).

The presence of the constraint $B \wedge B^* \rightarrow \bot$ in the set I of integrity constraints prevents the case when both B^* is in Δ (and thus B is assumed to be OUT in the labelling) and B is derivable from $T \cup \Delta$ (and thus B has to be labelled IN). Furthermore, the presence of a meta-level constraint demo(B)$\vee$demo(B^*) has the effect that, for each abductive solution Δ, either Δ contains the abducible proposition B^* or B is derivable from $T \cup \Delta$ (that is, each out-assumption B is either assumed OUT or proved IN).

Example 1(cont.)

To perform the second transformation, OUT(AB_QUAKER) and OUT(AB_REPUBLICAN) are replaced by AB_QUAKER* and AB_REPUBLICAN* in justifications (3), (4), (7) and (9) and the following constraints

(8) AB_QUAKER $\wedge$ AB_QUAKER* $\rightarrow \bot$

(9) AB_REPUBLICAN $\wedge$ AB_REPUBLICAN* $\rightarrow \bot$

(10) demo(AB_QUAKER) $\vee$ demo(AB_QUAKER*)

(11) demo(AB_REPUBLICAN) $\vee$ demo(AB_REPUBLICAN*)

are added. This set of justifications has two abductive solutions

Δ_1={AB_REPUBLICAN*} and Δ_2={AB_QUAKER*}.

Instead, the set Δ={AB_REPUBLICAN*,AB_QUAKER*} does not satisfy the object-level constraints, whereas the set Δ={} does not satisfy the meta-level constraints.

7 Conclusions

In this paper we have defined some possible (equivalent) characterizations for the justification-based TMS. In particular, a logic characterization of the TMS has been defined in terms of abduction. As regards it, in [7] it has been shown that, given a set of justifications, the basic ATMS can be used to compute all the abductive solutions of the corresponding abduction framework and, thus, all TMS labellings. In this way, by means of the defined translation and of a particular way of dealing with meta-level constraints, a non-monotonic ATMS can be obtained. In [7] a comparison is made with other proposals for a non-monotonic extension of assumption-based truth maintenance system (ATMS).

References

[1] J. Doyle, "A Truth Maintenance System," *Artificial Intelligence* **12** pp. 231-272 (1979).

[2] C. Elkan, "A Rational Reconstruction of Nonmonotonic Truth Maintenance Systems," *Artificial Intelligence* **43** pp. 219-234 (1990).

[3] K. Eshghi and R.A. Kowalski, "Abduction Compared with Negation by Failure," pp. 234-254 in *Proc. 6th Int. Conf. on Logic Programming*, (1989).

[4] Y. Fujiwara and S. Honiden, "Relating the TMS to Autoepistemic Logic," pp. 1199-1205 in *Proc. 11th IJCAI*, Detroit (August 1989).

[5] M. Gelfond and V. Lifschitz, "The Stable Model Semantics for Logic Programming," pp. 1070-1080 in *Proc. 5th Int. Conf. and Symposium on Logic Programming*, Seattle (1988).

[6] L. Giordano and A. Martelli, "Generalized Stable Models, Truth Maintenance and Conflict Resolution ," pp. 427-441 in *Proc. 7th Int. Conf. on Logic Programming*, Jerusalem (1990).

[7] L. Giordano and A. Martelli, "An Abductive Characterization of the TMS," pp. 308-313 in *Proc. 9th ECAI*, Stockholm (1990).

[8] L. Giordano and A. Martelli, "Three-valued Labellings for Truth Maintenance Systems," pp. 506-513 in *Proc. ISMIS*, Knoxville (1990).

[9] P.H. Morris, "Curing Anomalous Extensions," pp. 437-442 in *Proc. AAAI-87*, Seattle (July 1987).

[10] P.H. Morris, "Autoepistemic Stable Closures and Contradiction Resolution," in *Non-monotonic Reasoning, 2nd International Workshop*, Springer Verlag Lecture Notes in Computer Science 346 (June 1988).

[11] S.G. Pimentel and J.L. Cuadrado, "A Truth Maintenance System Based on Stable Models," pp. 274-290 in *Proc. NACLP90*, Cleveland (1989).

[12] M. Reinfrank and H. Freitag, "Rules and Justifications: a Uniform Approach to Reason Maintenance and Non-monotonic Inference," pp. 439-446 in *Proc. of the Int. Conf. on V Gen. Computer Systems*, Tokyo (1988).

[13] M. Reinfrank, O. Dressler, and G. Brewka, "On The Relation between Truth Maintenance and Autoepistemic Logic," pp. 1206-1212 in *Proc. 11th IJCAI*, Detroit (1989).

[14] R. Reiter, "A Logic for default reasoning," *Artificial Intelligence* 13 pp. 81-132 (1980).

[15] R. Reiter and J. DeKleer, "Foundations of Assumption-Based Truth Maintenance Systems: Preliminary Report," pp. 183-188 in *Proc. AAAI*, (1989).

A POSSIBILISTIC ASSUMPTION-BASED
TRUTH MAINTENANCE SYSTEM WITH UNCERTAIN JUSTIFICATIONS,
AND ITS APPLICATION TO BELIEF REVISION[*]

Didier DUBOIS, Jérôme LANG, Henri PRADE
Institut de Recherche en Informatique de Toulouse, Université Paul Sabatier
118, route de Narbonne, 31062 TOULOUSE Cedex – FRANCE

Abstract : In this paper we present an extension of the ATMS, called "possibilistic ATMS", where the management of uncertainty is integrated inside the basic capabilities of the ATMS. Uncertainty pervading justifications or grading assumptions is represented in the framework of possibility theory using necessity measures. The main interest of a possibilistic ATMS is to take advantage of the uncertainty pervading the available knowledge and rank-order environments in which a given proposition is true. Possibilistic ATMS offer a solution to the revision of uncertain knowledge bases by deleting the least certain piece(s) of knowledge that cause(s) the inconsistency. Moreover the functionalities of the possibilistic ATMS provide a simple procedure for computing the most "acceptable" maximal consistent sub-bases of a partially inconsistent knowledge base. The implementation of a possibilistic ATMS using a specially tailored typed-resolution is briefly discussed.

1. Introduction

ATMS [3, 4] are truth maintenance systems oriented towards hypothetical reasoning since they are able to determine under which set(s) of assumption(s) a given proposition is true (technically a set of assumption(s) under which a proposition is true is called an "environment" and the set of all these environments is called the "label" of the

---

[*] This paper is a thoroughly revised and extended version of a preliminary draft [10].

proposition). It is interesting to consider ATMS in connection with the treatment of uncertainty for three kinds of reasons : i) pieces of information in the knowledge base may be pervaded with uncertainty which leads to uncertain justifications, while some assumptions may be considered as less strong than others ; ii) it gives a natural way for rank-ordering the environments and thus for cutting down computational complexity by ignoring environments with a low certainty ; iii) it can offer a procedure for computing uncertainty measures (e.g. belief functions).

The works dealing with "uncertainty-handling" ATMS which have been presented until now and which are briefly reviewed in the following are only inspired by one of these three motivations usually. De Kleer and Williams [6], in a multiple faults diagnosis problem, compute the probability of a candidate (i.e. a configuration of faults) given the outcomes of the system and assuming that faults are mutually independent. Pearl [18], Provan [19], and Laskey and Lehner [16], among others, have independently incorporated belief functions into the ATMS ; their approaches are somewhat different but share the same basic features : first, a mass function is associated with each assumption ; then, for each proposition p we compute the belief Bel(p) of p by first computing the label of p symbolically (which can be done in the classical way), then we compute Bel(p) from Label(p) ; Provan computes Bel(p) by expressing logically Label(p) under the form of a formula containing only independent sub-formulas, assuming mutual independence of assumptions. Laskey-Lehner's and Provan's approaches differ essentially by their algorithm for the computation of Bel(p). Besides, Bernasconi et al. [1] have outlined the definition of an ATMS based on fuzzy logic in Lee [17]'s style (i.e. using a fully truth-functional multivalent logic based on max and min operations).

Possibilistic ATMS (or Π-ATMS for short) are also oriented towards hypothetical reasoning, but the assumptions or the justifications that they manipulate can receive an uncertainty weight. Uncertainty is represented in the framework of possibility theory. In possibilistic logic uncertain clauses are handled as such and then in possibilistic ATMS the management of uncertainty is not separated from the other classical capabilities of the ATMS. The certainty of each granule in the knowledge base (represented by a clause in possibilistic logic [11]) is evaluated under the form of a lower bound of a necessity measure. This uncertainty in the deduction process is propagated by means of an extended resolution principle. Uncertainty degrees are then naturally attached to the configurations of assumptions in which a given proposition is true ; one can also evaluate to what degree a given configuration of assumptions is inconsistent or compute the more or less certain consequences of a configuration of assumptions. This approach enables us to handle disjunctions and negations of assumptions without particular problem. Moreover, by rank-ordering configurations according to the degrees attached to them, Π–ATMS provides a way of limiting combinatorial explosion when using ATMS in practice. Possibility theory [23], [12] and in particular necessity measures agree with the ordinal nature of what we wish to represent (it enables us to distinguish between what is almost certain and what is less certain). Very recently, Wrzos-Kaminski and Wrzos-Kaminska [22] have defined ordered-ATMS by associating priorities to justifications ; their approach is very close to ours and share a lot of definitions (including labels' weak consistency and minimality, see section 3) and properties.

We present the basic definitions and results of possibilistic logic first. In Section 3 we give the basic definitions and functionalities of the Π–ATMS and illustrate them on an elementary example. Then Section 4 extends the notions of interpretation and extension to the possibilistic case, and show their possible use for the revision of uncertain knowledge bases. Section 5 presents an algorithm for the computation of labels and contradictory environments ("no-goods") based on an extension of the so-called CAT-correct resolution, initially developed by Cayrol and Tayrac [2, 21]. The conclusion emphasizes the characteristic features of possibilistic ATMS.

2. Possibilistic logic

2.1. Modeling uncertainty with possibility and necessity measures

Possibilistic logic [11, 7, 8] is an extension of classical logic where one manipulates propositional or first-order calculus closed formulas weighted by lower bounds of possibility or necessity degrees which belong to [0,1]. In this paper we restrict ourselves to a fragment of possibilistic logic, the "clausal possibilistic propositional logic", where the considered formulas are exclusively conjunctions of possibilistic propositional clauses (i.e. weighted propositional clauses).

A possibility measure Π satisfies the following axioms :

(i) $\Pi(\bot) = 0 ; \Pi(\top) = 1$
(ii) $\forall p, \forall q, \Pi(p \vee q) = \max(\Pi(p),\Pi(q))$

where $\perp$ and T denote contradiction and tautology respectively. We emphasize that we only have $\Pi(p \wedge q) \le \min(\Pi(p),\Pi(q))$ in the general case. More generally $\Pi(p \wedge q)$ is not a function of $\Pi(p)$ and $\Pi(q)$ only. This completely departs from fully truth-functional calculi like fuzzy logic [17]. A necessity measure is associated by duality with a possibility measure by $\forall p, N(p) = 1 - \Pi(\neg p)$. Axiom (ii) is then equivalent to $\forall p, \forall q, N(p \wedge q) = \min(N(p),N(q))$ and, as a consequence, letting $q = \neg p$, we get $N(p) > 0 \Rightarrow \Pi(p) = 1$. Moreover we only have $N(p \vee q) \ge \max(N(p),N(q))$ by duality. We adopt the following conventions :

- $N(p) = 1$ means that, given the available knowledge, p is certainly true ; conversely, if p is said to be true we can consider p as certain.
- $1 > N(p) > 0$ that p is somewhat certain and $\neg p$ not certain at all (since the axioms imply that $\forall p, \min(N(p), N(\neg p)) = 0$).
- $N(p) = N(\neg p) = 0$ (equivalent to $\Pi(p) = \Pi(\neg p) = 1$) corresponds to the case of total ignorance ; it expresses that, from the available knowledge, nothing enables us to say if p is rather true or rather false.
- $0 < \Pi(p) < 1$ (equivalent to $1 > N(\neg p) > 0$) means that p is somewhat impossible, i.e. that $\neg p$ is somewhat certain and p not certain at all.
- $\Pi(p) = 0$, means that p is certainly false.

Possibilistic logic is well-adapted to the representation of states of incomplete knowledge, since we can distinguish between the complete lack of certainty in the falsity of a proposition p ($N(\neg p) = 0$) and the total certainty that p is true ($N(p) = 1$). $N(p) = 1$ entails $N(\neg p) = 0$ but the converse is false. It contrasts with probability measures where $\text{Prob}(p) = 1$ is equivalent to $\text{Prob}(\neg p) = 0$. Possibilistic logic also contrasts with usual multiple-valued logics which are fully truth-functional and deal with fuzzy propositions [17], while possibility degrees apply to standard propositions belonging to a Boolean algebra and are compositional only with respect to disjunction (see [11] on this point) .

2.2. Possibilistic resolution

A necessity-valued formula is a first-order logic formula f to which a weight $\alpha \in [0,1]$ is attached, interpreted as a lower bound of its necessity measure. Thus, in the following we shall write $(f\ \alpha)$ as soon as the inequality $N(f) \ge \alpha$ is known. Let $c_1, ..., c_n$ be the clauses whose conjunction is equivalent to a propositional formula f, then (f α) is clearly equivalent to $\{(c_1\ \alpha), ..., (c_n\ \alpha)\}$ due to the basic axiom of necessity measures. Hence we can restrict ourselves to necessity-valued clauses. However possibilistic logic with both necessity-valued and possibility-valued clauses has been developed (e.g. [8]).

Resolution has been extended to possibilistic logic [11, 7]. The classical rule for propositional clauses is generalized by

$$\frac{(c\ \alpha) \qquad (c'\ \beta)}{(Res(c,c')\ min(\alpha,\beta))}$$

where Res(c,c') is a classical resolvent of the classical clauses c and c'. It can be shown that the lower bound obtained by this rule is the best possible one according to the axioms of necessity measures. The refutation method can be generalized to possibilistic logic [11, 7]. Indeed if we are interested in proving that a formula f is true, necessarily to some degree, we add in the knowledge base Σ the assumption $N(\neg f) = 1$, i.e. that f is false (with total certainty). Let Σ' be the new knowledge base obtained by adding to Σ the clauses issued from $\neg f$, with the weight 1. Then it can be proved that any weight attached to the empty clause produced by the extended resolution pattern from Σ' is a lower bound α of the necessity measure of the conclusion f. It entails the existence of "optimal refutations", i.e. derivations of an empty clause with a maximal weight.

2.3. Semantics and partial inconsistency

A semantics has been defined for possibilistic logic [8]. If f is a formula, M(f) the set of the models of f, then the models of (f α) will be defined by a fuzzy set M(f α) with a membership function $\mu_{M(f\ \alpha)}(I)=1$ if $I \in M(f)$

$$=1-\alpha \text{ if } I \in M(\neg f), \text{ where I is a (classical) interpretation.}$$

Then the fuzzy set of models of a set of weighted formulas $\Sigma = \{F_1, F_2, ..., F_n\}$, where F_i stands for $(f_i\ \alpha_i)$, is the intersection of the fuzzy sets $M(F_i)$, i.e.

$$\mu_{M(\Sigma)}(I) = min_{i=1,...,n}\ \mu_{M(F_i)}(I).$$

The consistency degree of Σ will be defined by $cons(\Sigma) = max_I\ \mu_{M(\Sigma)}(I)$; it estimates the degree to which the set of models of Σ is not empty. The quantity $Inc(\Sigma) = 1 - Cons(\Sigma)$ will be called degree of inconsistency of Σ.

Interestingly enough, this definition of the consistency of Σ (Cons(Σ) = 1) extends the usual notion of consistency in classical logic. Let Σ^* be the classical knowledge base obtained from Σ when we forget the weights of uncertainty. Then, as proved in [8], there is an equivalence between the inconsistency of Σ^* in the usual sense and the fact that the degree of inconsistency is positive. In other words, Σ^* is consistent $\Leftrightarrow$ Cons(Σ) = 1. It is also proved [7] that Inc(Σ) > 0 is equivalent to the fact that the assignment of weights in Σ is in contradiction with the basic axiom of necessity measures $N(p \wedge q) = \min(N(p), N(q))$.

Finally we say that a weighted formula F is a logical consequence of Σ if and only if $\forall I, \mu_{M(F)}(I) \geq \mu_{M(\Sigma)}(I)$, which will be written $\Sigma \vDash F$. Let us note that all these definitions subsume those of classical logic. We take the notation $\Sigma \vdash (f\ \beta)$ if and only if there exists a β'–refutation with $\beta' \geq \beta$, i.e. a deduction of $(\perp\ \beta')$, from the set of weighted clauses Σ' obtained by adding $N(\neg f) = 1$ to Σ. Then we have the following completeness theorem [8]: let Σ be a set of weighted clauses ; then $\Sigma \vdash (f\ \beta)$ if and only if $\Sigma \vDash (f\ \beta)$.

2.4. Hypothetical reasoning

As pointed out in [8], the weighted clause $(\neg p \vee q\ \alpha)$ is semantically equivalent to the weighted clause $(q\ \min(\alpha, v(p)))$ where $v(p)$ is the truth value of p, i.e. $v(p) = 1$ if p is true and $v(p) = 0$ if p is false. Indeed, for any uncertain proposition $(p\ \alpha)$ we can write $\mu_{M(p\ \alpha)}(I)$ under the form $\max(v_I(p), 1 - \alpha)$, where $v_I(p)$ is the truth-value assigned to p by interpretation I. Then obviously :

$$\forall I, \mu_{M(\neg p \vee q\ \alpha)}(I) = \max(v_I(\neg p \vee q), 1 - \alpha) = \max(1 - v_I(p), v_I(q), 1 - \alpha)$$
$$= \max(v_I(q), 1 - \min(v_I(p), \alpha)) = \mu_{M(q\ \min(v_I(p), \alpha))}(I)$$

The equivalence between the weighted clauses $(\neg p \vee \neg s \vee q\ \alpha)$ and $(\neg p \vee q\ \min(\alpha, v(s)))$ expresses that the rule "if p and s are true then q is certain to the degree α" means that "in an environment where s is true, if p is true then q is certain to the degree α" if we decide to consider s as an assumption. This equivalence leads to the following modified presentation of the resolution rule

$$\frac{(\neg p \vee q\ \min(\alpha, v(s)))\ (p \vee r\ \min(\beta, v(t)))}{(q \vee r\ \min(\alpha, v(s), \beta, v(t)))}$$

This enables us to express that if the clause $\neg p \vee q$ is certain to the degree α in an environment where s is true and if the clause $p \vee r$ is certain to the degree β in an environment where t is true, then the resolvent clause $q \vee r$ is certain to the degree $\min(\alpha,\beta)$ in an environment where s *and* t are true (since $v(s \wedge t) = \min(v(s),v(t))$). It turns out that when $\alpha = \beta = 1$, the above resolution rule is very close to the CAT-correct resolution rule [2], which separates the assumptions from the other literals by sorting them, and where resolution is restricted so as to get rid of the non-assumption literals.

It has been shown that if, adding to the knowledge base the clauses corresponding to $N(\neg p) = 1$, we obtain by resolution the empty clause with a strictly positive weight, then this weight is a lower bound of the necessity degree of p. The exploration of all proof paths leading to the empty clause will thus enable to determine the set of environments in which p is somewhat certain if all assumptions are carried over to the weight side, before running the refutation. This enables us to define in Sections 3 and 4 a possibilistic ATMS and to develop the associated basic procedures.

2.5. Example

Let Σ be the following set of propositional necessity-valued possibilistic clauses, concerning a given meeting about which we would like to make some predictions. The proposition Albert (respectively Betty, Chris, David, Eva) means that Albert (respectively Betty, Chris, David, Eva) will come to a given meeting ; the proposition begins-late (respectively quiet, productive) means that the meeting will begin late (resp. will be quiet, will be productive).

C1   ($\neg$Albert $\vee$ $\neg$Betty $\vee$ $\neg$Chris   0.7)
     "it is rather certain that Albert, Betty and Chris will not come together "
C2   ($\neg$David $\vee$ Chris   0.4)
     " it is somewhat certain that if David comes, then Chris also comes"
C3   ($\neg$Betty $\vee$ begins-late   0.3)
     " it is somewhat certain that if Betty comes, then the meeting will begin late"
C4   ($\neg$begins-late $\vee$ $\neg$Chris   0.3)
     " it is somewhat certain that if the meeting begins late, then Chris will not come"
C5   ($\neg$begins-late $\vee$ $\neg$quiet   0.5)

" it is relatively certain that if the meeting begins late, then the meeting will not be quiet"

C6 (¬Albert ∨ ¬David ∨ ¬quiet 0.6)
"it is rather certain that if Albert and David come, then the meeting will not be quiet"

C7 (¬Albert ∨ ¬Betty ∨ ¬David ∨ ¬quiet 0.9)
"it is almost certain that if Albert, Betty and David come, then the meeting will not be quiet"

C8 (Betty 0.2)
" it is weakly certain that Betty will come"

C9 (¬Albert ∨ ¬Eva ∨ productive 0.5)
"it is relatively certain that if Albert and Eva come, then the meeting will be productive"

C10 (¬Albert ∨ ¬Betty ∨ Chris ∨ ¬Eva ∨ productive 0.8)
"it is almost certain that if Albert, Betty and Eva come and Chris does not come then the meeting will be productive"

For example, the clause C1 means that $N(\neg\text{Albert} \vee \neg\text{Betty} \vee \neg\text{Chris}) \geq 0.7$. By resolution we can for example infer (¬Albert ∨ ¬Betty ∨ ¬David 0.4) from C1 and C2. It can be checked that Σ is consistent ; if we add "C11 : (David 1)" to Σ, then we can obtain ($\perp$ 0.2) from C1, C2, C3, C4, C8 and C11 ; hence we can conclude that $N(\neg\text{David}) \geq 0.2$, i.e. it is weakly certain that David will not come to the meeting. Clearly, the weights in the above example reflect an ordering of the propositions,in terms of certainty, and are used only as landmarks.

3. Basic principles and definitions of a possibilistic A.T.M.S.

Classical ATMS require that the clauses contained inside the knowledge base (justifications and disjunctions of assumptions) are certain ; we may wish to handle more or less uncertain information without losing the capacities of the ATMS. The basic principle of the Π–ATMS is to associate to each clause a weight α which is a lower bound of its necessity degree. Assumptions may also be weighted, i.e. the user or the inference engine may decide at any time to believe an assumption with a certainty degree that he/she will give. A Π–ATMS is able to answer the following questions :

(i) Under what configuration of the assumptions is the proposition p certain to the degree
     α ? (i.e., what assumptions shall we consider as true, and with what certainty degrees
     in order to have p certain to the degree α ?)

(ii) What is the inconsistency degree of a given configuration of assumptions ?

(iii) In a given configuration of assumptions, to what degree is each proposition certain ?

The kind of classical ATMS we extend here is Cayrol and Tayrac's [2, 21] generalized
ATMS, where each piece of information is represented by a (general) propositional clause,
which enables :

– a uniform representation for all pieces of knowledge (no differenciated storage and
  treatment between justifications and disjunctions of assumptions).
– the capability of handling negated assumptions as assumptions, i.e. environments and
  nogoods may contain negations of assumptions (they are called generalized
  environments and nogoods by Cayrol and Tayrac) ; this approach differs from De Kleer
  "NATMS" [5] where negated assumptions do not appear inside the environments.
– a simple and uniform algorithm for the computation of labels, based on a restricted
  resolution (see Section 5).

Environments

       First, we generalize the basic notions attached to the classical ATMS. Let Σ be a set of
necessity-valued clauses. Let E be a set of assumptions; the following definitions are useful:

–) [E α] is an <u>environment</u> of the proposition p if and only if $N(p) \geq \alpha$ is a logical
   consequence of $E \cup \Sigma$, where the assumptions of E are considered as certainly true (the
   certainty degree of the associated clauses is 1) ;

–) [E α] is an <u>α-environment</u> of p if and only if [E α] is an environment of p and if
   $\forall \alpha' > \alpha$, [E α'] is not an environment of p (α is maximal) ;

–) [E α] is an α–contradictory environment, or <u>α–nogood</u> if and only if $E \cup \Sigma$ is
   α–inconsistent (i.e. $E \cup \Sigma \models (\perp \alpha)$), with α maximal. We shall use the notation
   $nogood_\alpha E$. The α–nogood [E α] is said to be minimal if there is no β–nogood [E' β]
   such that $E \supset E'$ and $\alpha \leq \beta$.

Labels

       In order to define the label of a proposition p, we consider only non-weighted
assumptions (i.e. they will have the implicit weight 1). It can be shown that it is useless to
weight the assumptions inside the labels (this remark holds also for the base of no-goods).

The label of the proposition p, $L(p) = \{[E_i\ \alpha_i], i \in I\}$ is the only fuzzy subset of the set of the environments for which the four following properties hold :

- *(weak) consistency* : $\forall [E_i\ \alpha_i] \in L(p)$, $E_i \cup \Sigma$ is β-*inconsistent*, with $\beta < \alpha_i$ (i.e. $Inc(E_i \cup \Sigma) < \alpha_i$ in the sense of Section 2, the certainty degree associated to the E_i's being 1) ; it guarantees that either E_i is consistent (i.e. $\beta = 0$), or its inconsistency degree is anyway strictly less than the certainty with which p can be deduced from $E_i \cup \Sigma$ (i.e. we are sure to use a consistent sub-base of $E_i \cup \Sigma$ containing only formulas with weights greater than β, and from which it is possible to deduce p, see [8]).

- *soundness* : $L(p)$ is sound if and only if $\forall [E_i\ \alpha_i] \in L$ we have $E_i \cup \Sigma \vDash (p\ \alpha_i)$ where $\vDash$ has been defined in Section 2 ; i.e., $L(p)$ contains only environments of p.

- *completeness* : $L(p)$ is complete if and only if for every environment E' such that $E' \cup \Sigma \vDash (p\ \alpha')$ then $\exists i \in I$ such that $E_i \subset E'$ and $\alpha_i \geq \alpha'$, i.e., all minimal α-environments of p are present in $L(p)$.

- *minimality* : $L(p)$ is minimal if and only if it does not contain two environments $(E_1\ \alpha_1)$ and $(E_2\ \alpha_2)$ such that $E_1 \subset E_2$ and $\alpha_1 \geq \alpha_2$. It means that $L(p)$ only contains the most specific α-environments of p (i.e. all their assumptions are useful).

We emphasize that ranking environments according to their weight in the label of each proposition provides a way for limiting the consequences of combinatorial explosion (the problem was already pointed out by Provan [19] and Raiman [20]) : indeed when a label contains too many environments, the Π-ATMS can help the user by giving the environments with the greatest weight(s) only. However let us observe that these environments are also those with the greatest number of assumptions generally.

Example (continued) : we may consider the literals Albert, Betty, Chris, David and Eva as assumptions (abbreviated respectively by A, B, C, D, E), i.e. we wish to be able to fix the set of persons attending the meeting, in order to get it quiet, or productive, etc. In this case, the minimal nogoods are

$nogood_{0.7}\{A,B,C\}$; $nogood_{0.4}\{A,B,D\}$; $nogood_{0.4}\{D,\neg C\}$; $nogood_{0.3}\{B,C\}$; $nogood_{0.3}\{B,D\}$; $nogood_{0.2}\{\neg B\}$; $nogood_{0.2}\{C\}$; $nogood_{0.2}\{D\}$.

We now give examples of labels.

The label of *productive* is $\{\{A, E\}_{0.5}, \{A, B, \neg C, E\}_{0.8}\}$.

The label of *quiet* is $\{\}$, i.e. no configuration of assumptions enables to deduce that the meeting will be quiet with a strictly positive certainty degree.

The label of $\neg quiet$ is $\{\{\}_{0.2}, \{B\}_{0.3}, \{A,D\}_{0.6}, \{A,B,D\}_{0.9}\}$; let us make a few remarks :

- the presence of the empty 0.2 environment $\{\}_{0.2}$ in the label expresses that if no assumption is made, then we can already deduce ($\neg quiet\ 0.2$). We extend the classical terminology by saying that $\neg quiet$ is a 0.2–premisse.

- the 0.9–environment $\{A,B,D\}_{0.9}$ contains the 0.3–nogood $nogood_{0.3}\{B,D\}$; in a classical ATMS, such an environment would have been inhibited, since it would have been inconsistent ; however the label is weakly consistent ; this example show us that there is no equivalence between strong (i.e. classical) consistency and weak consistency (we have only consistency $\Rightarrow$ weak consistency). The same remark holds also for the nogood $nogood_{0.2}\{D\}$ contained in $\{A,D\}_{0.6}$ and in $\{A,B,D\}_{0.9}$.

- the environment $\{A,B,D\}$ contains the environment $\{A,D\}$ and nevertheless $\{A,D\}_{0.6}$ and $\{A,B,D\}_{0.9}$ are both in the label of $\neg quiet$ without violating the minimality of the label, because $\{A,D\}_{0.6}$ does not subsume $\{A,B,D\}_{0.9}$ whereas $\{A,D\}$ subsumes $\{A,B,D\}$ in classical logic and thus only $\{A,D\}$ would be kept in the label of $\neg quiet$ in a classical ATMS. Besides, the empty environment $\{\}$ subsuming any other one, it would remain alone in the label of $\neg quiet$ in a classical ATMS.

Consequently, due to the presence of uncertainty weights, the ATMS becomes more selective, and at the same time supplies richer symbolic information.

Let us suppose we add the clause C'11 : (Betty $\vee$ David 1) to $\Sigma = \{C1, ..., C10\}$, i.e. we are now absolutely certain that either Betty or David will come ; then the system Σ becomes 0.2–inconsistent, since ($\bot\ 0.2$) is derived by resolution from $\{C2, C3, C4, C8, C'11\}$. In consequence the new nogood base is : $nogood_1\{\neg C, \neg D\}$; $nogood_{0.7}\{A,B,C\}$; $nogood_{0.7}\{A,B,\neg D\}$; $nogood_{0.4}\{A,B\}$; $nogood_{0.4}\{\neg C\}$; $nogood_{0.3}\{B\}$; $nogood_{0.2}\{\}$. The fact that the empty environment is a 0.2–nogood expresses that Σ is 0.2–inconsistent. Consequently, all environments of a label having a membership degree less or equal to 0.2 are inhibited. In fact, the labels do not take into account the clause (Betty 0.2) which is "responsible" of the 0.2–inconsistency, since it is the least reliable clause involved in the inconsistency. The label of $\neg quiet$ is now $\{\{A,D\}_{0.6}, \{A,\neg C\}_{0.6}, \{A,B,D\}_{0.9}, \{A,B,\neg C\}_{0.9}\}$.

Contexts

To extend the notion of context, we now consider *weighted assumptions*. A weighted assumption is a couple (H α) where H is an assumption and $\alpha \in [0,1]$ is the certainty degree assigned to H.

The *context* associated with the set of weighted assumptions $\mathcal{E}$ is the set of all couples $(p, val_{\mathcal{E}}(p))$, where p is a proposition or an assumption, and $val_{\mathcal{E}}(p) = \sup\{\alpha, \mathcal{E} \cup \Sigma \models (p\ \alpha)\}$. Let us now give the following theorem :

Let $\mathcal{E}$ be a set of weighted assumptions. Let p be a proposition ; it can be shown that $\mathcal{E} \cup \Sigma \models (p\ \alpha)$ in possibilistic logic if and only if $\exists\ [E_i\ \alpha_i] \in$ Label (p) , $E_i = \{H_{i,1}, H_{i,2},..., H_{i,n}\}$ such that

(i) $\mathcal{E}^* \supset E_i$ where $\mathcal{E}^*$ is the classical set of assumptions obtained from $\mathcal{E}$ by ignoring the weights.

(ii) $\alpha \le \min(\alpha_i, \beta_1, \beta_2, ..., \beta_n)$ where $\beta_1, \beta_2, ..., \beta_n$ are the weights attached to $H_{i,1}, H_{i,2}, ..., H_{i,n}$ in $\mathcal{E}$.

(iii) $\alpha > \text{Inc}\ (\mathcal{E} \cup \Sigma)$.

The proof of the theorem is obvious using the results of the classical ATMS. This theorem gives an immediate algorithm to compute contexts, given the label of every proposition p :

> $\alpha\_\text{max} \leftarrow 0$;
> *For every* $[E_i\ \alpha_i] \in$ Label (p) *do*
> > *if* $\mathcal{E}^* \supset E_i$
> > *then* $\alpha\_\text{max} \leftarrow \max(\alpha\_\text{max}, \min(\alpha_i, \beta_1, \beta_2, ..., \beta_n))$ where
> > $\beta_1,.....,\beta_n$ are the weights attached to $H_{i,1},..., H_{i,n}$ in $\mathcal{E}$.
> *end*

Intuitively, for each environment of the label of p included in $\mathcal{E}^*$, the algorithm computes the degree of certainty with which this environment entails p ; this degree depends upon the justifications used in deriving p (via α_i) and the weights of the assumptions in this environment.

Example (continued) : let us consider the initial system $\Sigma = \{C1, ..., C10\}$ and let $\mathcal{E}$ be the set of weighted assumptions $\mathcal{E} = \{(A\ 0.8), (\neg C\ 0.9), (D\ 0.5), (E\ 0.7)\}$; then the inconsistency degree of $\mathcal{E} \cup \Sigma$ is 0.4 and the context of $\mathcal{E}$ is $\{(A\ 0.8), (\neg C\ 0.9), (D\ 0.5), (E\ 0.7), (\neg\text{quiet}\ 0.5), (\text{profitable}\ 0.5)\}$.

Ignored assumptions and environments

If we want to concentrate on significant environments, i.e. to hide environments with a weight ≤ α containing the assumption H, we add to the system the instruction *ignore (H α)*. The classical "ignore" instruction [4] corresponds to *ignore (H 1)*. The user may also choose to hide *all* environments with a weight below a threshold α.

4. Application to the revision of possibilistic knowledge bases

Classical ATMS enable us to compute all maximal consistent sub-bases of an inconsistent classical knowledge base, by associating a specific assumption to each formula and then by computing the "candidates" [6], i.e. the sets of assumptions whose deletion makes the knowledge base consistent ; roughly speaking, candidates are obtained as the conjunctions of assumptions where one assumption is selected in each minimal nogood. Maximal consistent sub-bases are then obtained from the candidates by complementation.

The revision process in possibilistic knowledge bases is somewhat more selective than in classical knowledge bases, since the weights enable the definition of a preference ordering on the set of maximal consistent knowledge bases. There is not a unique way of defining such an ordering, and we propose three of them in the following.

The first ordering is based on the computation, for each maximal consistent sub-base $\mathcal{B}_i$ of a possibilistic knowledge base $\mathcal{B}$, of its so-called acceptability degree [14], which is defined as the complement to 1 of the weight of the most certain formula which is not kept in $\mathcal{B}_i$, i.e.

$$\text{Acc}(\mathcal{B}_i) = 1 - \text{Max}\{\alpha, (f\ \alpha) \in \mathcal{B} - \mathcal{B}_i\}$$

The acceptability degree can be used either for selecting the preferred maximal consistent sub-base(s) (which maximize(s) it), or to grade the sub-bases in an approach which considers all the maximal consistent sub-bases for estimating various degrees of entailment from $\mathcal{B}$, for a given formula [14].

When several maximal consistent sub-bases have the same acceptability degree, this ordering can be refined into a second one, based on the idea that among a minimal subset of formulas involved in a contradiction, we throw out one of the formulas with the lowest weight in order to restore the consistency. This is the basic idea underlying epistemic entrenchment relations [15] whose numerical counterpart has been proved to be necessity measures [13]. This leads to the following definition: a sub-base $\mathcal{B}_i$ of a possibilistic knowledge base $\mathcal{B}$ is said to be *strongly maximal consistent* iff it is consistent and

$$\forall \, (f\,\alpha) \in \mathcal{B} - \mathcal{B}_i, \ \text{Inc}(\mathcal{B}_i \cup (f\,\alpha)) = \alpha.$$

Let us give an illustrative example : let $\mathcal{B}$ be the following possibilistic knowledge base :

$$\mathcal{B} = \{(p\ 0.9),\ (\neg p \vee q\ \ 0.8),\ (\neg q\ 0.7),\ (\neg p \vee r\ \ 0.6),\ (\neg p \vee \neg r\ \ 0.6),\ (\neg r \vee s\ \ 0.5),$$
$$(r \vee (t \wedge u)\ 0.4),\ (\neg s\ 0.3),\ (\neg t\ 0.2)\}$$

Among the maximal consistent sub-bases of $\mathcal{B}$ (in the classical sense), let us consider the four following ones (obviously other exist)

$$\mathcal{B}_1 = \mathcal{B} - \{(p\ 0.9)\}$$
$$\mathcal{B}_2 = \mathcal{B} - \{(\neg q\ 0.7),\ (\neg p \vee r\ \ 0.6),\ (r \vee (t \wedge u)\ 0.4)\}$$
$$\mathcal{B}_3 = \mathcal{B} - \{(\neg q\ 0.7),\ (\neg p \vee \neg r\ \ 0.6),\ (\neg s\ 0.3)\}$$
$$\mathcal{B}_4 = \mathcal{B} - \{(\neg q\ 0.7),\ (\neg p \vee r\ \ 0.6),\ (\neg t\ 0.2)\}$$

We have $\text{Acc}(\mathcal{B}_1) = 0.1$ and $\text{Acc}(\mathcal{B}_2) = \text{Acc}(\mathcal{B}_3) = \text{Acc}(\mathcal{B}_4) = 0.3$; $\mathcal{B}_3$ and $\mathcal{B}_4$ are strongly maximal consistent sub-bases of $\mathcal{B}$; $\mathcal{B}_2$ is not because $\text{Inc}(\mathcal{B}_2 \cup \{((r \vee (t \wedge u)\ 0.4)\}) = 0.3 < 0.4$.

In order to compute the maximal consistent knowledge sub-bases using the functionalities of a possibilistic ATMS, we transform the possibilistic knowledge base $\mathcal{B}$ into a set of uncertain justifications $\Sigma(\mathcal{B})$ by associating to each formula a specific assumption: in our previous example, the obtained set of justifications $\Sigma(\mathcal{B})$ is the following :

$(A_1 \rightarrow p\ 0.9)$ $(A_2 \rightarrow \neg p \vee q\ 0.8)$ $(A_3 \rightarrow \neg q\ 0.7)$

$(A_4 \rightarrow \neg p \vee r\ 0.6)$ $(A_5 \rightarrow \neg p \vee \neg r\ 0.6)$ $(A_6 \rightarrow \neg r \vee s\ 0.5)$

$(A_7 \rightarrow r \vee t\ 0.4)$ $(A_7 \rightarrow r \vee u\ 0.4)$ $(A_8 \rightarrow \neg s\ 0.3)$

$(A_9 \rightarrow \neg t\ 0.2)$

Note that the assumption A_7 controlling the 7th formula, controls two clauses in $\Sigma(\mathcal{B})$. When A_i is true (resp. false), the formula, i.e. one or more clauses, controlled by A_i is kept in the sub-base (resp. thrown out). In order to compute the strongly maximal consistent sub-bases of $\mathcal{B}$ we must compute the *strong candidates* of $\Sigma(\mathcal{B})$. A strong candidate is the set of assumptions attached to the formulas outside a strongly maximal consistent sub-base of $\mathcal{B}$. They can be obtained from the base of nogoods[1] as follows : the (minimal) nogoods are ranked according to their inconsistency degree (in decreasing order, i.e. starting from the most inconsistent one(s)), and the strong candidates are computed incrementally by "breaking" successively all nogoods in the list; given a nogood N_i in the list and a partial candidate C (i.e. a set of assumptions obtained by breaking the nogoods considered before N_i in the list), breaking N_i roughly[2] consists in

(i) doing nothing, if N_i is already broken, i.e. if an assumption of N_i appears in C ; or
(ii) adding to C one of the assumptions A_j of N_i such that the weight of the formulas associated to A_j is minimal among the assumptions of N_i ; if there are n such assumptions, then C splits into n partial candidates.

Then, once all nogoods have been broken, we get all strong candidates. Considering a strong candidate, the corresponding strong maximal consistent sub-base is obtained as the complement of the set of formulas attached to the assumption in the strong candidate.

Let us go back to our example : the minimal nogoods are the following :

$nogood_{0.7} \{A_1, A_2, A_3\}$ $nogood_{0.6} \{A_1, A_4, A_5\}$
$nogood_{0.3} \{A_1, A_4, A_6, A_8\}$ $nogood_{0.2} \{A_1, A_5, A_7, A_9\}$

Breaking out the 0.7-nogood gives only one partial candidate, $\{A_3\}$; then, breaking the 0.6-nogood splits the partial candidate into two new ones, $\{A_3, A_4\}$ and $\{A_3, A_5\}$; then, breaking the 0.3-nogood gives nothing new from $\{A_3, A_4\}$ since it already inhibits

---

[1] The base of nogoods is the set of minimal nogoods.

[2] In fact, step (ii) is more complicated in order to ensure the minimality of the candidates: if there are several nogoods with the same weight, they are treated together by expressing, for each nogood sharing no assumption with C, the assumptions with the lowest weight under the form of a logical disjunction, then transforming the conjunction of these disjunctions obtained for all non such nogoods into a disjunction of conjunctions; a new partial candidate is then obtained by adding one of these conjunctions to C.

the nogood (for it contains A_4), and gives $\{A_3,A_5,A_8\}$ from $\{A_3,A_5\}$; lastly, breaking the 0.2-nogood gives $\{A_3,A_4,A_9\}$ from $\{A_3,A_4\}$ and nothing new from $\{A_3,A_5,A_8\}$. Finally, we have computed two strong condidates which are $\{A_3,A_4,A_9\}$ and $\{A_3,A_5,A_8\}$. The two correspondent strongly maximal consistent sub-bases are obtained by taking the formulas of $\mathcal{B}$ which are not associated with an assumption of the candidate, i.e.

$$\mathcal{B}_3 = \mathcal{B} - \{(\neg q\ \ 0.7), (\neg p\vee\neg r\ \ 0.6), (\neg s\ \ 0.3)\}$$
$$\mathcal{B}_4 = \mathcal{B} - \{(\neg q\ \ 0.7), (\neg p\vee r\ \ 0.6), (\neg t\ \ 0.2)\}$$

It can be easily checked that $\mathcal{B}_1$ and $\mathcal{B}_2$, which are not computed by the algorithm, are not strongly maximal consistent sub-bases.

An orderingwhich is more selective than the previous one is the lexicographic ordering: to each candidate C we associate the multiset, denoted by list(C), of the weights of the justifications associated with the assumptions of C. In our example, to $\{A_1\}$ we associate (0.9), to $\{A_1,A_4,A_5\}$ we associate (0.9,0.6,0.6), etc. Then, if C_1 and C_2 are two candidates, we say that C_1 is lexicographically preferred to C_2, or $C_1 \leq_L C_2$, iff list(C_1) $\leq_L$ list(C_2), where $\leq_L$ is the usual lexicographic ordering, defined recursively by

list $(C_1) \leq_L$ list (C_2)
$\Leftrightarrow$list $(C_1) = \emptyset$
   or max(list(C_1)) < max(list(C_2))
   or (max(list(C_1)) = max(list(C_2))
     and list(C_1) - {max(list(C_1))} $\leq_L$ list(C_2) - {max(list(C_1))}

The minimal elements relatively to $\leq_L$ are called lexicographically optimal candidates, and the correspondent sub-bases are called lexicographically maximal consistent sub-bases. If $C_1$and C_2 are two candidates such that $C_1 \leq_L C_2$ then C_2 is a better candidate to deletion than C_1, since either the most reliable justification controlled by C_2 is strictly more reliable than the most reliable justification controlled by C_1, or these two most reliable justifications controlled respectively by C_1 and C_2 have the same weight, but the second most reliable justification controlled by C_2 is strictly more reliable than the second most reliable justification controlled by C_1, or they have the same weight and then we consider the third most reliable justification, etc.

It can be shown that the set of lexicographically maximal consistent sub-bases is included in the set of strongly maximal consistent sub-bases; thus this ordering is more refined than the previous one. The lexicographically optimal candidates can be computed from the nogood base by an algorithm similar to the previous one. In our example, we have list $(\{A_3,A_4,A_9\}) = (0.7,0.6,0.2)$ and list $(\{A_3,A_5,A_8\})= (0.7,0.6,0.3)$; thus, the only lexicographically optimal candidate is $\{A_3,A_4,A_9\}$ and the only lexicographically maximal consistent sub-base is $\mathcal{B}_4$.

5. Basic algorithms of a possibilistic ATMS

The implementation of our possibilistic ATMS is based on a straightforward generalization to possibilistic logic of the works of Cayrol and Tayrac [2, 21]. It presents the following features :

– all pieces of information of the knowledge base are stored under the form of general (non-Horn) weighted clauses, which enables to represent all kinds of information in an homogeneous way.
– negated assumptions are naturally taken into account, and they may appear in environments, nogoods, labels and contexts.
– as seen in Section 3, the main task of an ATMS (possibilistic or classical) is to compute the label of each proposition of interest and the minimal nogoods (since the knowledge of the labels and of the nogood base enables the Π–ATMS to answer the different kinds of requests). The computation of labels and nogoods is made by using a restriction of possibilistic resolution, the CAT-correct possibilistic resolution. A clause with typed antecedent, or CAT [2] is a clause containing no negative non-assumption literal (by convention, typed literals are assumptions). For example, $(\neg A \vee B \vee c\ \alpha)$, $(\neg A \vee B\ \alpha)$, $(\neg A \vee B \vee c \vee d\ \alpha)$ are CATs whereas $(\neg a \vee B \vee c\ \alpha)$ is not. The deduction of a CAT whose non-assumption literal is d enables to deduce an α–environment of d ; for example, $(\neg A \vee B \vee d\ \alpha)$ enables to add $\{A,\neg B\}_\alpha$ to the label of d (if it was not already there) ; similarly, the deduction of a CAT containing no non-assumption literal enables to deduce an α–nogood. CAT-correct possibilistic resolution is then defined as follows : let O be a total ordering on the set of non-assumption atoms, and let C1 and C2 be two possibilistic clauses ; then the CAT-correct possibilistic resolution consists in applying the possibilistic resolution principle between C1 and C2 if and only if :

        (i)   C1 and C2 are CATs.

or   (ii)   C1 is a CAT and C2 is a non-CAT which is resolved with respect to the smallest (relatively to O) non-assumption negative literal.

Each time a new clause is introduced into the system, a search tree is built (depth-first or breadth-first) in order to deduce all possible CATs ; after the introduction of the new clause and after each resolution step, the set of clauses is minimized by suppressing first the tautologies, then the subsumed clauses, a clause (c α) subsuming a clause (c' β) if only if $\alpha > \beta$ and c implies c'.

It can be proved that the use of CAT-correct possibilistic resolution is complete for the computation of labels and nogoods (which comes immediately from the completeness of the CAT-correct resolution in the classical case [2]). A possibilistic ATMS based on CAT-correct possibilistic resolution is currently being implemented.

6. Conclusion

The approach presented in this paper differs from the ones mentioned in the introduction and which handle uncertainty, on several points :

First, the ATMS with embedded belief functions enable us to rank interpretations (i.e. maximal consistent environments), as they intend to do, but they cannot handle the uncertainty pervading the knowledge base if any, i.e. the justifications. They hold the justifications as classical knowledge (i.e. certain) and, putting weights on the assumptions, they deduce the weights attached to the other propositions. Our approach does not attach any a priori weight to each proposition (assumptions or non-assumptions) but assigns a certainty degree to the clauses contained in the knowledge base (not only justifications, but also disjunctions of assumptions and nogoods specified by the user) ; then, taking into account this uncertain knowledge, we establish a mapping from certainty degrees assigned to assumptions to the certainty degrees of the propositions (i.e. the consequences of the assignment).

Secondly, in the other approaches, truth maintenance and uncertainty management are completely separated, i.e. the label of a proposition p is first computed, then Bel(p) is computed (of course, taking into account Label(p)). Our approach completely integrates the uncertainty management into the truth maintenance system, by assigning a weight to each environment of a proposition. Besides, the handling of weights will be done during the computation of labels, since certainty weights are present inside the label.

Thirdly, the main purpose of introducing uncertainty into A.T.M.S. is the ability of ranking solutions (i.e. interpretations) and eliminating solutions which are too uncertain. Hence the precise values of certainty degrees are not as important as their ordering. Possibility theory offers a framework where the ordering of the uncertainty degrees is more important than their precise values, and which requires easier computations (only min and max operations are used) than the general Dempster-Shafer approach. Furthermore, the weights assigned to nogoods are always available and no extra computations are required in order to renormalize results.

Fourthly, in Provan's model, the belief of the proposition p is first computed formally by rewriting the label of p into an "independent form" and then computed numerically ; if we decide to change the weight of an assumption, the formal expression of the label of p remains unchanged and the re-computation of Bel(p) is immediate ; however this is not the case if the label of p changes (which may happen each time we add a new justification) : then we have to transform again the expression of the label of p ; in the possibilistic model, both changes of weights or labels lead to almost no more computations than in De Kleer's original model.

Lastly, the other models cannot handle disjunctions of assumptions ; besides, Provan's model needs to consider the assumptions as independent as long as they are not mutually exclusive (i.e. not containing any nogood). Possibilistic ATMS do not require this assumption, and can handle disjunctions of assumptions, as well as negated assumptions.

In summary, possibilistic ATMS proposes a joint handling of assumptions and uncertainty relative to a knowledge base, in the framework of possibilistic logic, by ordering the environments of a proposition according to the certainty with which it can be deduced from each of them. The fact that possibilistic logic remains on many points close to classical logic facilitates the extension of efficient procedures, such as those based on CAT-correct resolution for the computation of labels, nogoods and contexts.

Possibilistic ATMS can be applied to truth maintenance problems in presence of uncertainty, to default reasoning, to fault diagnosis (see [9]), or to generation of (the most plausible) explanations.

Acknowledgements : The authors would like to thank Michel Cayrol and Pierre Tayrac for many fruitful discussions about ATMS and CAT-correct resolution. This work has been supported by the European ESPRIT Basic Research Action number 3085 entitled Defeasible Reasoning and Uncertainty Management Systems (DRUMS). Support from THOMSON-SIMSA-CINTRA is also gratefully acknowledged.

References

[1] Bernasconi C., Rivoira S., Termini S. On the notion of uncertain belief revision systems, Extended Abstracts of the Third International Conference on Information Processing and Management of Uncertainty in Knowledge-based Systems, Paris, 1990, 458–460.

[2] Cayrol M., Tayrac P. ARC : un ATMS basé sur la résolution CAT-correcte. Revue d'Intelligence Artificielle (Hermès, Paris), 3(3), 1989, 19–39.

[3] De Kleer J. An assumption-based TMS. Artificial Intelligence, 28, 1986, 127–162.

[4] De Kleer J. Extending the ATMS. Artificial Intelligence, 28, 1986, 163–196.

[5] De Kleer J. A general labeling algorithm for assumption-based truth maintenance, Proc. of the Nat. Conf. on Artificial Intelligence, Saint Paul, Minnesota, Aug. 21–26, 1988, 188–192.

[6] De Kleer J., Williams B. Diagnosing multiple faults. Artificial Intelligence, 32, 1987, 97–130.

[7] Dubois D., Lang J., Prade H. Theorem proving under uncertainty – A possibility theory-based approach. Proc. of the 10th Inter. Joint Conf. on Artificial Intelligence, Milano, August, 1987, 984–986.

[8] Dubois D., Lang J., Prade H. Automated reasoning using possibilistic logic : semantics, belief revision and variable certainty weights. Proc. of the 5th Workshop on Uncertainty in Artificial Intelligence, Windsor, Ontario, 1989, 81–87.

[9] Dubois D., Lang J., Prade H. Gestion d'hypothèses en logique possibiliste : un exemple d'application au diagnostic. Proc. of the 10th Inter. Conf. Workshop on Expert Systems and their Applications, Avignon, France, May 28–June 1st, 1990, 299–313.

[10] Dubois D., Lang J., Prade H. Handling uncertain knowledge in an ATMS using possibilistic logic. In : Methodologies for Intelligent Systems, 5 (Z.W. Ras, M. Zemankova, M.L. Emrich, eds.), North-Holland, Amsterdam, 1990, 252-259.

[11] Dubois D., Prade H. Necessity measures and the resolution principle. IEEE Trans. Systems, Man and Cybernetics, 17, 1987, 474–478.

[12] Dubois D., Prade H. (with the collaboration of Farreny H., Martin-Clouaire R., Testemale C.) Possibility Theory – An Approach to Computerized Processing of Uncertainty. Plenum Press, New York, 1988.

[13] Dubois D., Prade H. Epistemic entrenchment and possibilistic logic. In Tech. Report IRIT/90-2/R, IRIT, Univ. P. Sabatier, Toulouse, France, 1990. Artificial Intelligence, to appear.

[14] Dubois D., Prade H. Reasoning with inconsistent information in a possibilistic setting. Proc. of the 9th Europ. Conf. on Artificial Intelligence Stockholm, Sweden, Aug. 6–10, 1990, 259–261.

[15] Gärdenfors P. Knowledge in Flux – Modeling the Dynamics of Epistemic States. The MIT Press, Cambridge, Mass., 1988.

[16] Laskey K.B., Lehner P.E. Belief maintenance ; an integrated approach to uncertainty management. Proc. of the 7th Nat. Conf. of Amer. for Artificial Intelligence, Saint Paul, Minnesota, Aug. 21–26, 1988, 210–214.

[17] Lee R.C.T. Fuzzy logic and the resolution principle. Journal of ACM, 19, 1972, 109–119.

[18] Pearl J., Probabilistic Reasoning in Intelligent Systems : Networks of Plausible Inference. Morgan Kaufmann Publ. Inc., San Mateo, Ca., 1988.

[19] Provan G.M. An analysis of ATMS-based techniques for computing Dempster-Shafer belief functions. Proc of the 9th Joint Conf. on Artificial Intelligence, Detroit, Aug. 20–25, 1989, 1115–1120.

[20] Raiman O. Two heuristics integrating probabilities and logic : a preliminary report on parsimonious search. In : Computational Intelligence II (F. Gardin, G. Mauri, M.G. Filippini, eds.), North-Holland, Amsterdam, 1990, 61-68.

[21] Tayrac P. ARC : an extended ATMS based on directed CAT-correct resolution. See in this volume.

[22] Wrzos-Kaminski J., Wrzos-Kaminska A. Explicit ordering of defaults in ATMS. Proc. of the 9th Europ. Conf. on Artificial Intelligence, Stockholm, Sweden, Aug. 6–10, 1990, 714–719.

[23] Zadeh L.A. Fuzzy sets as a basis for a theory of possibility. Fuzzy Sets and Systems, 1, 1978, 3–28.

ARC: AN EXTENDED ATMS BASED ON DIRECTED CAT-CORRECT RESOLUTION

Pierre TAYRAC

Institut de Recherche en Informatique de Toulouse, Université Paul Sabatier
118, Route de Narbonne 31062 Toulouse Cédex - FRANCE

New professional address:
Société CRIL, Innopole Labège, BP O5, 31 312 Labège - FRANCE

Abstract

This article describes an original resolution strategy (RCD: "Résolution CAT-correcte Dirigée") which is defined in propositionnal logic. This strategy represents a restriction of the application of "resolution principle" [12] and is specially designed to infer particular Horn clauses called CATCL ("Clauses à Antécédents Typés et Conséquents Limités").

We show that all significant clauses for an ATMS (Assumption-based Truth Maintenance System [4, 5, 6]) can be considered CATCL clauses under certain conditions and thus define an ATMS based on this resolution strategy, named ARC ("ATMS basé sur la Résolution CAT-correcte dirigée").

The ARC system retains all the advantages of conventional ATMS, allows the manipulation of general clauses (not only Horn clauses or disjunctions of assumptions), and integrates the new concept of "required label" which permits an improvement in performances.

1. Introduction

Most "intelligent" systems use classical logic to represent and process knowledge. This has lead to a great amount of development in improved methods of resolution which are generally based on the "Principle of Resolution" [12], [8], [15], [14]. However, the computational complexity of resolution requires the introduction of certain restrictive processes which improve efficiency while remaining complete.

We propose a new method of restriction based on the division of the language alphabet into two classes. This dichotomy has its origin in the ATMS which we are currently developing. This new strategy, which is defined in propositional logic, was specially designed to be used in the ATMS.

We first expose this strategy of resolution before explaining its use in the ATMS and its consequences.

2. A new strategy of resolution: RCD with clash

We propose a new strategy of resolution which is named: directed CAT-correct resolution with clash, or RCD ("Résolution CAT-correcte Dirigée") with clash, or simply RCD.

This strategy is based on the division of data[1] into two groups: $\mathcal{T}$ and $\mathcal{NT}$ (respectively Typed and uN-Typed). $\mathcal{T} \cup \mathcal{NT}$ corresponds to the language alphabet.

The division is completely arbitrary and typing is used simply to differentiate the two groups. There is no relation between this sort of typing and "typed data" generally used in computer terminology.

The definition of RCD requires the introduction of the notion of CAT clauses ("Clauses à Antécédents Typés" or "Clauses with Typed Antecedent").

This definition refer to the antecedent and consequent sides of a clause with respect to implicative clause form [10]. The clause $A \vee \neg B \vee C \vee \neg D$ can be written B D -> A C, where {B, D} is the antecedent and {A, C} is the consequence. The clause B D -> A C may also be represented by {B, D} -> {A, C}.

---

[1] Every atomic proposition is called a datum.

Definition

α is a CAT clause, if and only if: $T \supseteq$ Antecedent(α).

Example

If the language alphabet is: {A, B, c, d, e} with the set of typed data T: {A, B} and the set of un-typed data $\mathcal{NT}$: {c, d, e}, then the following clauses:

    -> A c,

    A ->,

    A B -> e d,

are CAT clauses, contrary to the next clauses:

    c ->,

    A B d -> x,

whose antecedent side includes at least one un-typed data.

RCD strategy is original in that it tries to produce particular clauses as opposed to most other resolution strategies which simply test sets of clauses for consistency.

We previously proposed a strategy, named CAT-correct resolution, which ensures the inference of every CAT logically entailed from the initial set of clauses [1, 2].

Both RCD and CAT-correct resolution use the principle of resolution to produce a specific type of clause. RCD strategy represents an improvement of CAT-correct resolution in that it is more efficient. This lies in the fact that RCD produces fewer clauses than CAT-correct resolution.

RCD is designed to deduce particular CATs. These clauses are named CATCL (CAT with Limited Consequent), and represent CATs whose the consequent side is either empty or a singleton element of a third parameter: the set L. Thus the definition of CATCL clauses depends on three parameters: T, $\mathcal{NT}$ (see above), and L.

Definition

α is a CATCL clause, if and only if:

  - $T \supseteq$ Antecedent(α),

  - $L \supseteq$ Consequent(α), and

  - |Consequent(α)| ≤ 1.

Example

If T={A, B}, $\mathcal{NT}$={a, b, c}, and L={B, c},

the clauses:

    A -> B,

    A -> c,

    B ->,

are CATCL, in contrast with the following clauses which are not:

a ->,

A -> b,

-> B c.

2.1. Definition of RCD

RCD is based on the use of the principle of resolution, and ensures the deduction of every minimal CATCL (not subsumed and which is not a tautology) which can be logically inferred from the initial set of clauses.

The application of RCD requires the definition of the parameters T, NT and L (previously presented). Furthermore, it is necessary to define a particular complete ordering O on $T \cup NT$, such that each un-typed datum is less than each typed datum.

Definition

A complete ordering O on $NT \cup T$ is RCD-correct if and only if $\forall x \in NT, \forall y \in T$ $x<y$ according to O.

Example

If $T=\{A, B, C\}$, $NT=\{d, e, f\}$, then the complete orderings

A < d < e < f < B < C,

A < d < B < C < e < f,

are not RCD-correct since in both cases there exists a typed data which is less than an un-typed data. Conversely the following complete orderings are RCD-correct:

d < e < f < A < B < C,

d < e < f < B < A < C,

e < f < d < B < A < C.

Thus the use of RCD depends on: T the set of typed data, NT the set of un-typed data, L a subset of $T \cup NT$, and O a complete RCD-correct ordering on $NT \cup T$.

The application of RCD is split up into two resolution processes:

typed RCD,

execution of RCD-clash.

Definition of typed RCD

The binary typed RCD consists of the application of the resolution principle between two clauses α1 and α2 of the form:

$$α1: \mathcal{A}1 \rightarrow \{x\} \cup \mathcal{B}1, \quad α2: \mathcal{A}2 \cup \{x\} \rightarrow \mathcal{B}2$$

under the following conditions:
1) α1 is a CAT;
2) α2 is a CATCL;
3) x is either the first datum in $\{x\}\cup\mathcal{B}1$ (w.r.t. $\mathcal{O}$), or the second datum in $\{x\}\cup\mathcal{B}1$ if the first one is member of $\mathcal{L}$;[1]
4) $|NTD^2(Consequent(α1)\cup Consequent(α2))| \leq 1$.

Remark: The datum x is necessarily typed[3] since α1 and α2 are CAT clauses.

Example
Let us suppose $\mathcal{T}=\{A, B, C\}$, $\mathcal{NT}=\{a, b, c\}$, $\mathcal{O}$: a < b < c < A < B < C, $\mathcal{L}=\{a\}$ and the following initial set of clauses:

A -> b B,
B -> a,
C -> B,
c B ->,

only the resolution between the clauses C -> B and B -> a is a typed RCD:

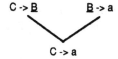

Execution of RCD-clash

The definition of RCD-clash depends on the notion of a primitive instance of a clause.

Definition
An instance α of a clause is primitive if and only if α is not the resolvent of a typed RCD.

---

[1] the rank of data in $\{x\}\cup\mathcal{B}1$ is defined by $\mathcal{O}$.
[2] NTD(X) represents the set of uN-Typed Data of X.
[3] Which explains the name: typed RCD.

According to this definition: each instance of the initial clause base and each instance of clauses which result from the execution of an RCD-clash, is primitive.

We use the term primitive instance of a clause instead of primitive clause because two instances of a same clause can be primitive and non-primitive respectively.

<u>Example</u>
If $T=\{A, B\}$, $NT=\{a, b\}$, O: $a < b < A < B$ and the clause base includes:

    A -> a,
    a -> b,
    A -> B,
    B -> b,

then the resolvent $\alpha 1$: A -> b of the clauses A -> <u>B</u> and <u>B</u> -> b is not a primitive instance because the resolution which allows its inference is a typed RCD.

In contrast the resolvent $\alpha 2$: A -> b of the clauses A -> <u>a</u> and <u>a</u> -> b is a primitive instance.

A clause can thereby have a primitive and a non-primitive instance.

Definition

An ordered and finite set of clauses $\{\alpha, \beta 1, ..., \beta q\}$ where $q \geq 1$, is a RCD-clash under the following conditions:

    1. $\beta 1, ..., \beta q$ are primitive instances of CATs;
    2. Antecedent(α) exactly includes q un-typed data $x1...xq$, such that $xi < xi+1$ according to O, $\forall i \in [1, q-1]$;
    3. $\forall i \in [1, q]$, xi is either the first datum in Consequent(βi), or the second datum in Consequent(βi) if the first one is a member of L;

<u>Example</u>
If $T=\{A, B, C\}$, $NT=\{a, b, c, d\}$, $L=\{c\}$, O: $a < b < c < d < A < B < C$, and the initial set of clauses is:

    a b -> d,
    A -> a c C,
    A -> b,
    c ->,

only the set {a b -> d, A -> a d C, A -> b} is a RCD-clash.

The execution of a clash consists of q applications of the resolution principle (q is the number of un-typed data included in the antecedent side of the non-CAT clause). Since each resolved datum is un-typed, none of the q un-typed data can be part of the antecedent side of the last resolvent.

If the clash is of the form $\{\alpha, \beta 1...\beta q\}$ $(q \geq 1)$ and $x1..xq$ are the un-typed data on the antecedent side of α such that for all i: $xi < xi+1$ (w.r.t. a complete RCD-correct ordering), then exactly one CAT clause can be deduced by q applications of the resolution principle.

Let $\alpha 1 = \alpha$.

For each $i = 1..q$, we apply the principle of resolution to the clauses βi and αi such that xi is the resolved datum. Let $\alpha i+1$ be the resolvent.

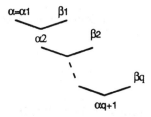

The resolvent $\alpha q+1$ is a CAT clause which is a primitive instance by definition.

Definition of RCD with clash

The directed CAT-correct resolution with clash consists of
1. the determination of all possible clashes and their execution,
2. the application of all typed RCD.

Example:

Let $T = \{A, B, C, D\}$, $NT = \{a, b, c\}$, $L = \{c\}$ and $O: a < b < c < A < B < C < D$, with initial clauses:

    A -> a,
    B -> C,
    D -> b c
    a b C -> c.

None of these four clauses is CATCL.

We shall apply directed CAT-correct resolution with clash and thereby deduce all possible CATCL clauses.

There is only one possible RCD-clash: $\{a b C \to c, A \to a, D \to b c\}$. Its execution consists of the following applications of resolution principle:

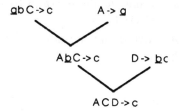

Only one application of typed RCD is feasible:

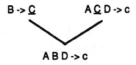

The resolvent A B D -> c is not a primitive instance of clause, contrary to the other instances in this example.

2.2. Deletion strategy with RCD

This new strategy of resolution is compatible with the deletion strategy [9] which consists of the removal of every tautology (clauses including a common datum on the antecedent and consequent sides), and also every subsumed clause (a clause $\alpha1$ is subsumed in the set of clauses $\mathcal{BC}$, if there exists in $\mathcal{BC}$ a clause $\alpha2$ such that each literal of $\alpha2$ appears in $\alpha1$) from the set of clauses.

Nevertheless, one process must be added so as to preserve the completeness of RCD for the deduction of CATCL: each time a primitive instance α of clause is subsumed, it is necessary to ensure that there exists in the current set of clauses, a primitive instance of a clause which subsumes α. In this way, an instance of clause can become primitive by minimization.

Example
Let $\mathcal{T}=\{A\}$, $\mathcal{NT}=\{a, b\}$, $\mathcal{L}=\{a, b\}$ and O: a < b < A with the clauses:
    A -> a,
    -> A,
    a -> b.
These initial clauses are primitive instances.

The application of the principle of resolution between the two clauses $\underline{A}$ -> a and -> $\underline{A}$, is a typed RCD. The resolvent -> a, which subsumes a primitive instance of the clause A -> a, becomes primitive by minimization.

Since the instance -> a is primitive, the set {a -> b, -> a} is a clash. Its execution allows the inference of the CATCL: -> b.

If -> a had not been primitive by minimization, it would have been impossible to deduce the CATCL -> b.

2.3. Completeness of RCD

We have shown the completeness of the application with minimization of directed CAT-correct resolution with clash for the deduction of CATCL: every CATCL clause (deduced by systematic application of the resolution principle) which is neither a tautology nor a subsumed clause, is deduced by the application with minimization of directed CAT-correct resolution with clash.

This theoretical result is proven in [13].

2.4. Incremental use of RCD

We have also proved [13] that the resolution strategy RCD remains complete for the deduction of the minimal CATCL when it is used in an incremental manner.

So, if we produced a clause base BC' by the application of RCD on an initial clause base BC and if α denotes a new clause, it is sufficient to apply RCD on $BC \cup \{\alpha\}$ so as to deduce the minimal CATCL of $BC \cup \{\alpha\}$.

3. ARC: an ATMS based on RCD with clash

We expose in this section how the strategy RCD can be used to build an ATMS. To do this we show that the clauses inferred by the application of RCD (in certain conditions) are significant for a Truth Maintenance System.

First, let us briefly recall the main characteristics of an ATMS (Assumption-based Truth Maintenance System [4, 5]).

This system computes every nogood and the label of each datum according to the set of assumptions and an initial set BC of justifications (Horn clauses) and disjunctions of assumptions.

A nogood is a minimal environment (set of assumptions) which logically entails $\perp$ (the false value) according to BC.

Definitions

An environment $\mathcal{E}$ is a nogood if and only if $\mathcal{E} \cup \mathcal{BC} \models \bot$ and $\nexists$ $\mathcal{E}'$ such that $\mathcal{E} \neq \mathcal{E}'$, $\mathcal{E} \supset \mathcal{E}'$ and $\mathcal{E} \cup \mathcal{BC} \models \bot$.

An environment $\mathcal{E}$ is coherent if and only if there does not exist a nogood $\mathcal{N}$ such that $\mathcal{E} \supseteq \mathcal{N}$.

<u>Example</u>

If only the data A, B and C are assumptions and if the clause base $\mathcal{BC}$ includes:

   A b ->,

   B -> b,

then the environment {A, B} is a nogood because the empty clause is entailed from {A, B} $\cup \mathcal{BC}$ and it does not exist an incoherent environment strictly included in {A, B}.

As the environment {A, B} is incoherent, every environment which includes it (for example {A, B, C}) is incoherent too.

To manage the truth value of a datum d, the ATMS associates d with a set containing all coherent environments $\mathcal{E}$ such that $\mathcal{E} \cup \mathcal{BC} \models$ d. The sets $\mathcal{E}$ are called the environments of d. The association of data with environments is performed by means of special set of environments called the label.

Definition

The label of a datum d is the minimal[1] set of every coherent environment $\mathcal{E}$ such that $\mathcal{E} \cup \mathcal{BC} \models$ d.

We can easily prove that each datum has one and only one label.

<u>Example</u>

If the data A and B are the only assumptions and the clause base $\mathcal{BC}$ includes:

   A d -> c,

   A -> c,

   B -> d,

   c -> d,

the label of A is: {{A}}, because {A} $\cup \mathcal{BC} \models$ A,

the label of B is: {{B}},

the label of c is: {{A}},

   (the environment {A, B} does not belong to this label because it is not minimal)

the label of d is: {{A}, {B}}.

---

[1] Each environment $\mathcal{E}$ of a label L is such that no other environment of L is included in $\mathcal{E}$.

As a consequence of the basic properties of labels, the ATMS can determine if a datum d is true under an environment E (we say that d is true with respect to E). It is sufficient that an environment of d be included in E to deduce the truth of d.

The set of data which are true with respect to an environment E is called the context of E.

<u>Example</u>
If we consider the labels of the previous example, we have the following contexts.
The context of the environment {A} is: {A, c, d}.
The context of the environment {B} is: {B, d}.
The context of the environment {A, B} is: {A, B, c, d}.
The context of the environment {} is: {}.

3.1. Using RCD in the ATMS: ARC

After we recall the main characteristics of an ATMS, we show the resolution strategy RCD is specially adapted to the ATMS and can be used to conceive an extended ATMS. This system is named ARC ("ATMS basé sur la Résolution CAT-correcte dirigée").

We first define the notion of "implicate" and "minimal implicate" which are useful to describe the significant clauses for an ATMS.

Definitions
A clause α is an implicate of BC if and only if $BC \models \alpha$.
α is a minimal implicate of BC, if and only if α is an implicate of BC and there does not exist an implicate α' of BC which strictly subsumes α.

We can prove that an environment E is incoherent if and only if the clause $E \rightarrow$ is an implicate of BC and E is a nogood if and only if the clause $E \rightarrow$ is a minimal implicate of BC.

Likewise, a set of assumptions E is an environment of a datum d if and only if the clause $E \rightarrow d$ is an implicate of BC. E belongs to the label of d if and only if $E \rightarrow d$ is an minimal implicate of BC.

<u>Example</u>
If A, B and C are assumptions and the clause base BC includes:
    A -> a,
    a B -> b,

b C ->,
the label of A is: {{A}},
the label of B is: {{B}},
the label of a is: {{A}},
the label of b is: {{A, B}},
the environment {A, B, C} is a nogood.

Every environment of a label or every nogood is computed from the minimal implicates of $\mathcal{BC}$:

A -> A (denotes an environment of the label of A),
B -> B (denotes an environment of the label of B),
A -> a (denotes an environment of the label of a),
a B -> b,
b C ->,
A B -> b (denotes an environment of the label of b),
a B C ->,
A B C -> (denotes a nogood).

Thus all significant clauses (nogoods and label environments) contain only assumptions on their antecedent side, and their consequent side contains at most one datum. These clauses are CATCL when $\mathcal{T}$ denotes the set of assumptions and L is the initial alphabet. We can thereby apply RCD with minimization so as to compute all nogoods and all label environments.

If $\mathcal{BC}'$ denotes the set of clauses resulting from the application with minimization of RCD on $\mathcal{BC}$, we have demonstrated that:

- $\mathcal{E}$ is a nogood if and only if the clause ($\mathcal{E}$ ->) is a member of $\mathcal{BC}'$;
- the label of a datum d is: {$\mathcal{E}$/($\mathcal{E}$ -> d) $\in$ $\mathcal{BC}'$, $\mathcal{E}$ an environment}. Moreover, when d is an assumption, the environment {d} is a member of its label if and only if the environment {} does not belong to it and {d} is coherent (this addition of environment is due to the fact that the clause which denotes the environment {d} for an assumption d is a tautology (d -> d) and tautologies are not deduced by applying with minimization RCD with clash).

Example
If data A, B, C are assumptions[1] ($\mathcal{T}$={A, B, C}, $\mathcal{NT}$={a}), L={a, A, B, C}, O: a < A < B < C, and the initial set of clauses $\mathcal{BC}$ is:

A -> B,

---

[1] Throughout this text capital letters will designate assumptions and small letters will designate other data.

B -> a,

a C ->,

the clause base resulting from the application with minimization of RCD includes:

A -> B,

A -> a,

a C ->,

B -> a,

A C ->,

B C ->.

The label of a is {{A}, {B}}.

The label of A is {{A}}.

The label of B is {{A}, {B}}.

The label of C is {{C}}.

There are two nogoods: {A, C} and {B, C}.

In an ATMS based on directed CAT-correct resolution with clash, conventional processes such as the label computation algorithm [4] and the hyper-resolution rules [5] are no longer necessary. They are replaced by the application of RCD with minimization.

3.2. Consequences of the use of RCD

3.2.1. The concept of "required label"

The use of RCD to infer "interesting" clauses (nogoods and label environments) allows the application of an original concept named "required label" which improves performances. It can be used when the labels of all data are not necessary, that is when only labels of certain data are useful.

On applying RCD, it is possible to state the labels of data in which we are interested: every clause which denotes environments of a label of a datum d is necessarily deduced only if d is member of the parameter L.

Experimental observation has shown [13] that a restriction of L produces a considerable increase in the efficiency of the resolution process when RCD is applied on a clause base involving either non-Horn clauses or justifications for assumptions.

We can note that every nogood is necessarily inferred, since a clause which corresponds to a nogood is a CATCL for every value of L.

3.2.2. Processing of general clauses

The use of the principle of resolution means that binary resolution is performed between two clauses regardless of their type (Horn clause or not). Thus every clause can be used directly, which is impossible in J. de Kleer's ATMS. Logical implications involving several consequent data can be encoded in a conventional ATMS, but require the creation of new assumptions, justifications, and a disjunction of assumptions [5]. In ARC, the same processing is performed directly, without requiring the creation of new data.

3.2.3. Homogeneity in information storage

In the classical ATMS, information is stored in four different areas depending on the clause type: justifications, disjunctions of assumptions, nogoods, and environments. The use of directed CAT-correct resolution enables the storage of information in a single area (clause base), and thereby eliminating the node[1] associated with each datum. Environments are represented by clauses containing only assumptions on the antecedent side and a single datum on the consequent side; nogoods become clauses with only assumptions on the antecedent side and no data on the consequent side.

3.3. Processing in ARC

ARC performs two main tasks:

1) Minimization of the clause base,
2) Application of RCD.

---

[1] Nodes are no longer necessary since the label algorithm [de Kleer, 86a] is not used in ARC.

3.3.1. Minimization of the clause base

This is performed at the creation of each new clause. It consists in removing tautologies and subsumed clauses [9].

Example:
The clause c -> A b will be selected in preference to c d -> A b, and only the first clause will be recorded in the system.

This algorithm permits:

a) the maintenance of label coherency (every environment of the label is coherent).
Incoherent environments are removed by this algorithm, (if $\mathcal{N}$ is a nogood and $\mathcal{E}$ an environment of a datum d such that $\mathcal{E} \supseteq \mathcal{N}$, then the clause characterizing the nogood $\mathcal{N}$ subsumes the clause corresponding to the environment $\mathcal{E}$ of d).

b) the maintenance of label and nogood minimality.

3.3.2. Application of RCD

This is performed at the introduction of every new clause. It consists of the deduction of all possible new clauses by applying typed RCD or executing RCD-clash.
This resolution strategy is employed in an incremental manner and applied with minimization (use of deletion strategy).

4. Related work

In the construction of an ATMS based on the resolution principle, Reiter and de Kleer propose to restructure an ATMS based on a clause management system (CMS) [11] by defining the "support" and "explanation" of a clause: the support of a clause α w.r.t. a set of clauses $\mathcal{BC}$ is any clause δ such that $\mathcal{BC} \models \delta \vee \alpha$ and $\mathcal{BC} \not\models \delta$. The explanation is defined to be the negation of the support.
An ATMS can be thus constructed upon a CMS. We note that each environment of a datum corresponds to the explanation of the unit clause containing this datum).

The use of directed CAT-correct resolution is similar to this approach but a most important difference lies in the fact that the Reiter/de Kleer system requires the computation of all minimal implicates[1] whereas ARC only needs clauses which are CATCL and minimal implicates of $\mathcal{BC}$.

5. Conclusion

The ARC, based on directed CAT-correct resolution with clash, retains all the advantages of a standard ATMS, i.e. efficient management of contexts, and conflicts, default logic, etc. [5].

One of the principal characteristics of ARC lies in the fact that this system allows the use of general clauses, and thus considerably decreases the number of assertions and new data introduced into the ATMS. A second advantage is that application of directed CAT-correct resolution in the ATMS produces homogeneity in information storage. Finally, experimental observation has shown that system performance is notably improved by the use of the concept "required label". We have observed that the restriction of the set of labels to compute, in the case of a set of clauses which contains justifications and disjunctions of assumptions, allows to considerably increase the performance in comparison to the classical ATMS.

Finally, we note that directed CAT-correct resolution with clash, unlike classical strategies ("Semantic resolution", "Lock resolution" etc [3]) is not designed to prove whether a set of clauses is unsatisfiable or not (although it is capable of this). RCD simply tries to deduce special clauses (named CATCL).

ACKNOWLEDGEMENTS

I would like to express my thanks to Claudette Testemale-Cayrol, Robert Wigetman and specially to Michel Cayrol for his help and direction during my Ph.D. research.

---

[1] No algorithm is proposed in [Reiter and de Kleer, 87] to compute all minimal implicates.

REFERENCES

[1] Cayrol and Tayrac, Les résolutions CAT-correcte et CCT-correcte, la résolution CAT-correcte dans l'ATMS, "Colloque international sur l'informatique cognitive des organisations", Québec 89.

[2] Cayrol et Tayrac, CAT-correct and CCT-correct resolution, CAT-correct resolution in ATMS, submited to Artificial Intelligence.

[3] Chang and Lee, Symbolic Logic and Mechanical Theorem Proving, Computer Science and Applied Mathematics (1973).

[4] de Kleer, An Assumption-based TMS, Artificial Intelligence 28 (1986) 127-162.

[5] de Kleer, Extending the ATMS, Artificial Intelligence 28 (1986) 163-196.

[6] de Kleer, Problem Solving with the ATMS, Artificial Intelligence 28 (1986) 197-224.

[7] de Kleer, A general labeling algorithm for assumption-based truth maintenance, Proceedings of the National Conference on Artificial Intelligence, Saint Paul, MN (August 1988), 188-192.

[8] Kean and Tsiknis, An incremental method for generating prime implicants/implicates, University of British Columbia Technical Report TR-88-16 (1988).

[9] Kowalski, Studies in the completeness and efficiency of theorem proving by resolution, Ph.D. Thesis Univ. of Edinburgh, Scotland (1970).

[10] Maier D. and Warren D. S., Computing with Logic. The Benjamin/Cummings Publishing Company, Inc. (1988).

[11] Reiter and de Kleer, Foundations of assumption-based truth maintenance system. Preliminary report. Proc. of Amer. Assoc. for Artificial Intelligence Conf. (AAAI-87), Seatle, 183-188.

[12] Robinson, Automatic deduction with Hyper-resolution. Intern. J. Comput. Math. 1 (227 - 234).

[13] Tayrac, Etude de nouvelles stratégies de résolution, Application à l'ATMS, Ph.D. Thesis Univ. Paul Sabatier of Toulouse, France, June 1990.

[14] Tison, Generalized Consensus Theory and Application to the Minimisation of Boolean Functions, IEEE Transaction on Electronic Computers, EC-16, 4, August 67, pp 446-456.

[15] Tsiknis and Kean, Clause Management Systems, University of British Columbia, Technical report TR-88-21 (1988).

On logical foundations of the ATMS

Yasushi FUJIWARA
Shinichi HONIDEN

Systems & Software Engineering Laboratory
Toshiba Corporation
70 Yanagicho, Saiwai-ku
Kawasaki 210, JAPAN

1. Introduction

In this paper, we shall clarify the semantics of the ATMS in terms of propositional Horn logic. The label update algorithm will be shown to be correct with respect to the least fixpoint semantics of Horn logic.

Doyle's TMS [4] and de Kleer's ATMS [2] are two representative truth maintenance systems. Their merits and demerits are complementary. In the original paper of Doyle, his main intention seemed to be to put nonmonotonic reasoning into practical use. The TMS allows full nonmonotonic justifications and has a great expressive power. However, the TMS keeps one consistent context at a time and is inefficient on account of frequent backtracking. The ATMS aims at efficient search and can process multiple contexts simultaneously. Because of these advantages, the ATMS is widely used in AI reasoning systems. But it can treat monotonic justifications only and its expressive power is insufficient.

There are several proposals of the ATMS architecture which allow nonmonotonic justifications [3,6], but their descriptions are algorithmic and without semantics. We shall describe the semantics of the basic ATMS *completely*. We hope that this result may shed some light on attempts at implementing nonmonotonic ATMS architectures.

On the other hand, it has been pointed out that the ATMS can be very inefficient for large databases [8]. In order to improve the performance several parallel implementations are proposed [5,12], but ATMS performance is highly problem-specific and for problems for which the ATMS is inherently ill-suited, there seems little room where parallelism can be of help [9,13]. We hope that our result may also serve as a rigid background for the discussion on ATMS efficiencies of various problems.

2. Preliminaries

In this section, we first give a preliminary discussion on Horn logic. Justifications of the ATMS will be translated into propositional Horn clauses. Next we define the notion of upper closed sets. It will play the crucial role in treating labels and nogoods.

2.1. Propositional Horn logic

We now give a brief account of the least fixpoint semantics of Horn logic. Horn logic is well known as the mathematical foundation of logic programming [7]. Here we treat propositional case only.

We suppose that atomic propositions are drawn from a finite set N. A literal is an atomic proposition or its negation. For any truth assignment I, there is a corresponding subset of N consisting of atomic propositions whose truth values with respect to I are 1. Conversely, given a subset M of N, there is a corresponding truth assignment which assigns 1 to an atomic proposition n if and only if n belongs to M. This identification will be used throughout.

A Horn clause is a formula of the form $x_1 \wedge \ldots \wedge x_s \to y$, where $x_1,\ldots,x_s$ and y are atomic propositions, $s \geq 0$. Let P be a set of Horn clauses and M be a truth assignment. We shall call M a model of P if M assigns 1 to all the formulas which belong to P. Then the set of all the models of P has the following property.

Proposition 1. Let P be a set of Horn clauses. If L and M are models of P, the intersection $L \cap M$ is also a model of P.

As the whole set N is always a model of P, the set of all the models of P is non-empty. Thus, the intersection M_P of all the models of P is again a model of P by Proposition 1. We call M_P the least model of P because it is the least with respect to set inclusion.

Define the operator T_P on 2^N (the power set of N) by
$$T_P(M) = \{\, y \in N \mid (x_1 \wedge \ldots \wedge x_s \to y) \in P \text{ and } \{x_1,\ldots,x_s\} \subset M \,\}.$$
The set $T_P(M)$ consists of conclusions which are obtainable by applying a rule from P only once. It is easily observed that M is a model of P if and only if $T_P(M) \subset M$.

The following theorem due to van Emden and Kowalski [14] shows that M_P is the set of logical consequences of P. It strongly suggests that M_P is the "canonical" model of P.

Theorem 1. 1) The operator T_P is monotonic, i.e. if $L \supset M$ then $T_P(L) \supset T_P(M)$.

2) M_P is the least fixpoint of T_P and $M_P = \bigcup_{i \geq 0}(T_P)^i(\emptyset)$.

2.2. Upper closed sets

An ATMS label is employed in order to distinguish whether a node holds or not under the given environment. It represents a subset of a Boolean algebra, which we shall call an upper closed set. We need several properties of upper closed sets in discussion of the label update procedure.

Definition 1. A subset S of 2^A is called *upper closed* if it satisfies the following condition: If $E \in S$ and $E \subset E' (\subset A)$, then $E' \in S$.

Let A be a finite set of atomic propositions. For any subset I of A, denote by V_I the corresponding truth assignment. It is easily observed that, for any subset S of 2^A, there exists a formula p such that $I \in S$ if and only if $V_I(p) = 1$. We shall call p a characteristic formula of S and denote it by ch(S). Ch(S) is uniquely determined up to logical equivalence. (In this paper, we denote the logical equivalence relation by $\equiv$.)

A *prime implicant* [1] for a formula f is a conjunction of literals α which implies f, but which does not imply f if any literal in α is deleted.

For any subset $E = \{a_1,...,a_n\}$ of A, we denote by c(E) the conjunction $a_1 \wedge ... \wedge a_n$. In the case that E is empty, we put c(E) = true. Then we easily see that the characteristic formula of an upper closed set has the following property.

Proposition 2. Suppose that a subset S of 2^A is upper closed.
1) The mapping $E \rightarrow c(E)$ gives a one-to-one correspondence between the following sets.
    (i) The set of minimal elements of S.
    (ii) The set of prime implicants of the formula ch(S).
2) A prime implicant decomposition $ch(S) \equiv \bigvee_\lambda p_\lambda$, where p_λ ranges over all the prime implicants of ch(S), is irredundant. Consequently, the prime implicant decomposition of ch(S) is unique.

Conversely, let p be a formula such that $p \equiv \bigvee_{\lambda \in \Lambda} c(E_\lambda)$. Then the subset of 2^A defined by $\{ E \in 2^A \mid V_E(p) = 1 \} = \{ F \mid F \supset E_\lambda \text{ for some } \lambda \in \Lambda \}$. is upper closed.

Let S be a subset of 2^A. Then there exists the least upper closed set among all the upper closed sets that contain S. It will be called *the upper closure* of S and denoted by ucl(S). Obviously we have $\text{ucl}(S) = \{ F \in 2^A \mid F \supset E \text{ for some } E \in S \}$.

The following technical lemma will be used repeatedly.

Lemma 1. 1) Suppose that S, S_1 and T are upper closed sets with $S \backslash S_1 \subset T \subset S$. Let $\bigvee_{\lambda \in \Lambda} c(E_\lambda)$ be the prime implicant decomposition of ch(T). Then the following are equivalent.

    (i) $T = \text{ucl}(S \backslash S_1)$.

    (ii) $E_\lambda \notin S_1$ for all $\lambda \in \Lambda$.

2) Let S and S_1 be upper closed and $\text{ch}(S) \equiv \bigvee_{\mu \in M} c(E_\mu)$ be the prime implicant decomposition of ch(S). Then we have $\text{ch}(\text{ucl}(S \backslash S_1)) \equiv \bigvee_{\mu \in M'} c(E_\mu)$, where $M' = M \backslash \{ \lambda \in M \mid E_\lambda \in S_1 \}$.

Proof. 1) We first show the implication (i) $\Rightarrow$ (ii). Suppose that $E_\kappa \in S_1$ for some $\kappa \in \Lambda$. Let us consider the upper closed set T' with the characteristic formula $\bigvee_{\lambda \in \Lambda \backslash \{\kappa\}} c(E_\lambda)$. Then we get $S \backslash S_1 \subset T'$ as follows: Let $E \in S \backslash S_1$. Since $S \backslash S_1 \subset T$, we observe that $E \supset E_\lambda$ for some $\lambda \in \Lambda$. If $E \supset E_\kappa$, we have $E \in S_1$, a contradiction. Thus, we know that $E \supset E_\lambda$ for some $\lambda \in \Lambda \backslash \{\kappa\}$, hence $E \in T'$. By the definition of the upper closure, we get $\text{ucl}(S \backslash S_1) \subset T'$. On the other hand, we see that $T' \subset T$ and $T' \neq T$. Thus, $\text{ucl}(S \backslash S_1) \neq T$.

We now show the other implication. By the definition, we have $\text{ucl}(S \backslash S_1) \subset T$. On the other hand, as $T \subset S$, we have $E_\lambda \in S$ for all $\lambda \in \Lambda$. By ii), we have $E_\lambda \in S \backslash S_1$ for all $\lambda \in \Lambda$. Notice that $\text{ucl}(S \backslash S_1) = \{ F \mid F \supset E \text{ for some } E \in S \backslash S_1 \}$ and that $T = \{ F \mid F \supset E_\lambda \text{ for some } \lambda \in \Lambda \}$. Thus, we observe that $T \subset \text{ucl}(S \backslash S_1)$, hence $T = \text{ucl}(S \backslash S_1)$.

2) Let M' be as above and T denote the upper closed set with the characteristic formula $\bigvee_{\mu \in M'} c(E_\mu)$. Then T satisfies the condition that $S \backslash S_1 \subset T \subset S$ and (ii) of 1). Thus, by 1), we get $T = \text{ucl}(S \backslash S_1)$. Hence, we conclude that $\text{ch}(\text{ucl}(S \backslash S_1)) \equiv \bigvee_{\mu \in M'} c(E_\mu)$.   Q.E.D.

3. The ATMS

The ATMS adopts the conventional view of problem solving. An ATMS is a subsystem of a reasoning system. The whole reasoning system consists of a problem solver and an ATMS. The problem solver transmits every inference made to the ATMS. The ATMS manages justifications and labels and answers what data are believed or not when asked. Unlike Doyle's TMS which is based on justifications only, the ATMS can treat assumptions, too. By using this facility, the ATMS can process multiple contexts.

3.1. The formalism of the ATMS

We here give a formulation of de Kleer's ATMS and define a translation rule from the ATMS to propositional Horn logic.

Definition 2. *An ATMS is a quadruple* $K = (N, A, J, C)$ such that

1) N is a finite set (The elements of N will be called *nodes.*).

2) A is a subset of N (The elements of A will be called *assumption nodes.*).

3) J is a subset of $N \times 2^N$ (The elements of J will be called *(ordinary) justifications.*).

4) C is a subset of 2^N (The elements of C will be called *nogood justifications.*).

Let $K = (N, A, J, C)$ be an ATMS. To a justification $j = (n, \{x_1,...,x_s\})$, we attach a Horn clause $x_1 \wedge ... \wedge x_s \rightarrow n$, which we shall denote also by j. We shall call n the consequent node of j. For the set of justifications J, we shall denote the set of corresponding Horn clauses also by J.

A subset of A will be called *an environment*. A node n is said to hold in an environment E if n belongs to the least model $M_{J \cup E}$ of $J \cup E$. $M_{J \cup E}$ is called *the context* with the characterizing environment E. For a node $n \in N$, we define a set $l(J,n)$ by $l(J,n) = \{ E \mid n \in M_{J \cup E} \}$. An environment E is called *inconsistent* if there exists a nogood justification $c = (\{x_1,...,x_s\}) \in C$ such that $x_i \in M_{J \cup E}$ for all i. The set consisting of all inconsistent environments will be denoted by $i(J,C)$.

Lemma 2. The sets $l(J,n)$ and $i(J,C)$ are upper closed.

Now we define labels and nogoods. Let n be a node. We are interested in the set $l(J,n) \backslash i(J,C)$ of consistent environments whose contexts contain n. Although the set $l(J,n)$ is upper closed, $l(J,n) \backslash i(J,C)$ is not in general. Instead, we consider its upper closure $m(J,C,n) = ucl(l(J,n)\backslash i(J,C))$ and the characteristic formula $p(J,C,n) \equiv$ ch(m(J,C,n)) of m(J,C,n).

Definition 3. Let $K = (N,A,J,C)$ be an ATMS and n be a node. Let $p(J,C,n) \equiv V_{\lambda \in \Lambda} c(F_\lambda)$ be the prime implicant decomposition of $p(J,C,n)$. Then the set $\{ F_\lambda \mid \lambda \in \Lambda \}$ is called the *label* of n.

The label defined above will be shown to be a consistent, sound, complete and minimal label in de Kleer's sense.

Definition 4. Let $K = (N,A,J,C)$ be an ATMS. Let $ch(i(J,C)) \equiv V_{\mu \in M} c(E_\mu)$ be the prime implicant decomposition of $ch(i(J,C))$. Then the sets E_μ are called *nogoods*.

Notice that, in the definition of nogoods ordinary justifications and nogood justifications are treated separately. In particular, nogoods cannot be computed from ordinary labels only. But we can restore enough information of $l(J,n)\backslash i(J,C)$ because the equality $l(J,n)\backslash i(J,C) = ucl(l(J,n)\backslash i(J,C))\backslash i(J,C)$ holds.

In the rest of this paper, we prove that the label update procedure preserves labels and nogoods in the above sense, which in turn means that our formulation of the ATMS is correct.

3.2. The label update procedure

Let us consider the situation that a new (ordinary or nogood) justification is added. Then we must update labels and nogoods. In [2], de Kleer presented a label update algorithm without proof. The label update facility of the ATMS is indispensable for its practical use. It is somewhat curious that the algorithm which is used so broadly is without the proof of its correctness. In addition, the correctness proof may shed some light on attempts at extending the basic ATMS algorithm.

Suppose, for example, an ordinary justification j is added. We shall show that the label update procedure is exactly an algorithm which computes the formulas $p(J \cup \{j\},C,n)$ and $ch(i(J \cup \{j\},C))$ from $p(J,C,n)$ and $ch(i(J,C))$. This in turn implies that the semantics of the ATMS we have given is correct.

We first consider the case that a nogood justification c is added. Then we can calculate the formula $ch(i(J,C \cup \{c\}))$ from $ch(i(J,C))$ and $p(J,C,n)$ as follows: Let c =

($\{x_1,...,x_s\}$). Notice that $E \in i(J,C \cup \{c\})$ if and only if $E \in i(J,C)$ or $x_i \in M_{J \cup E}$ for all i. Thus, we conclude that $ch(i(J,C \cup \{c\})) \equiv ch(i(J,C)) \vee \wedge_i ch(l(J,x_i)) \equiv \wedge_i(ch(i(J,C)) \vee ch(l(J,x_i)))$. On the other hand, by the definition of $m(J,C,x_i)$, we easily observe that $ch(i(J,C)) \vee ch(l(J,x_i)) \equiv ch(i(J,C)) \vee p(J,C,x_i)$ for all i. Hence, we obtain $ch(i(J, C \cup \{c\})) \equiv \wedge_i(ch(i(J,C)) \vee p(J,C,x_i)) \equiv ch(i(J,C)) \vee \wedge_i p(J,C,x_i)$.

We can also determine the formula $p(J,C \cup \{c\},n)$ as follows: Let $p(J,C,n) \equiv \vee_{\lambda \in \Lambda} c(F_\lambda)$ be the prime implicant decomposition. Then, by Lemma 1 the prime implicant decomposition of $p(J,C \cup \{c\},n)$ is $p(J,C \cup \{c\},n) \equiv \vee_{\lambda \in \Lambda'} c(F_\lambda)$, where $\Lambda' = \Lambda \setminus \{ \lambda \in \Lambda \mid F_\lambda \in i(J,C \cup \{c\}) \}$.

We now consider the case that an ordinary justification j is added. The following proposition, which is an immediate consequence of the least fixpoint semantics of Horn logic, is crucial to prove the correctness.

Proposition 3. Let J, E be as above and j be a justification. Then, we have $M_{J \cup \{j\} \cup E} = \cup_{i \geq 0}(T_{J \cup \{j\} \cup E})^i(M_{J \cup E})$.

Proof. Notice that $M_{J \cup \{j\} \cup E} \supset M_{J \cup E}$. By Theorem 1, we have $M_{J \cup \{j\} \cup E} \supset \cup_{i \geq 0}(T_{J \cup \{j\} \cup E})^i(M_{J \cup E}) \supset \cup_{i \geq 0}(T_{J \cup \{j\} \cup E})^i(\emptyset) = M_{J \cup \{j\} \cup E}$. Thus, we get $M_{J \cup \{j\} \cup E} = \cup_{i \geq 0}(T_{J \cup \{j\} \cup E})^i(M_{J \cup E})$. Q.E.D.

Let J be a set of justifications and j be a justification. We calculate the new characteristic formula $ch(l(J \cup \{j\},n))$ from formulas $ch(l(J,m))$, where m ranges over nodes. We first introduce auxiliary sets. For a nonnegative integer s and a node n, we define the set $\underline{l}(s,J,j,n)$ by $\underline{l}(s,J,j,n) = \{ E \mid n \in (T_{J \cup \{j\} \cup E})^s(M_{J \cup E}) \}$. Obviously, $\underline{l}(s,J,j,n)$ is upper closed and $\underline{l}(0,J,j,n) = l(J,n)$.

The following proposition shows that $ch(\underline{l}(s+1,J,j,n))$ can be computed from formulas $ch(\underline{l}(s,J,j,m))$, where m ranges over nodes.

Proposition 4. Let n be a node and $J_n = \{ j_k \}$ denote the subset of $J \cup \{ j \}$ consisting of all the justifications j_k whose consequent node is n. We denote by m_{ki} the i-th node of the justification j_k, i.e. $j_k = (m_{k1} \wedge ... \wedge m_{ki} \wedge ... \wedge m_{k\mu k} \rightarrow n)$. Then, for any integer $s \geq 0$, we have

$$ch(\underline{l}(s+1,J,j,n)) \equiv n \vee \vee_k \wedge_i ch(\underline{l}(s,J,j,m_{ki})) \text{ (if n is an assumption node)}$$
$$\equiv \vee_k \wedge_i ch(\underline{l}(s,J,j,m_{ki})) \text{ (if n is not an assumption node)}.$$

Proof. Notice that $(T_{J\cup\{j\}\cup E})^{s+1}(M_{J\cup E}) = E \cup (T_{J\cup\{j\}})(T_{J\cup\{j\}\cup E})^s(M_{J\cup E})$. Thus, a node n lies in $(T_{J\cup\{j\}\cup E})^{s+1}(M_{J\cup E})$ if and only if it belongs to the environment E or there exists $j_k = (m_{k1}\wedge...\wedge m_{k\mu k} \to n) \in J\cup\{j\}$ such that $m_{ki} \in (T_{J\cup\{j\}\cup E})^s(M_{J\cup E})$ for all $1 \le i \le \mu_k$. Thus, if n is an assumption, for any environment E, we have $V_E(ch(\underline{l}(s+1,J,j,n))) = V_E(n \vee \bigvee_{k}\wedge_i ch(\underline{l}(s,J,j,m_{ki})))$. Similarly, if n is not an assumption, for any environment E, $V_E(ch(\underline{l}(s+1,J,j,n))) = V_E(\bigvee_{k}\wedge_i ch(\underline{l}(s,J,j,m_{ki})))$.

Q.E.D.

The following theorem, which is an immediate consequence of Proposition 3, shows that the auxiliary set $\underline{l}(s,J,j,n)$ eventually coincides with the set $l(J\cup\{j\},n)$. (Notice that we have assumed that N is finite.)

Proposition 5. 1) There exists an integer $s \ge 0$ such that $\underline{l}(s+1,J,j,n) = \underline{l}(s,J,j,n)$ for all n.
2) Let s be as in 1). Then we have $l(J\cup\{j\},n) = \underline{l}(s,J,j,n)$ for all n.

For an integer $s \ge 0$, we denote by $\underline{i}(s,J,j,C)$ the set consisting of environments E such that there exists $c = (\{x_1,...,x_s\}) \in C$ with $x_i \in (T_{J\cup\{j\}\cup E})^s(M_{J\cup E})$ for all i.

Let s be a nonnegative integer and n be a node. We define the upper closed set $\underline{m}(s,J,j,C,n)$ by $\underline{m}(s,J,j,C,n) = ucl(\underline{l}(s,J,j,n)\backslash\underline{i}(s,J,j,C))$ and the formula $\underline{p}(s,J,j,C,n)$ by $\underline{p}(s,J,j,C,n) \equiv ch(\underline{m}(s,J,j,C,n))$. Notice that $\underline{m}(0,J,j,C,n) = m(J,C,n)$ and that $\underline{p}(0,J,j,C,n) \equiv p(J,C,n)$.

We can now prove the correctness of the label update algorithm.

Theorem 2. 1) For a node n, let $J_n = \{ j_k \}$ and $j_k = (m_{k1}\wedge...\wedge m_{ki}\wedge...\wedge m_{k\mu k} \to n)$ be as in Proposition 4. Let $s \ge 0$ be an integer and $\bigvee_{\lambda\in\Lambda}c(E_\lambda)$ be the prime implicant decomposition of the formula defined as follows:
$\quad n \vee \bigvee_{k}\wedge_i\underline{p}(s,J,j,C,m_{ki})$ (if n is an assumption node)
$\quad \bigvee_{k}\wedge_i\underline{p}(s,J,j,C,m_{ki})$ (if n is not an assumption node).
Then we have $ch(ucl(\underline{l}(s+1,J,j,n)\backslash\underline{i}(s,J,j,C))) \equiv \bigvee_{\lambda\in\Lambda'}c(E_\lambda)$, where $\Lambda' = \Lambda\backslash\{ \lambda \in \Lambda \,|\, E_\lambda \in \underline{i}(s,J,j,C) \}$.
2) Let $C = \{ c_k \}$ and $c_k = (\{x_{k1},...,x_{ki},...,x_{kvk}\})$. Then we have $ch(\underline{i}(s+1,J,j,C)) \equiv ch(\underline{i}(s,J,j,C)) \vee \bigvee_{k}\wedge_i ch(ucl(\underline{l}(s+1,J,j,x_{ki})\backslash\underline{i}(s,J,j,C)))$.
3) Let $ch(ucl(\underline{l}(s+1,J,j,n)\backslash\underline{i}(s,J,j,C))) \equiv \bigvee_{\lambda\in\Lambda'}c(E_\lambda)$ be as in 1). Then $\underline{p}(s+1,J,j,C,n) \equiv \bigvee_{\lambda\in\Lambda''}c(E_\lambda)$, where $\Lambda'' = \Lambda'\backslash\{ \lambda \in \Lambda' \,|\, E_\lambda \in \underline{i}(s+1,J,j,C) \}$.

Proof. 1) Let T be the upper closed set with the characteristic formula $\bigvee_{\lambda\in\Lambda}c(E_\lambda)$ as above. Comparing this with $ch(\underline{l}(s+1,J,j,n))$ of Proposition 4, we observe that

$\underline{l}(s+1,J,j,n)\backslash\underline{i}(s,J,j,C) \subset T \subset \underline{l}(s+1,J,j,n)$ as follows: First let us prove $\underline{l}(s+1,J,j,n)\backslash\underline{i}(s,J,j,C) \subset T$. Suppose that $E \in \underline{l}(s+1,J,j,n)\backslash\underline{i}(s,J,j,C)$. If n is an assumption node, by Proposition 4, we know that $n \in E$ or there exists $j_k = (m_{k1}\wedge...\wedge m_{k\mu k} \to n) \in J \cup \{j\}$ with $m_{ki} \in (T_{J\cup\{j\}\cup E})^s(M_{J\cup E})$ for all $1 \le i \le \mu_k$. If $n \in E$, we easily see that $E \in T$. Suppose $n \notin E$ and let j_k be the justification as above. Then we have $E \in \underline{l}(s,J,j,m_{ki})\backslash\underline{i}(s,J,j,C)$ for all $1 \le i \le \mu_k$. Thus, we observe that $V_E(n \vee V_{k\wedge i}\underline{p}(s,J,j,C,m_{ki})) = 1$, hence $E \in T$. The case that n is not an assumption node is similar. We now show the second inclusion $T \subset \underline{l}(s+1,J,j,n)$. We consider the case that n is an assumption node. Suppose $E \in T$. Then $n \in E$ or there exists $j_k = (m_{k1}\wedge ... \wedge m_{k\mu k} \to n) \in J \cup \{j\}$ such that $E \in ucl(\underline{l}(s,J,j,m_{ki})\backslash\underline{i}(s,J,j,C))$ for all $1 \le i \le \mu_k$. Notice that $ucl(\underline{l}(s,J,j,m_{ki})\backslash\underline{i}(s,J,j,C)) \subset \underline{l}(s,J,j,m_{ki})$. By Proposition 4, we see that $E \in \underline{l}(s+1,J,j,n)$. The case that n is not an assumption node is similar. Thus, the above inclusion is established.

Applying Lemma 1 to the inclusion $\underline{l}(s+1,J,j,n)\backslash\underline{i}(s,J,j,C) \subset T \subset \underline{l}(s+1,J,j,n)$, we conclude that $ch(ucl(\underline{l}(s+1,J,j,n)\backslash\underline{i}(s,J,j,C))) \equiv V_{\lambda\in\Lambda'}c(E_\lambda)$, where Λ and Λ' are defined as above.

2) Let T' be the upper closed with the characteristic formula
$$ch(\underline{i}(s,J,j,C)) \vee V_{k\wedge i}ch(ucl(\underline{l}(s+1,J,j,x_{ki})\backslash\underline{i}(s,J,j,C))).$$
We shall show that $\underline{i}(s+1,J,j,C) = T'$. Let us first consider the inclusion $\underline{i}(s+1,J,j,C) \subset T'$. Suppose $E \in \underline{i}(s+1,J,j,C)$. If $E \in \underline{i}(s,J,j,C)$, we immediately have $E \in T'$. If $E \notin \underline{i}(s,J,j,C)$, by the definition there is a nogood justification $c_k = (\{x_{k1},...,x_{ki},...,x_{kvk}\}) \in C$ such that $x_{ki} \in (T_{J\cup\{j\}\cup E})^{s+1}(M_{J\cup E})$ for all i. Thus, $E \in \underline{l}(s+1,J,j,x_{ki})\backslash\underline{i}(s,J,j,C)$ for all i. This shows that $E \in T'$.

Let us show $T' \subset \underline{i}(s+1,J,j,C)$. Suppose $E \in T'\backslash \underline{i}(s,J,j,C)$. There exists $c_k = (\{x_{k1},...,x_{ki},...,x_{kvk}\}) \in C$ such that $E \in ucl(\underline{l}(s+1,J,j,x_{ki})\backslash\underline{i}(s,J,j,C)) \subset \underline{l}(s+1,J,j,x_{ki})$. Thus, $x_{ki} \in (T_{J\cup\{j\}\cup E})^{s+1}(M_{J\cup E})$ for all i. This implies $E \in \underline{i}(s+1,J,j,C)$.

3) This is an immediate consequence of Lemma 1. $\qquad$ Q.E.D.

The following theorem guarantees the correctness and the termination of the label update procedure.

Theorem 3. 1) Let $s \ge 0$ be an integer. Then the following conditions are equivalent.

    (i) $ch(ucl(\underline{l}(s+1,J,j,n)\backslash\underline{i}(s,J,j,C))) \equiv \underline{p}(s,J,j,C,n)$ for all n.

    (ii) $ch(\underline{i}(s+1,J,j,C)) \equiv ch(\underline{i}(s,J,j,C))$ and $\underline{p}(s+1,J,j,C,n) \equiv \underline{p}(s,J,j,C,n)$ for all n.

2) There exists an integer $s \ge 0$ which satisfies the condition (i) (hence also (ii)) of 1).

3) Let s be an integer as in 2). Then $ch(i(J\cup\{j\},C)) \equiv ch(\underline{i}(s,J,j,C))$ and $p(J\cup\{j\},C,n) \equiv \underline{p}(s,J,j,C,n)$ for any node n.

Proof. 1) The implication (ii) $\Rightarrow$ (i) is obvious. Suppose that s satisfies (i). Then, by 2) of Theorem 2, we easily observe that $ch(\underline{i}(s+1,J,j,C)) \equiv ch(\underline{i}(s,J,j,C))$. Hence, we have $\underline{p}(s+1,J,j,C,n) \equiv ch(ucl(\underline{l}(s+1,J,j,n)\backslash\underline{i}(s,J,j,C)))$ for all n. By the assumption, we get $\underline{p}(s+1,J,j,C,n) \equiv ch(ucl(\underline{l}(s+1,J,j,n)\backslash\underline{i}(s,J,j,C))) \equiv \underline{p}(s,J,j,C,n)$.

2) Let s be a nonnegative integer as in Proposition 5. Notice that we also have $\underline{i}(s+1,J,j,C) = \underline{i}(s,J,j,C)$. This implies our claim.

3) Let s be an integer such that $ch(\underline{i}(s+1,J,j,C)) \equiv ch(\underline{i}(s,J,j,C))$ and that $\underline{p}(s+1,J,j,C,n) \equiv \underline{p}(s,J,j,C,n)$ for any node n. Then, by Theorem 2, for any integer t $\geq$ s, we have $ch(\underline{i}(t,J,j,C)) \equiv ch(\underline{i}(s,J,j,C))$ and $\underline{p}(t,J,j,C,n) \equiv \underline{p}(s,J,j,C,n)$ for any node n. On the other hand, for a sufficiently large t, we have $ch(i(J \cup \{j\},C)) \equiv ch(\underline{i}(t,J,j,C))$ and $p(J \cup \{j\},C,n) \equiv \underline{p}(t,J,j,C,n)$ for any node n by Proposition 5. Combining these, we conclude the above statement.   Q.E.D.

4. Comparison with related work

There have been several attempts at formalizing the description of the ATMS. In particular, Reiter and de Kleer [11] proposed a generalization of the ATMS, a Clause Management System (CMS) and gave to it the semantics based on prime implicants. But there seems to be no proof of the correctness of the algorithm based on the semantics. Also their CMS cannot be fully accommodated to nonmonotonicity.

In this note, we have exhibited the declarative semantics of the ATMS in terms of propositional Horn logic and have given a thorough proof of the correctness of the label update algorithm with respect to the semantics. Recently, close relationship between nonmonotonic reasoning and logic programming is discovered [10]. This relationship suggests that our technique can also be applied to the analysis of nonmonotonic ATMSs.

Conclusion

We have exhibited the declarative semantics of the ATMS in terms of propositional Horn logic. In particular, we have proved the correctness of its label update algorithm with respect to the semantics. It can serve as a rigid background for the discussion on ATMS computational efficiencies of the various actual problems.

Reference

1. Birkhoff, G and Bartee, T. C., Modern applied algebra, McGraw-Hill, New York, 1970.

2. de Kleer, J., An assumption-based truth maintenance system, Artificial Intelligence 28, pp.127~162, 1986.

3. de Kleer, J., Extending the ATMS, Artificial Intelligence 28, pp.163~196, 1986.

4. Doyle, J., A truth maintenance system, Artificial Intelligence 12, pp.231~272, 1979.

5. Dixon, M and de Kleer, J., Massively parallel assumption-based truth maintenance, in Proc. of AAAI-88, 1, pp.199~204.

6. Dressler, O., An extended basic ATMS, in Proc. of 2nd International workshop on non-monotonic reasoning, pp.143~163, Springer LNCS 346, Springer Verlag, Berlin, 1989.

7. Lloyd, J. W., Foundations of logic programming, Springer Verlag, New York, 1984.

8. Provan, G. M., Efficiency analysis of multiple-context TMSs in scene representation, in Proc. of AAAI-87, 1, pp.173~177.

9. Provan, G. M., The computational complexity of multiple-context truth maintenance systems, in Proc. of 9-th ECAI, pp.522~527, 1990.

10. Przymusinski, T., On the relation between logic programming and nonmonotonic reasoning, in Proc. of AAAI-88, 2, pp.444~448.

11. Reiter, R and de Kleer, J., Foundations of assumption-based truth maintenance systems: preliminary report, in Proc. of AAAI-87, 1, pp.183~188.

12. Rothberg, E and Gupta, A., Experiences implementing a parallel ATMS on a shared-memory multiprocessor, in Proc. of 11-th IJCAI, 1, pp.199~205, 1989.

13. Selman, B and Levesque, H. J., Abduction and default reasoning: a computational core, in Proc. of AAAI-90, 1, pp.343~348.

14. van Emden, M. H and Kowalski, R. A., The semantics of predicate logic as a programming language, J. of ACM 23, 4, pp.733~742, 1976.

A SKEPTICAL SEMANTICS FOR TRUTH MAINTENANCE

Cees Witteveen
Department of Mathematics and Computer Science
Delft University of Technology
Julianalaan 132 , 2628 BL Delft, The Netherlands
witt@dutiae.tudelft.nl

Abstract

To generalize the 2-valued stable model semantics for truth maintenance, we introduce a 3-valued stable model semantics. Unlike the 2-valued semantics, this semantics can be given compositional properties. In particular we show that a canonical model (the skeptical model) can be derived as a composition of 3-valued interpretations.
The skeptical model can also be characterized by a fixpoint construction. We show that using this construction, the skeptical model can be computed in $O(n^2)$.
Finally, since the skeptical model turns out to be not a straightforward generalization of the 2-valued stable model semantics, we investigate a possible alternative. Although we can find another canonical model, this alternative model seems to be difficult to compute.

1 Introduction and Motivation

The ability to maintain a coherent and consistent set of beliefs and to revise them when contradictions occur, is a major characteristic of intelligent reasoning systems.
One of the contexts in which the maintenance and revision of beliefs has been studied extensively is the field of Truth Maintenance Systems (TMSs) (e.g. [1, 2, 4, 7, 10, 12]). In this paper, we restrict our attention to the Doyle-style or *justification-based* TMS.

Basically, a TMS is a supporting system of a general reasoning system. The reasoning system communicates inferences to the TMS in the form of propositional arguments, called *justifications*, for statements or *beliefs*. The TMS maintains a *dependency network* of such justifications and the beliefs they connect. The primary task of a TMS is to provide for a coherent and consistent interpretation of these beliefs and to update the belief status after the addition of new arguments.

To capture the idea of such a set of coherent and consistent set of beliefs, the *grounded* or *stable* model semantics ([5, 6]) has been proposed. This semantics, however, has some clear disadvantages:

- it is *not canonical*: it is well-known ([5, 6, 12]) that a TMS network may have more than one stable model or even no 2-stable model at all.

- it is *not tractable*: finding a stable model is NP-hard ([5]). Hence, a TMS using this semantics is not likely to be of practical interest.

Therefore, we propose a 3-valued generalisation of the stable model semantics for truth-maintenance.

First of all, we show that such a semantics has compositional properties and we will discuss a Stacking Lemma stating that stability can be preserved in combining *3-valued* stable models. This lemma then will be used to derive a canonical, information minimizing, 3-valued model for truth maintenance, called the *skeptical* model.

One of the important aspects of the skeptical model is its *tractability*. We will show a simple $O(n^2)$ algorithm to construct the skeptical model for an arbitrary TMS.

Although the skeptical model is canonical and easy to compute, it also has a disadvantage: in case a TMS has a unique 2-valued stable model, this model is not always identical to the skeptical model.

Therefore, we will discuss an alternative semantics, removing this discrepancy. This alternative, however, does not seem to be easy to compute.

The paper is organized as follows. In Section 2, we briefly introduce the necessary terminology. In Section 3, we discuss partial interpretations, stable partial interpretations and models as a generalization of the stable model semantics. In Section 4, we introduce the skeptical model and give an algorithm to compute it. Finally, in Section 5, we present an alternative to the skeptical model.

2 Preliminaries

By the perceived correspondence between truth-maintenance and propositional logic programming ([5]), we will use some notational conventions from logic programming in the sense of [9].

By a TMS dependency network we mean a tuple $\mathcal{D} = (N, J)$ where N is a finite set of propositional atoms and J a finite set of justifications, each justification j being a directed formula of the form

$$\alpha \wedge \beta \rightarrow c$$

where α stands for a conjunction of positive literals in the body of the justification, β for a conjunction of negative literals and c is a propositional atom. It can be interpreted as : "c can be believed if every a_i in α is believed and none of the b_j in β is believed".

To avoid cumbersome notations, we will also use α and β to denote the *set* of literals occurring in the conjunction. We will use $A(j)$ to denote the *antecedent* $\alpha \wedge \beta$ of j and $C(j)$ to denote the *consequent* c of j. For a given wff ϕ, $At(\phi)$ will denote the set of atoms occurring in ϕ.

We say that a network $\mathcal{D} = (N, J)$ is *monotonic* if every justification is of the form $j = \alpha \rightarrow \beta$, i.e. the body of j does not contain any negative literal. *Non-monotonic* networks indicate the general case.

The task of a TMS is to give a suitable interpretation of the network $\mathcal{D} = (N, J)$. An *interpretation I of $\mathcal{D}$* is an arbitrary subset $I \subseteq N$, denoting the set of nodes believed. Since an interpretation I can be conceived as a simple truth-assignment to propositional atoms, we will use $I(a) = t$ (or $I \models a$) iff $a \in I$. For propositions ϕ over N, $I \models \phi$ is defined in a standard recursive way. Note that if ϕ is the empty conjunction, $I \models \phi$ for every interpretation I.

An interpretation I is said to *satisfy* a justification $j = \alpha \wedge \beta \rightarrow c$, abbreviated

$I \models j$, if $I \models \alpha \wedge \beta$ implies $I \models c$. An interpretation I is said to be a *model* of $\mathcal{D}$ if $I \models j$, for every justification $j \in J$.

In case of monotonic networks, where each justification is of the form $j = \alpha \rightarrow c$, the intended semantics of the network $\mathcal{D} = (N, J)$ is given by the *minimal model* of $\mathcal{D}$. As a standard result (see [9]), we mention that this model equals the intersection of all propositional models of $\mathcal{D}$ and also can be characterized as the least fixpoint $lfp(T)$ of the *immediate consequence* operator $T : 2^N \rightarrow 2^N$

$$T(I) = \{c \mid \alpha \rightarrow c \in J, I \models \alpha\}$$

For nonmonotonic truth maintenance the *stable model* semantics offers a natural generalization of the minimal model semantics:

Definition 2.1 (Gelfond 88,Elkan90) *Let* $\mathcal{D} = (N, J)$ *be a network. Then* M *is a 2-valued stable model, abbreviated 2-stable model, of* $\mathcal{D}$ *iff* M *is the unique minimal model of the derived network* $\mathcal{D} = (N, J(M))$ *where* $J(M) = \{\alpha \rightarrow c \mid \alpha \wedge \beta \rightarrow c \in J, M \models \beta\}$ ∎

It can easily be proven that M is a 2-stable model of $\mathcal{D}$ iff, for every $c \in M$, a valid and well-founded argument for c can be given. That means, for every such a c, there is a sequence $(c_1, c_2, \ldots, c_n)$ such that $c_i \in M$ for $i = 1, 2, \ldots n$, $c_n = c$ and for every c_i there exists a justification $\alpha_i \wedge \beta_i \rightarrow c_i$ in J such that $M(\alpha_i \wedge \beta_i) = t$ and $\alpha_i \subseteq \{c_1, c_2, \ldots, c_{i-1}\}$. Therefore, a 2-stable model also have been called *well-founded* or *grounded* models.

The equivalence between grounded and 2-stable models is captured in the following useful lemma:

Lemma 2.2 M *is a grounded model of* $\mathcal{D} = (N, J)$ *iff* M *is the least fixpoint of the operator* T_M *defined as*

$$T_M(I) = \{c \mid \alpha \wedge \beta \rightarrow c \in J, I \models \alpha, M \models \beta\}$$

Although the 2-stable model semantics offers an elegant generalization of the fairly standard minimal model semantics, we have some objections against this semantics.

Intuitively, a satisfactory semantics for nonmonotonic systems should at least be *universal* in the sense that it would give a suitable meaning to every network and *unique* in the sense that not more than one meaning is given to a network. Last but not least, we should keep in mind that the idea of truth maintenance is to render assistance to a reasoning system in an efficient way. This means that the interpretation process should be tractable. Hence, we would require a canonical model to be easy to compute.

The 2-stable model semantics does not satisfy these requirements, since it is well-known that a network may have one, more than one, or no 2-stable model at all. For example, $\mathcal{D}_1 = (\{a, b\}, \{\neg b \rightarrow a\})$ has a unique 2-stable model $M = \{a\}$, while $\mathcal{D}_2 = (\{a\}, \{\neg a \rightarrow a\})$ does not have a 2-stable model and $\mathcal{D}_3 = (\{a, b\}, \{\neg b \rightarrow a, \neg a \rightarrow b\})$ has two 2-stable models $M_1 = \{a\}$ and $M_2 = \{b\}$.

Also, finding a 2-stable model has been proven to be NP-hard, so there is little hope for a tractable model construction process.

The solution to these problems can be found if we are prepared to give up the idea of a *complete* evaluation of beliefs. Instead of it, we propose a partial semantics based on 3-valued logic.

3 Three-valued interpretations and models

A *3-valued* or *partial* interpretation I of $\mathcal{D}$ is a tuple $I = (I_t, I_f)$ where I_t and I_f are disjoint subsets of N. I_t is called the true-set of I, I_f the false-set. The *kernel of* I, $Ker(I)$, is the set $I_t \cup I_f$ and the set of unknowns is the set $I_u = N - Ker(I)$. The *empty interpretation* $I = (\emptyset, \emptyset)$ will be abbreviated by $\emptyset^2$.

A partial interpretation I can be interpreted as a truth-assignment $N \rightarrow \{t, u, f\}$ as follows : $I(a) = t$ iff $a \in I_t$, $I(a) = f$ iff $a \in I_f$ and $I(a) = u$, else. We will use two partial orderings for the set $\{t, u, f\}$ of truth-values. The *truth ordering* $<_t$ defined by

$$f <_t u <_t t$$

is used to evaluate the truth-value of wffs. The connective $\wedge$ is interpreted as the (finite) meet under the $<_t$ ordering and $\neg$ is defined by $\neg t = f$, $\neg f = t$

and $\neg u = u$. This gives us for these operations the interpretation given in Kleene's strong 3-valued logic ([8, 13]).

We will also use $<_t$ to define the satisfaction relation for justifications: an interpretation I is said to *satisfy* a justification $\alpha \wedge \beta \rightarrow c \in J$ iff $I(\alpha \wedge \beta) \leq_t I(c)^1$, where $\leq_t$ is the reflexive closure of $<_t$.

I is said to be a *3-valued model* of $\mathcal{D} = (N, J)$ if I satisfies every $j \in J$. In the sequel, we will use "model" to stand for "3-valued model".

Besides a truth-ordering, we also use the *knowledge* ordering $<_k$:

$$u <_k f \, , \; u <_k t$$

This ordering will be used to compare partial interpretations and models. This ordering can be extended to an ordering $\sqsubseteq_k$ of partial interpretations by defining

$$I \sqsubseteq_k I' \quad \text{iff} \quad I(a) \leq_k I'(a) \text{ for every } a \in N$$

where $\leq_k$ is the reflexive closure of $<_k$. We say that I' is the *(knowledge)-extension* of I. Note, that $I \sqsubseteq_k I'$ implies that $Ker(I) \subseteq Ker(I')$.

Given a set $\mathcal{I}$ of partial interpretations, a $\sqsubseteq_k$-minimal interpretation is an interpretation $I \in \mathcal{I}$ such that for all $I' \in \mathcal{I}$, $I' \sqsubseteq_k I$ implies $I' = I$.

We will need the following operations on partial interpretations :

Definition 3.1 *The intersection $\sqcap_k$ of two partial interpretations I and I', denoted as $I \sqcap_k I'$, is the partial interpretation defined by*

$$(I \sqcap_k I')(a) = I(a) \wedge_k I'(a) \quad \text{for all } a \in N$$

where $\wedge_k$ is the meet under the $<_k$ ordering. ∎

Partial interpretations I and I' such that $I \sqcap_k I' = \emptyset^2$ are called *disjunct* interpretations.

---

[1]This is equivalent to the Lukasiewicz interpretation of the conditional

Definition 3.2 *If I and I' are disjunct partial interpretations, the* **union** *of I and I', denoted as $I \sqcup I'$, is defined as*

$$(I \sqcup_k I')(a) = I(a) \vee_k I'(a) \quad \text{for all } a \in N$$

where $\vee_k$ is the join under the $<_k$ ordering. ∎

It is easy to see that both operations are well-defined and that the following relations do hold : $I \sqsubseteq_k (I \sqcup_k I')$ and $(I' \sqcap_k I) \sqsubseteq_k I'$.

3.1 Stable partial interpretations

The kernel $\text{Ker}(I)$ of a partial interpretation I for $\mathcal{D}$ is a complete 2-valued interpretation of a subnetwork of $\mathcal{D}$. Therefore, we can distinguish two subnetworks of $\mathcal{D} = (N, J)$, *induced by I*:

- the network $\mathcal{D}$ *restricted to I*, denoted by $\mathcal{D}_I$, containing only atoms occurring in $\text{Ker}(I)$ and only those justifications $j \in J$ such that $At(j) \subseteq \text{Ker}(I)$. Note, that I is a complete, 2-valued interpretation for this restricted network, i.e. I_t is the set of atoms believed and $I_f = N_I - I_t$ the set of atoms not believed.

- the network $\mathcal{D}$ *modulo I*, denoted by $\mathcal{D}^{-I}$, the network $\mathcal{D}$ reduces to given the partial interpretation I. It contains the remaining part of the network, after the influence of I on $\mathcal{D}$ has been taken into account.

We give the corresponding formal definitions:

Definition 3.3 *The network $\mathcal{D}$* **restricted to** *I is the network $\mathcal{D}_I = (N_I, J_I)$, where $N_I = Ker(I)$ and $J_I = \{\, j \in J \mid At(j) \subseteq Ker(I) \,\}$* ∎

Definition 3.4 *The network $\mathcal{D}$* **modulo** *I, denoted as $\mathcal{D}^{-I}$, is the network (N^{-I}, J^{-I}) where $N^{-I} = N - Ker(I)$ and J^{-I} is the set of justifications*

$$j^{-I} = (\alpha - I_t) \wedge (\beta - I_f) \to c$$

for which there exists a justification $j = \alpha \wedge \beta \to c \in J$ such that $c \notin Ker(I)$ and $I(\alpha \wedge \beta) > f$. ∎

Note that for every network and partial interpretation I, $\mathcal{D}_I$ and $\mathcal{D}^{-I}$ are disjunct networks, i.e. $N_I \cap N_{-I} = \emptyset$ and $J_I \cap J^{-I} = \emptyset$. Moreover, for disjunct interpretations I and I' we have $(\mathcal{D}^{-I})^{-I'} = \mathcal{D}^{-(I \sqcup_k I')}$.

Example 3.5 Consider the network $\mathcal{D} = (N, J)$ with $N = \{a, b, c, d, e, f\}$ and the set of justifications J :

$$\neg a \rightarrow b \qquad \neg d \rightarrow c$$
$$\neg b \rightarrow a \qquad e \rightarrow f$$
$$b \wedge \neg c \rightarrow e \qquad f \rightarrow a$$
$$\neg c \rightarrow d$$

Let $I = (\{a, c\}, \{d\})$ be a partial interpretation. Then $\mathcal{D}_I = (\{a, c, d\}, \{\neg c \rightarrow d, \neg d \rightarrow c\})$ and $\mathcal{D}^{-I} = (\{b, e, f\}, \{e \rightarrow f\})$. Note that $b \rightarrow e$ does not occur in $\mathcal{D}^{-I}$ since $I(\neg c) = f$, so $I(b \wedge \neg c) = f$, implying that the justification cannot be used to justify e. ∎

The idea of conceiving a partial interpretation as a complete interpretation of a subnetwork immediately leads to a first, simple generalization of the notion of a 2-stable model:

Definition 3.6 *A partial interpretation I of $\mathcal{D}$ is a* **3-valued stable interpretation**, *abbreviated* **3-stable interpretation**, *of $\mathcal{D}$ if I is a 2-valued stable model of $\mathcal{D}_I$.* ∎

Clearly, if I is a 3-stable interpretation and $Ker(I) = N$, this definition reduces to the definition of a 2-valued stable model of $\mathcal{D}$.

It turns out that this simple notion of of a 3-stable interpretation is the right approach to a compositional 3-valued stable semantics of TMS.

3.2 Compositional aspects

It is easy to see that a partial interpretation I of $\mathcal{D}$ and a partial interpretation I' of $\mathcal{D}^{-I}$ can be combined: the partial interpretation $I \sqcup_k I'$ is well-defined, since $I \sqcap_k I' = \emptyset^2$. In general, however, stability will not be preserved in combining partial interpretations :

Example 3.7 Consider the network $\mathcal{D} = (\{a, b\}, \{\to a, \ a \to b\})$. The partial interpretation $I = (\emptyset, \{b\})$ is a 3-stable interpretation of $\mathcal{D}$ and $I' = (\{a\}, \emptyset)$ is a 3-stable interpretation of $\mathcal{D}^{-I}$. However, $I \sqcup_k I' = (\{a\}, \{b\})$ is not a stable (partial) model of $\mathcal{D}$. ∎

The cause of this deficiency is the possible occurrence of justifications in $J_{I \sqcup I'}$ that are absent in both J_I and $J_{I'}$.

To prevent such justifications from influencing the combination of such partial interpretations, we add the following property to ensure that stability will be compositional:

Definition 3.8 *Let I be a partial interpretation of a network $\mathcal{D} = (N, J)$. Then I is called* **false complete,** *abbreviated to* **f-complete,** *for $\mathcal{D}$ if $I(c) = f$ implies that for all $j = \alpha \wedge \beta \to c \in J$, $I(\alpha \wedge \beta) = f$.* ∎

Remark. Note that a 3-stable interpretation I of $\mathcal{D}$ which is also f-complete for $\mathcal{D}$ needs not to be a 3-valued model of $\mathcal{D}$. For it is possible that there is a justification $\alpha \wedge \beta \to c \in J$, such that $I(\alpha \wedge \beta) = t$, while $c \notin Ker(I)$, hence $I(c) = u < I(\alpha \wedge \beta)$. ∎

The following result shows that 3-stability can be preserved in combining f-complete 3-stable interpretations, giving this semantics a compositional flavor:

Lemma 3.9 (Stacking lemma) *If I is an f-complete 3-stable interpretation of $\mathcal{D} = (N, J)$ and I' is an f-complete stable partial interpretation of $\mathcal{D}^{-I}$, then $I \sqcup_k I'$ is an f-complete 3-stable interpretation of $\mathcal{D}$.*

Note that, given $I \sqcup_k I'$ as an f-complete 3-stable interpretation of $\mathcal{D}$, the Stacking Lemma again can be applied on $I \sqcup_k I'$ and an f-complete 3-stable interpretation I'' of $\mathcal{D}^{-(I \sqcup_k I')}$ to form an f-complete 3-stable interpretation $I \sqcup_k I' \sqcup_k I''$.

If, after such a composition M of 3-stable interpretations, the remaining network $\mathcal{D}^{-M}$ is the empty network, by definition of 3-stable interpretations, M is a 2-stable model of $\mathcal{D}$.

So the Stacking Lemma can be used to show that a 2-stable model can be composed of disjunct 3-stable interpretations.

Therefore, in a sense, 2-stable models occur as the result of a *limit composition* of 3-stable interpretations. We will show that a more general notion of a limit composition can be used to characterize *3-valued stable models*.

3.3   Three-valued stable models

To give a second generalization of the 2-stable model semantics, we introduce the notion of a 3-valued stable model, abbreviated **3-stable** model.

Note that in the definition of a 2-stable model, we used a set of *reduced* justifications $J(M)$, where M was a 2-valued interpretation, i.e. a subset of N.

In case $M = (M_t, M_f)$ is a partial interpretation for $\mathcal{D} = (N, J)$, we use two reductions of J:

1. $J(M, t) = \{\alpha \to c \mid \alpha \wedge \beta \to c \in J, M(\beta) = t\}$

2. $J(M, u) = \{\alpha \to c \mid \alpha \wedge \beta \to c \in J, M(\beta) \geq_t u\}$

Now we can define a 3-stable model as follows:

Definition 3.10 $M = (M_t, M_f)$ *is a 3-stable model of* $\mathcal{D} = (N, J)$ *iff*

1. *M_t is the least 2-valued model of*
   $\mathcal{D}(M, t) = (N, J(M, t))$

2. *$N - M_f = M_t \cup M_u$ is the least 2-valued model of*
   $\mathcal{D}(M, u) = (N, J(M, u))$ ∎

Clearly, this definition reduces to Definition 2.1 if the partial interpretation is *complete*: in that case $Ker(M) = N$, and case 1 and case 2 will coincide[2].

There is a special relation between 3-stable interpretations and 3-stable models. In fact, the following "Characterization Theorem" shows that a 3-stable model can be conceived as a special composition of 3-stable interpretations:

---

[2]The definition of 3-valued stable models appearing in [11] is completely equivalent to the definition presented here.

Theorem 3.11 *M is a 3-stable model of $\mathcal{D}$ iff*

1. *M is an f-complete 3-stable interpretation of $\mathcal{D}$.*

2. *$\emptyset^2$ is a 3-stable model of $\mathcal{D}^{-M}$.*

To check that $\emptyset^2$ is a 3-stable model of a network $\mathcal{D}$ is easy: the reductions $J(\emptyset^2, t)$ and $J(\emptyset^2, u)$ are equal to

1. $J(\emptyset^2, t) = \{ j \mid j = \alpha \rightarrow c \in J \}$

2. $J(\emptyset^2, u) = \{ \alpha \rightarrow c \mid \alpha \wedge \beta \rightarrow c \in J \}$

Hence, according to Definition 3.10, we have to check that

1. $\emptyset$ is the least 2-valued model of
   $\mathcal{D}(\emptyset^2, t) = (\, N, J(\emptyset^2, t) \,)$

2. N is the least 2-valued model of
   $\mathcal{D}(\emptyset^2, u) = (\, N, J(\emptyset^2, u) \,)$

In the next section, we will see that the derived networks $\mathcal{D}(\emptyset^2, t)$ and $\mathcal{D}(\emptyset^2, u)$ also can be used to *construct* 3-stable models.

It should be clear that the Stacking Lemma and the Characterization Theorem together are the key to a compositional semantics for truth maintenance: starting with 3-stable interpretations, the Stacking Lemma guarantees that they can be combined to interpretations, preserving stability. The Characterization Theorem tells us in which case such a 3-stable interpretation is a 3-stable model of $\mathcal{D}$. Hence, a 3-stable model can be viewed as a kind of *limit* composition of f-complete 3-stable interpretations.

4   The Skeptical model

It is not difficult to show that every TMS has at least one 3-stable model. To obtain a canonical model, we have to select a special 3-stable model. In this section, we show that the 3-valued semantics gives us back the advantages the semantics of monotonic TMS systems had: for every TMS $\mathcal{D}$ there exists a unique $\sqsubset_k$-minimal 3-stable model of $\mathcal{D}$, we will call the *skeptical model*. To show that besides the canonical properties, this semantics also offers tractability, we will analyze the complexity of computing the skeptical model and show that the $\sqsubset_k$-minimal model can be obtained in quadratic time. For proofs of the results stated here and full details of constructions, we refer to [15, 16].

4.1 Characterizing the skeptical model

For 3-stable models, the following results can be easily obtained:

Proposition 4.1 *Every TMS network $\mathcal{D}$ has at least one 3-stable model.*

Proposition 4.2 *The intersection of all 3-stable models of $\mathcal{D}$ is a 3-stable model of $\mathcal{D}$.*

Since the intersection of two partial interpretations I and I' results in a partial interpretation $I \sqcap_k I'$ whose kernel equals $Ker(I) \cap Ker(I')$, it is not difficult to see that the intersection of all 3-stable models is a unique $\sqsubset_k$-minimal 3-stable model of $\mathcal{D}$.

Example 4.3 Let $\mathcal{D} = (N, J)$, $N = \{a, b\}$ and $J = \{\neg a \rightarrow b, \neg b \rightarrow a\}$. $\mathcal{D}$ has three 3-stable models:

$$M_1 = (\{a\}, \{b\})$$
$$M_2 = (\{b\}, \{a\})$$
$$M_3 = \emptyset^2$$

The $\sqsubset_k$-minimal 3-stable model is M_3 and M_3 is also equal to the $\sqcap_k$ intersection of all 3-stable models of $\mathcal{D}$. ∎

Remark. Note that the $\sqsubset_k$-minimal *stable* model does not always correspond to the also uniquely defined $\sqsubset_k$-minimal model of a network. For example $\mathcal{D} = (\{a\}, \{a \rightarrow a\})$ has a unique $\sqsubset_k$-minimal model $\emptyset^2$, but the unique $\sqsubset_k$-*minimal 3-stable* model is $(\emptyset, \{a\})$. ∎

In the semantics for logic programming, the $\sqsubseteq_k$-minimal stable model has been baptized as the *well-founded model* ([11]). Since this namegiving will cause a possible confusion in truth maintenance, we propose to call it the *skeptical model*.

The skeptical model offers a solution to the problems encountered in the 2-stable model semantics:

- *universality*
  By Proposition 4.1, every network has a 3-stable model, hence by Proposition 4.2, the $\sqsubseteq_k$-minimal 3-stable model also exists.

- *uniqueness*
  by Proposition 4.2, the $\sqsubseteq_k$-minimal 3-stable model is unique.

In the next section, we will show that the skeptical model is also easy to compute.

4.2 Computing the Skeptical Model

In [16, 17] we have shown that the Characterization Theorem can be used to derive the Skeptical model. A key result is the following lemma:

Lemma 4.4 *Let $\mathcal{D} = (N, J)$ be an arbirary dependency network. Let M_1 be the minimal 2-valued model of the monotonic network $\mathcal{D}(\emptyset^2, t) = (N, J(\emptyset^2, t))$ and M_2 be the minimal 2-valued model of the monotonic network $\mathcal{D}(\emptyset^2, u) = (N, J(\emptyset^2, u))$.*
Then

1. *$(M_1, N - M_2)$ is an f-complete 3-stable interpretation of $\mathcal{D}$.*

2. *$(M_1, N - M_2) \sqsubseteq_k M_{sk}$, where M_{sk} is the skeptical model of $\mathcal{D}$.*

This lemma, together with the Stacking Lemma and the Characterization Theorem almost immediately implies that the skeptical model of a TMS $\mathcal{D}$ is equivalent to the least fixed point of the operator $TT_{\mathcal{D}}$ defined as :

$$TT_{\mathcal{D}}(I) = I \sqcup_k (M_1(\mathcal{D}^{-I}), N^{-I} - M_2(\mathcal{D}^{-I}))$$

where

- $M_1(\mathcal{D}^{-I})$ is the least 2-valued model of the monotonic network $\mathcal{D}^{-I}(\emptyset^2, t) = (N^{-I}, J^{-I}(\emptyset^2, t))$

- $M_2(\mathcal{D}^{-I})$ is the least model of the monotonic network $\mathcal{D}^{-I}(\emptyset^2, u) = (N^{-I}, J^{-I}(\emptyset^2, u))$

Let $TT_{\mathcal{D}}^{\uparrow 0} = \emptyset^2$ and $TT_{\mathcal{D}}^{\uparrow k+1} = TT_{\mathcal{D}}(TT_{\mathcal{D}}^{\uparrow k})$. Then we have :

Theorem 4.5 *lfp*$(TT_{\mathcal{D}})$ *is the unique* $\sqsubseteq_k$-*minimal stable partial model of* $\mathcal{D}$.

We will analyze the complexity of finding $lfp(TT)$.
Note that each application of TT on a network $\mathcal{D}$, given a partial interpretation M requires

1. the computation of $\mathcal{D}$ modulo M and

2. the computation of two minimal models $M_1(\mathcal{D}^{-M})$ and $M_2(\mathcal{D}^{-M})$ for two monotonic subnetworks of $\mathcal{D}^{-M}$.

First of all, it is easy to see that the the computation of the networks modulo the partial interpretations can be performed in a cumulative way such that the total cost of these "modulo" operations will be $O(|\mathcal{D}|)$, where $|\mathcal{D}|$ denotes the size of the network.
The interesting part concerns the computation of M_1 and M_2. Notice, that a monotonic dependency network can be conceived as a set of Horn clauses. In [3], linear-time algorithms have been given to find a least truth-assignment, i.e. a minimal model for such a set of Horn clauses. Hence, for every monotonic network $\mathcal{D} = (N, J)$, there exists a function $MIN(\mathcal{D})$ computing a 2-valued minimal model M for $\mathcal{D}$ in a time linear in the size $|\mathcal{D}|$ of the network $\mathcal{D}$.
Then, the least fixpoint $lfp(TT_{\mathcal{D}})$ of $\mathcal{D} = (N, J)$ can be computed as follows:

```
begin
    M := (∅, ∅);
    repeat
        μ := (MIN(N, J₁), N − MIN(N, J₂));
        M := M ⊔ μ;
        N := N⁻μ, J := J⁻μ;
    until μ = (∅, ∅)
    lfp(TT_D) := M
end
```

Since $MIN(\mathcal{D})$ is computable in linear time, it is not difficult to see that every iteration step takes not more than $O(|\mathcal{D}|)$ time. Furthermore, before $lfp(TT_\mathcal{D})$ has been found, in every iteration step at least one atom is added to $Ker(M)$ and removed from N. So the number of nodes in the remaining part of the network is strictly decreasing and therefore, the number of iteration steps cannot be more than $|N|$, the number of nodes of the original network $\mathcal{D}$. This implies a worst case of $O(|N| \times |\mathcal{D}|)$ to find the least fixpoint $lfp(TT_\mathcal{D})$.

5 An alternative to the skeptical model semantics

The skeptical model M_{sk} of a TMS $\mathcal{D}$ can be interpreted as an information minimizing model. As an interesting property for truth maintenance, it can be shown that not only the set of all its true beliefs is contained in the true-belief set of every 3-stable model of $\mathcal{D}$, but also that every grounded argument for such a belief valid in M_{sk} is a grounded argument valid in every other 3-stable model of $\mathcal{D}$. So the skeptical model captures the idea of common justified belief.

The skeptical model, however, is not able to capture this idea completely. In case a TMS has a unique 2-stable model, this model is not always equal to the skeptical model. Therefore, the skeptical semantics is not a straightforward generalization of the 2-valued stable model semantics.

Example 5.1 Let $\mathcal{D} = (\{a, b, c\}, \{\neg a \rightarrow b, \neg b \rightarrow a, \neg b \wedge \neg c \rightarrow c\})$. The unique 2-stable model of $\mathcal{D}$ is $M_1 = (\{b\}, \{a, c\})$, while the skeptical model equals $M_2 = (\emptyset, \emptyset)$. ∎

The reason is that the skeptical model equals the intersection of *all* 3-stable models of a network $\mathcal{D}$:

$$M_{sk} = \sqcap_k \{ \ M \mid M \text{ is a 3-stable model of } \mathcal{D} \}$$

To obtain an alternative for the skeptical semantics we could define a partial interpretation I_m as

$$I_m = \sqcap_k \{ \ M \mid M \text{ is a } \sqsubseteq_k\text{-maximal 3-stable model of } \mathcal{D} \}$$

for in that case, I_m would be equal to the unique 2-stable model of $\mathcal{D}$ if such a stable model exists.

There is, however, a problem with I_m, since the intersection of all $\sqsubseteq_k$-maximal 3-stable models does not need to be a 3-stable model.

Therefore, let us concentrate on 3-stable models that are subinterpretations of I_m. First of all, note that $M_{sk} \sqsubseteq_k I_m$ is a unique $\sqsubseteq_k$-minimal 3-stable model. On the other hand we can distinguish a $\sqsubseteq_k$-maximal 3-stable model $M_{ms} \sqsubseteq_k I_m$.

The following Lemma shows that such a model M_{ms} is unique.

Lemma 5.2 *Let M and M' be 3-stable models of $\mathcal{D}$. If M and M' are both $\sqsubseteq_k$-maximal subinterpretations of I_m, then $M = M'$.*

Since the skeptical model is a $\sqcap_k$-minimal model, let us call this alternative model the $\sqcap_k$-maximal or *maximal skeptical* model M_{ms}.

Example 5.3 Let $\mathcal{D} = (\{a, b, c\}, \{\neg a \rightarrow b, \neg b \rightarrow a, \neg b \wedge \neg c \rightarrow c\})$. The maximal skeptical model of $\mathcal{D}$ is $M_{ms} = (\{b\}, \{a, c\})$, while the skeptical model equals $M_{sk} = (\emptyset, \emptyset)$. ∎

The following result is immediate:

Theorem 5.4 *Let M be the unique 2-stable model of a network $\mathcal{D} = (N, J)$. Then $M_{ms} = (M, N - M)$, i.e. the maximal skeptical model and the unique 2-stable model coincide.*

Since M_{ms} always exists and is uniquely defined, we could propose it as a serious alternative to the skeptical semantics. There is, however, little hope that M_{ms} can be computed efficiently: it can be proven, that the decision problem COMPLETE M_{ms} : Given an arbitrary $\mathcal{D}$, is M_{ms} a complete model of $\mathcal{D}$? can be reduced to the UNIQUE SAT problem defined as: Given an instance of SAT, does this instance have a unique solution ? In [14], it has been proven that finding a solution to UNIQUE SAT is as hard as finding a solution to the NP-complete SAT problem, under randomized reductions.

Remark. Both the skeptical model and the maximal skeptical model can be seen as special cases of so-called *immune* interpretations and models ([17]).

Definition 5.5 *A partial interpretation I of $\mathcal{D}$ is called* immune *if I is the unique 3-stable interpretation of $(\mathcal{D}^{-(I'-I)})$ for all extensions I' of I.* ∎

Analogously, an immune model of $\mathcal{D}$ is defined as an immune interpretation which is a 3-stable model of $\mathcal{D}$ as well.
Intuitively, immunity means that I remains the unique 2-stable model of the subnetwork determined by its kernel $Ker(I)$, whatever interpretation is given to atoms outside this subnetwork. ∎

References

[1] Brewka, G., Nonmonotonic Reasoning - From Theoretical Foundations Towards Efficient Computation, thesis University of Hamburg, 1989

[2] Charniak, E., Riesbeck C., and McDermott, D., *Artificial Intelligence Programming*, L.E. Erlbaum, Baltimore, 1979.

[3] Dowling, W. and Gallier, J., Linear Time Algorithms for Testing the Satisfiability of Propositional Horn Formulae, *Journal of Logic Programming* 3 (1984), 267-284.

[4] Doyle, J., A Truth Maintenance System, *Artificial Intelligence* 12, 1979

[5] Elkan, Ch., Logical Characterizations of Nonmonotonic TMSs, in: Kreczmar, A. and G. Mirkowska, (eds) *Mathematical Foundations of Computer Science 1989*, Springer Heidelberg, 1989, pp. 218-224.

[6] Gelfond, M., and Lifschitz, V., The Stable Model Semantics for Logic Programming. In : *Fifth International Conference Symposium on Logic Programming*, pp. 1070-1080, 1988.

[7] Goodwin, J. , An Improved Algorithm for Non-Monotonic Dependency Net Update. LITH-MAT-R-82-23, Linkoeping University 1982.

[8] Kleene, S., Introduction of metamathematics, Van Nostrand, 1952.

[9] Lloyd, J.W., *Foundations of Logic Programming*, Springer Verlag, Heidelberg, 1987

[10] Petrie, C.J., Revised Dependency-Directed Backtracking for Default Reasoning, Proc. AAAI, 1987.

[11] Przymusinska, H., and Przymusinski, T., Semantic Issues in Deductive Databases and Logic Programs, in : *Formal Techniques in Artificial Intelligence, A Sourcebook* R.B. Banerji (ed.), Elsevier, Amsterdam, 1990, pp 321-367.

[12] Reinfrank, M., Fundamentals and Logical Foundations of Truth Maintenance, Linköping Studies in Science and Technology. Dissertations no. 221, Linköping University, 1989.

[13] Turner, R., *Logics for Artificial Intelligence*, Ellis Horwood Ltd, Chichester, 1987.

[14] Valiant,L.G., Vazirani, V.V., NP is as easy as detecting unique solutions, *Theoretical Computer Science* 47 (1986) 85-93.

[15] Witteveen, C., Fixpoint Semantics for Truth Maintenance, TWI-report 90-85, Faculty of Technical Mathematics and Computer Science, Delft University of Technology, Delft, 1990

[16] Witteveen, C., Partial Semantics for Truth Maintenance, to appear as TWI-Report, Department of Mathematics and Computer Science, Delft University of Technology, 1990.

[17] Witteveen, C., Partial Semantics for Truth Maintenance, in : J.W. van Eyk(ed.), Proceedings of JELIA90, LNCAI, Springer Heidelberg, 1990, (to appear).

Semantic Accounts of Belief Revision

Peter Jackson & John Pais
McDonnell Douglas Research Laboratories
Dept 225, Bldg 105/2, Mailcode 1065165
P.O. Box 516, St. Louis, MO 63166, USA

Abstract

We present a semantic approach to belief revision, called BERYL, which is based on counterfactual logic. We compare our approach to alternative accounts of belief revision and argue for the importance of certain logical properties, such as syntax-independence and preservation. Finally, we suggest that the revision-based approach to truth maintenance has a number of advantages over justification- and assumption-based methods.

1 Introduction

Among the various approaches to truth maintenance that have been advocated in the literature, a distinction (due to de Kleer, 1984) is usually drawn between those that are *justification-based* (JTMS) and those that are *assumption-based* (ATMS).

A JTMS is a mechanism for ensuring consistency in a single view of the world which is incomplete and may require belief update in the light of new information. Dependencies record reasons for believing or disbelieving in certain propositions on the basis of what is currently known. If a contradiction is discovered by dependency-directed backtracking, the user is invited to disable some part of the justification structure. Exemplars of this approach include Doyle (1980) and McAllester (1980).

An ATMS represents multiple views of the world under different assumption sets with a view to identifying all those views which satisfy some problem-specific constraints. Assumptions are then reasons for believing (or expecting) certain propositions to be true in a given context. Contexts that turn out to be inconsistent (*nogoods*) are eliminated from further consideration. The main exemplars are due to de Kleer (1986) and Martins & Shapiro (1988).

In this paper, we consider another class of TMS, which we shall call *revision-based* (RTMS). An RTMS is primarily a mechanism for computing belief change in the face of both change in the world and change in the amount of information available about the world. Although this does not rule out a role for dependencies or assumptions, the central idea is to compute the minimum revision required of a theory in order to accommodate new information. Another distinguishing feature of the RTMS approach is that it usually identifies the culprits responsible for a contradiction and automatically excises them from the theory. Exemplars include Ginsberg (1986), Winslett (1988), Dalal (1988) and Jackson (1989), and the main thrust of this paper is a comparison of the four approaches.

We argue that Ginsberg's Possible Worlds Approach (PWA) to belief revision through counterfactual implication suffers from a number of defects which are the result of confusing proof theory and model theory. In particular, logically equivalent theories do not have identical counterfactual consequences. This paper presents a semantics for counterfactual implication based on Jackson (1989) in which propositions are treated as operations on sets of possible worlds. Logically equivalent theories have identical consequences in the model theory, which validates most of the belief revision postulates of Gärdenfors (1988) and satisfies an axiomatization of the counterfactual logic C (see *e.g.*, Bell, 1990). We show that our semantics is closer to the intent of PWA than the correction proposed by Winslett's (1988) Possible Models Approach (PMA), because it shares more of PWA's desirable properties.

Finally, we compare BERYL with Dalal's (1988) approach in some depth. We show that these systems are founded on different notions of what constitutes a minimum revision. Examples are used to clarify this difference, and we make some suggestions concerning which method might be best suited to which kind of application.

2 PWA, PMA and Revise

Counterfactuals are conditional statements in which the antecedent is deemed to be false, *e.g.*, 'If Waldo were rich, he'd live in Las Vegas.' Considered as material conditionals, all such statements are trivially true; thus 'If Waldo were rich, he'd live in Milwaukee' would also be a true statement, if Waldo were not rich. Yet the intention seems to be something like: 'if things were more or less as they are, except that Waldo were rich, he'd be living in Las Vegas,' which rules out living in Milwaukee. It is customary to write a counterfactual conditional of the general form 'if ψ then ϕ' as '$\psi > \phi$' rather than '$\psi \supset \phi$', in order to preserve this distinction.

Counterfactuals are not truth-functional because they can only be evaluated relative to (i) some theory of what the world is like, and (ii) some notions about what the world *would* be like if certain things were to change. Informally, we want $\psi > \phi$ to be true if and only if ϕ is true in all those plausible worlds where ψ holds which are most similar to the current world. From a formal point of view, the problem is to specify what we mean by 'plausible' and 'similar.'

The link with belief revision is as follows. Assuming that $\psi > \phi$ holds with respect to an agent's beliefs, if that agent subsequently gets new information to the effect that ψ while still in the same belief state, then the agent should also accept ϕ. Thus if I believe that ϕ would be the case if ψ *were* the case, then if I learn that ψ *is* the case I should accept ϕ too, all other things being equal.

Ginsberg's (1986) paper was perhaps the first to demonstrate the relevance of counterfactual reasoning to a range of AI applications. Its scope is considerable, including a brief review of the philosophical literature, an account of counterfactual implication that has become known as the Possible Worlds Approach (PWA), a discussion of implementation issues, and a survey of applications as diverse as planning, diagnosis, and simulation. In this paper, we shall be concerned only with the account of counterfactual implication, which we feel to be flawed in corrigible ways.

Ginsberg's construction for counterfactuals consists of an initial set S of sentences, a predicate B on 2^S, and a partial order $<$ on 2^S which extends set inclusion and respects B. S is a theory of the world, B is a 'bad world' predicate which declares some states of affairs to be implausible, and $<$ is a comparator of possible worlds along the plausibility dimension. The definition of plausible, similar worlds is as follows.

<u>Definition 1</u>. A *possible world for* ψ *in* S is any subset T of S such that $T \not\models \neg\psi$, $\neg B(T)$, and T is maximal with respect to $<$, given these restrictions. The set of such worlds, $W(\psi, S)$, is

$$\{T \subseteq S \mid T \not\models \neg\psi \wedge \neg B(T) \wedge \{U \subseteq S \mid T < U \wedge U \not\models \neg\psi \wedge \neg B(U)\} = \emptyset\}.$$

A counterfactual $\psi > \phi$ is now true w.r.t. S iff $T \cup \{\psi\} \models \phi$ for all $T \in W(\psi, S)$. ‖

In treating 2^S as a set of possible worlds, Ginsberg encourages us to confuse syntactic objects, such as sets of sentences, with semantic objects, such as models. It is rather dangerous to treat arbitrary theories as 'partial possible worlds' because theories are more complex than models, *e.g.*, they have a consequence structure. Ginsberg notes that logically equivalent theories do not have identical counterfactual consequences in PWA.

The problem is that everything depends on the syntactic representation of S. For example, if $S = \{p \wedge q\}$, then PWA will excise $p \wedge q$ from the revised theory when revising by $\neg p$, so $\neg p > q$ will not hold. On the other hand, if $T = \{p, q\}$, then $\neg p > q$ would hold, even though S and T are logically equivalent.

Winslett's PMA attempted to regularize the model theory of counterfactual consequence. Given a set of formulas S and a theory T, PMA computes a set of models Incorporate(S, M) produced by incorporating S into T, where M is a model of T. Incorporation is essentially a process of moving from M to a model M' that satisfies S and 'differs minimally' from M. The models of the revision of T by S are computed by aggregating all the models that result from incorporating S into each model of T. The formal definition can be expressed as follows.

<u>Definition 2</u>. Let T be a theory with protected formulas $T^* \subset T$, let M be a model of T, and let S be a set of formulas. Incorporate(S, M) is the set of all models M' such that

(i) $M' \models S$ and $M' \models T^*$; and
(ii) no other model satisfying (i) differs from M on fewer atoms,

where 'fewer' is defined by set inclusion. If Models(T) is the set of all models of T, then the set of models of the revised theory is given by:

$$\cup_{M \in \text{Models}(T)} \text{Incorporate}(S, M). \qquad \qquad \|$$

It is easy to verify that logically equivalent theories have identical counterfactual consequences in PMA. We return to Winslett's construction in Section 5, where we conduct a systematic analysis of its properties with respect to certain belief revision postulates and compare it with the alternative accounts considered in this paper.

Dalal's (1988) revision function can be seen as a specialization of PMA. The semantics was originally presented in terms of a generalization operator over sets of formulas; here we give a 'Winslett style' definition which we think is much clearer, particularly for the purposes of comparison. The main departure from PMA is that Dalal's function exhibits a preference for minimum *cardinality* change.

<u>Definition 3</u>. Let T be a theory, let Models(T) be the set of all models of T, and let S be a set of formulas. The *revision of T by S*, written Revise(T, S), is the set of all models M' such that: (i) $M' \models S$; and (ii) no other model satisfying (i) differs from *any* model M of T on fewer atoms, where 'fewer' is defined in terms of cardinality, *i.e.*, the number of atoms involved. $\qquad \|$

We return to the Revise function in Section 6, where we argue that a particular monotonicity property renders it unsuitable for certain applications of nonmonotonic reasoning.

3 Possible world semantics for counterfactuals

In this section, we present a semantic account of belief revision (BERYL) which is also based on counterfactual logic. Like PMA and Revise, it is intended to correct the syntax dependency of earlier accounts, such as Ginsberg's PWA, which have no model theory. However, we shall use examples and analysis to show that BERYL is closer to being a 'minimum revision' of PWA than the other two systems, and therefore preserves more of its desirable properties.

Our account assumes a propositional language L, defined over a finite alphabet A. We use the following notation. Letters in various ranges stand for propositional constants in this alphabet $(p, q, r, ...)$, propositional metavariables standing for any formula of L $(\psi, \phi, \chi, ...)$, theories or arbitrary sets of such formulas $(S, T, U, ...)$ and possible worlds $(w, v, u, ...)$.

Given a finite alphabet A, we can construct $2^{|A|}$ interpretations over it, and consider each of these interpretations as a possible world. Let the set of interpretations be W. A *theory*, $S \subset L$, describes a set of worlds, $W_S \subseteq W$, containing the models of S, *i.e.*, just those interpretations which satisfy S. We do not assume that S is necessarily consistent or closed under deduction. As usual, if S is a theory, then $W_S = W_{Cn(S)}$, where $Cn(S)$ denotes the logical closure of S. If S is inconsistent, then $W_S = \emptyset$.

A possible world w is represented by a set of atomic propositions, $[\psi_1, ..., \psi_n]$; we use square brackets as a notational device to distinguish models from sets of arbitrary formulas. If ψ is an atom, then $w \models \psi$ iff $\psi \in w$, and if $\psi \notin w$ then $w \models \neg\psi$. Satisfaction conditions for a compound statement follow the normal truth-functional recursion on its complexity. The world [] denotes the interpretation under which all atomic formulas based on the propositonal letters in A are false.

Using this convention, it is easier to analyze the comparative relationship 'u differs from v on fewer atoms than w under set inclusion,' where u, v and w are models or possible worlds. We first met this relation in the definition of PMA, and we shall use it in our own definitions, where it will be represented by the notation $u <_v w$. If we consider models as sets of atomic formulas, then $u <_v w$ says that the symmetric set difference between u and v is a proper subset of the symmetric set difference between v and w. Similarly, 'u differs from v on fewer atoms than w under cardinality' means that the symmetric set difference between u and v is of smaller cardinality than the symmetric set difference between v and w.

The semantics that we shall give for counterfactuals of the form $\psi > \phi$ with respect to a theory S depends upon a very simple idea. A proposition ψ is considered as a *revision function*, $\psi: 2^W \rightarrow 2^W$, that applies to W_S to return those worlds where ψ holds which are most similar to some world in W_S. $\psi > \phi$ is then a consequence of S just in case ϕ holds in each of these worlds. This 'comparative similarity' approach is orginally due to Lewis (1973, Ch.2).

For example, if $S = \{p \supset q\}$, then arguably $p(W_S)$ should be the set of worlds where p holds which are most similar to some world in W_S. If $A = \{p, q\}$, then $W_S = \{[], [q], [p, q]\}$, and $p(W_S)$ ought to return $\{[p, q]\}$, the only model of $\{p, p \supset q\}$.

This example is rather straightforward. p is consistent with S, and we did not place any restrictions upon the range of p; *i.e.*, all worlds in which p held were deemed to be plausible. But we are most interested in the case where p is inconsistent with S. What general principles should propositions considered as revision functions observe? Here are a number of suggestions, most of which can be found elsewhere in the literature. Each of them is based upon a case analysis of the logical properties of ψ and S and the logical relationships that might hold between them. We state these principles informally here to motivate the definitions that will follow shortly. Later, in Section 5, we review some of the original suggestions from the literature in a more formal setting, notably those of Gärdenfors (1988).

(P1) If S *is inconsistent*, then every proposition already follows from it. Hence it is impossible to revise S by any proposition whatsoever and obtain anything other than S. Thus $\psi(W_S) = W_S = \emptyset$ for all ψ.

(P2) If ψ *is inconsistent*, then it has no models, so $\psi(W_S) = W_{\{\psi\}} = \emptyset$.

The rest of the principles assume that S and ψ are consistent in themselves (but not necessarily with each other).

(P3) If S *logically implies* ψ, then there is no need to change W_S. Else, some revision must be effected, otherwise there will be a world in $\psi(W_S)$ which is not a model of ψ.

(P4) If ψ *is consistent with* S but does not follow from it, then we compute the new set of worlds $\psi(W_S) = W_{\{\psi\}} \cap W_S$, containing all the worlds which satisfy $S \cup \{\psi\}$.

(P5) If ψ *is inconsistent with S*, then we compute some minimum revision $\psi(W_S)$ of W_S such that $\psi(W_S) \subseteq W_{\{\psi\}}$. This inclusion must hold if ψ is to be true at every world in $\psi(W_S)$.

Finally, we follow Ginsberg and Winslett in protecting some propositions in a special set $S^* \subset S$ whose truth we deem to be unalterable. In applications, such propositions normally correspond to domain axioms, *e.g.*, fundamental physical principles of the real world. Their use is more than a matter of implementation, so we need principles for revisions involving them.

(P6) If ψ *is inconsistent with S**, then we cannot accept ψ, and so $\psi(W_S) = W_S$.

(P7) If ψ *is inconsistent with S but consistent with S**, then $\psi(W_S) \subseteq (W_{\{\psi\}} \cap W_{S*})$.

Our revision function is specified in Definitions 5-7, and it satisfies each of the principles **P1-P5** (see Section 5 for proofs). Definition 5 outlines what it means for one world to be close (or similar) to another. Definition 6 gives the revision operation itself, based on the idea of *closest* worlds, and Definition 7 defines counterfactual consequence in terms of this operation. We incorporate protected propositions separately at the end of the section, and the modified system satisfies **P6** and **P7**.

In our presentation of BERYL, we use the notion of a world lattice.

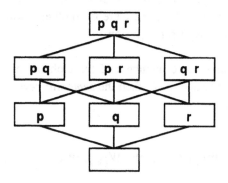

Figure 1. A world lattice for the alphabet $\{p, q, r\}$.

Definition 4. If $S \subset L$ and $B \subseteq A$ contains those members of the alphabet of L occurring in S and ψ, then $\Lambda_B = (2^B, \subset)$ is a *world lattice* for B, where '$\subset$' denotes the proper subset relation.   ‖

Figure 1 shows the world lattice for $B = \{p, q, r\}$. The greatest element of the lattice represents the possible world $[p, q, r]$ where each atomic formula derived from a propositional letter in B is deemed to be true. The least element represents the world $[]$, in which each such formula is false.

Definition 5. Let $\Lambda_B = (2^B, \subset)$ and $W, V \subseteq 2^B$ with $W \cap V = \emptyset$. Then $v \in V$ is among the *neighbours* of $w \in W$, written $N(v, w)$ iff

    (i) $v \in \mathbf{B}_w(V)$ *or*
    (ii) $\mathbf{B}_w(V) = \emptyset$ and $\neg(\exists u)(u <_w v)$

where $\mathbf{B}_w(V) = \{v \in V \mid \text{glb}(v, w) \text{ or } \text{lub}(v, w)\}$
and $u <_w v$ iff u differs from w on fewer atoms than v under set inclusion.

The *set of closest worlds in V to W*, written $V \Leftarrow W$, is given by

$$V \Leftarrow W = \{v \in V \mid (\exists w \in W)N(v, w)\}.$$ ‖

The intuitive reading of Definition 5 is as follows. v is a neighbour of w if and only if: (i) v is a greatest lower bound (glb) or least upper bound (lub) of w in the lattice; *or* (ii) there is no other world in V that is a glb or lub of w, and there is no other world u in V that differs from w on fewer atoms than v under set inclusion.

Definition 6. If $S \subset L, \psi \in L, B \subseteq A$ contains those members of the alphabet of L occurring in either S or ψ, and Λ_B is a world lattice for B, then the *semantic revision* of S by ψ, written $\psi(W_S)$, is given as follows:

    (i) if $W_S = \emptyset$, then $\psi(W_S) = \emptyset$, else
    (ii) if $W_{\{\psi\}} \cap W_S \neq \emptyset$, then $\psi(W_S) = W_{\{\psi\}} \cap W_S$, else $W_{\{\psi\}} \Leftarrow W_S$.   ‖

(i) defines $\emptyset$ as the fixed point of the revision operator. It is the model of every inconsistent theory and cannot be revised, since it already entails every proposition. (ii) states that if ψ is consistent with S, then we simply intersect their models, otherwise we compute the set of those worlds in $W_{\{\psi\}}$ that are closest to some world in W_S by Definition 6.

<u>Definition 7</u>. $\psi > \phi$ is a counterfactual consequence of S iff $w \models \phi$ for all $w \in \psi(W_S)$.

Let us agree to call the logic of Definitions 5-7 'Belief Revision Logic', using the failed acronym BERYL for short. It is easy to demonstrate the following result.

<u>Theorem 1</u>. If S and T are equivalent theories, then for all propositions ψ and ϕ, $\psi > \phi$ is a counterfactual consequence of S in BERYL iff $\psi > \phi$ is a counterfactual consequence of T.

Proof. Follows straightforwardly from Definitions 5-7. If the antecedent holds, then $W_S = W_T$. Thus $w \models \phi$ for all $w \in \psi(W_S)$ iff $w \models \phi$ for all $w \in \psi(W_T)$.   ‖

Given a set $S^* \subset S$ of protected propositions, we restrict the range of all functions ψ to the set $W_{\{\psi\}} \cap W_{S^*}$. Worlds in $W_{\{\psi\}}$ but not in W_{S^*} are deemed implausible, regardless of how close they are to worlds in W_{S^*}. If $v \in W_{\{\psi\}}$ is the closest world to some $w \in W_S$, but $v \notin W_{S^*}$, then the closest world $u \in W_{\{\psi\}}$ to v that satisfies S^* is the closest world to w. We shall not weary the reader by recapitulating the definitions, but see Sections 4 and 5 for examples. Section 5 shows that this modification has only minor consequences for the formal properties of the revision function.

4 A crucial example

In the long version of her 1988 paper, Winslett argued against what she called the 'Gärdenfors semantics' (Gärdenfors & Makinson, 1988), which would require that

$$\text{Incorporate}(\psi, \mathbf{Cn}(T)) = \mathbf{Cn}(\mathbf{Cn}(T) \cup \{\psi\})$$

if $T \cup \{\psi\}$ is consistent (see our **P4**). The claim is that PWA's use of this principle leads to a difficulty with the ramification problem when reasoning about actions, and cites a specific example (her Example 3, Section 5.1). We reconstruct this example below, and show that the Gärdenfors semantics is *not* the cause of this difficulty; rather, it is due to the syntax-dependency of PWA.

Example 1. The original example is based on reasoning about actions in a room containing a TV and two ventilation ducts. Let d denote 'the TV is on duct1', e denote 'the TV is on duct2', and f denote 'the TV is on the floor.' We insist that the TV be either on duct1, on duct2, or on the floor, and can only occupy one place at a time. Thus the propositions in the set

$$S^* = \{d \vee e \vee f, d \supset \neg e, d \supset \neg f, e \supset \neg f\}$$

are each protected against revision. This means that every world in the set

$$X = 2^B - W_{S^*} = \{[d, e, f], [d, e], [d, f], [e, f], []\}$$

is 'bad,' reverting to Ginsberg's terminology. Suppose that

$$S = S^* \cup \{\neg d, \neg e, f\}.$$

If we now revise by the sequence of three actions: (i) $d \vee e$, (ii) d, and (iii) $\neg d$, then PWA gets the counterintuitive result that e is in the revised theory, *i.e.*, that the TV ends up on duct2, even though all we should be able to deduce is that the TV is not on duct1. This is the result that Winslett blames on the Gärdenfors semantics.

If we examine PWA's derivation in detail, we see that the blame for this outcome lies elsewhere. After revision by $d \vee e$, S becomes $S' = S^* \cup \{d \vee e\}$. After revision by d, S' becomes $S'' = S^* \cup \{d \vee e, d\}$. Further revision by $\neg d$ finally leaves us with $S^* \cup \{d \vee e, \neg d\}$ which logically implies e.

However, the fault lies not with the handling of the consistent case, in step (ii), but in the fact that we allow $d \vee e$ to loiter in the revised theory, once d is true. To see why this causes problems recall that, if $p \in S$ for any proposition p, then $p \vee q \in \text{Cn}(S)$ for *any* proposition q. Thus, once p becomes false, we can draw any conclusion whatever!

BERYL's solution is described below and shown in Figure 2. This example also serves to illustrate how we handle protected propositions.

The way to read Figure 2 is as follows. We begin at world $[f]$, the only model of S. The first revision by $d \vee e$ takes us from $[f]$ to $[d]$ and $[e]$. Although both $[d, f]$ and $[d, f]$ are close to $[f]$ and satisfy $d \vee e$, each of these worlds is 'bad,' because each allows the TV to be in more than one place at a time. So we are forced to move on to $[d]$ and $[e]$, since the range of $d \vee e$, considered as a revision function, is restricted to $W_{\{\psi\}} \cap W_{S^*}$. The second revision by d simply rules out $[e]$, leaving $[d]$. The final revision by $\neg d$ takes us to $[e]$ and $[f]$ via the bad world $[]$. $[]$ is bad because the TV must be somewhere. Thus the TV ends up either on duct2 or on the floor.

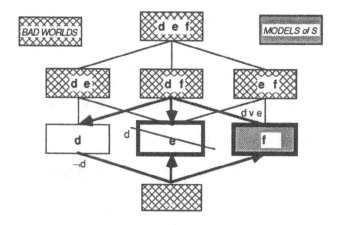

Figure 2. World lattice for Example 1

In summary:

$(d \vee e)(W_S) = \{[d], [e]\}$
$d((d \vee e)(W_S)) = \{[d]\}$
$\neg d(d(d \vee e)(W_S))) = \{[e], [f]\}.$

The point is that BERYL's result is the same as PMA's, despite our use of the Gärdenfors semantics in Definition 6.　　　　　　　　　‖

5 BERYL and the Gärdenfors postulates

Gärdenfors (1988, Ch. 3) argues for a number of postulates (**K*1-K*8**) that a syntactic belief revision function ought to satisfy. If we render the postulates in the BERYL notation, then we can translate them into *semantic* constraints upon $\psi(W_S)$ and see which ones BERYL satisfies. We also recapitulate this analysis for the other three systems to facilitate a formal comparison between them.

In Gärdenfors' notation, K represents a belief set, *i.e.*, a set of sentences closed under logical consequence, while K^*_A represents the revision of K by the sentence A and K^+_A represents the expansion of K by A, *i.e.*, the result of adding A to K. The following theorem proves the easier results first, by showing that BERYL satisfies all but one of the postulates **K*1-K*6**.

Theorem 2. BERYL satisfies the postulates **K*1-K*6**, except for **K*5**.

Proof.

K*1. For any sentence A, and any belief set K, K^*_A is a belief set. The corresponding semantic constraint is that, for any sentence ψ, $\psi: 2^W \to 2^W$. BERYL satisfies this postulate in a straightforward manner, since revision functions are total. Recall that $\psi(W_S) = \emptyset$ if either $W_S = \emptyset$ or $W_{\{\psi\}} = \emptyset$.

K*2. $A \in K^*_A$. BERYL satisfies $\psi(W_S) \subseteq W_{\{\psi\}}$, which is the corresponding semantic constraint.

K*3. $K^*_A \subseteq K^+_A$. We can guarantee that $(W_S \cap W_{\{\psi\}}) \subseteq \psi(W_S)$ for BERYL. For if $S \models \neg\psi$, then the postulate is trivially satisfied, else $\psi(W_S) = W_S \cap W_{\{\psi\}}$ by Definition 6.

K*4. If $\neg A \notin K$, then $K^+_A \subseteq K^*_A$. The corresponding semantic constraint is as follows: If $(W_S \cap W_{\{\psi\}}) \neq \emptyset$, then $\psi(W_S) \subseteq (W_S \cap W_{\{\psi\}})$. If $(W_S \cap W_{\{\psi\}}) \neq \emptyset$, then $\psi(W_S) = W_S \cap W_{\{\psi\}}$ by Definition 6, so BERYL satisfies this postulate.

K*5. $K^*_A = K_\perp$ iff $\vdash \neg A$. The corresponding semantic constraint, $\psi(W_S) = \emptyset$ if and only if $\models \neg\psi$, is *not* satisfied in the case where $W_S = \emptyset$.

K*6. If $\vdash A \equiv B$, then $K^*_A = K^*_B$. The corresponding semantic constraint is as follows: If $\models \psi \equiv \phi$, then $\psi(W_S) = \phi(W_S)$. It is easy to see that Definition 5 enforces this constraint, since $W_{\{\psi\}} = W_{\{\phi\}}$. ‖

With regard to **K*5**, it seems unnatural to insist that revision will always result in a consistent theory just because the revising proposition is consistent. (In fact, Gärdenfors' postulates implicitly assume that K is consistent.) However, it is easy to see that BERYL satisfies the weaker postulate:

K*5w. $\psi(W_S) = \emptyset$ if and only if S or ψ is inconsistent.

If we have a set of protected propositions, $S^* \subset S$, then we must also allow $\psi(W_S) = \emptyset$ if $S^* \cup \{\psi\}$ is inconsistent.

Referring back to the informal 'principles' outlined in Section 3, **P4** corresponds to **K*4** and **P5** corresponds to **K*2**. The rest of the principles follow trivially from the BERYL definitions.

Theorem 3. BERYL satisfies **K*7**: $K^*_{A \wedge B} \subseteq (K^*_A)^+_B$, which is equivalent to the semantic constraint: $\psi(W_S) \cap W_{\{\phi\}} \subseteq (\psi \wedge \phi)(W_S)$.

Proof. Let $R = (\psi \wedge \phi)(W_S)$ stand for the revision, let $I = \psi(W_S) \cap W_{\{\phi\}}$ stand for the intersection, and let $V = W_{\{\psi, \phi\}}$.

We begin by giving an outline of the proof. If **K*7** is false, then the following proposition must be true:

(1) $(\exists v \in I)(v \notin R)$.

Further, propositions (2) and (3) follow from Definition 6.

(2) $(\forall v \in V)(v \in I \supset (\exists w \in W_S)N_1(v, w))$.

(3) $(\forall v \in V)(v \notin R \supset (\forall w \in W_S)\neg N_2(v, w))$.

These propositions deserve some explanation. It is necessary to index the N predicate in each formula, since its denotation depends upon the revising proposition, *i.e.*, upon the context of worlds competing to be in the revision. Thus $N_1(v, w)$ says that v is among the closest worlds to some world w in W_S with respect to the revising proposition ψ, *i.e.*, in the context of $W_{\{\psi\}}$, while $\neg N_2(v, w)$ says that v is *not* among the closest worlds to *any* world $w \in W_S$ with respect to revising proposition $(\psi \wedge \phi)$.

To prove **K*7**, it suffices to establish propositions (2) and (3) and show that they are jointly inconsistent with (1).

Proposition (2): By Definition 5, for any $x \in \psi(W_S)$, there is some $w \in W_S$ such that x is a glb or lub of w, or x differs from w on fewer atoms under set inclusion than any other world in $W_{\{\psi\}}$. But I contains just those worlds in $\psi(W_S)$ that also satisfy ϕ, so these worlds also satisfy Definition 5 and have the properties ascribed to the arbitrary world x.

Proposition (3): If $v \notin R$, then v is not a glb or lub of w, by the first clause of Definition 5. By the second clause, there must be another world $u \in V$ such that either (i) u is a glb or lub of w, or (ii) u differs from w on fewer atoms under set inclusion than v. In any event, $N_2(v, w)$ does not hold for any world $w \in W_S$.

Now we demonstrate the contradiction between propositions (1), (2) and (3). By hypothesis, there is at least one world in I that is not in R; let this world be a. It follows from (2) and $a \in I$ that

(4) $(\exists w \in W_S)N_1(a, w)$,

and it follows from (3) and $a \notin R$ that

(5) $(\forall w \in W_S)\neg N_2(a, w)$.

If $(\exists w \in W_S)(N_1(a, w))$ holds, then a is a neighbour of some world w in W_S in the context of $W_{\{\psi\}}$. On the other hand, $(\forall w \in W_S)(\neg N_2(a, w))$ states that a is not a neighbour of any world in W_S in the context of $W_{\{\psi, \phi\}}$. This means that there must be some other world, $b \in W_{\{\psi, \phi\}}$, which prevents a from being a neighbour of w in the new context. But $W_{\{\psi, \phi\}} \subseteq W_{\{\psi\}}$, so there can be no such b. Hence the formulas (4) and (5) are inconsistent. We have therefore shown that propositions (2) and (3) are jointly inconsistent with the assumption that $K*7$ is false. Since (2) and (3) follow from our definitions, $K*7$ must hold.   ‖

It turns out (see Example 2 for a counterexample) that BERYL does not satisfy the final postulate $K*8$: If $\neg B \notin K*_A$, then $(K*_A)^+_B \subseteq K*_{A \wedge B}$, which is equivalent to the semantic constraint:

$$(\psi \wedge \phi)(W_S) \subseteq \psi(W_S) \cap W_{\{\phi\}}, \text{ if } \psi(W_S) \cap W_{\{\phi\}} \neq \emptyset.$$

Example 2. Let $S = \{\neg(p \equiv q), q \equiv r, r \equiv s\}$, $\psi = \neg p \wedge \neg q \wedge \neg r$ and $\phi = \neg p \wedge \neg q \wedge (\neg r \vee s)$, then $W_S = \{[p], [q, r, s]\}$, $W_{\{\phi\}} = \{[r, s], [s], []\}$, and

$$W_{\{\psi\}} = W_{\{\psi, \phi\}} = W_{\{\psi\}} \cap W_{\{\phi\}} = (\psi \wedge \phi)(W_S) = \psi(W_S) = \{[s], []\}$$
$$\phi(W_S) = \{[r, s], []\}.$$

Thus $\phi(W_S) \cap W_{\{\psi\}} = \{[]\} \neq \emptyset$, which is not a superset of $(\psi \wedge \phi)(W_S)$, and $K*8$ does not hold.   ‖

This result is contrary to a mistaken claim for the formulation of BERYL described in Jackson (1989). Elsewhere (Pais & Jackson, 1990), we argue that $K*8$ is incompatible with a number of defensible notions of what a 'minimal revision' should be. We will only summarize a part of the argument here.

Since $W_{\{\psi, \phi\}} \subseteq W_{\{\phi\}}$, it can be seen that $K*8$ is a kind of monotonicity condition, where we focus on the models of the revising proposition, instead of on the models of the theory being revised. As we show later in Theorem 7, BERYL provides a semantics for a nonmonotonic logic, in the sense that the counterfactual consequences of a theory do not merely accumulate as that theory expands. In failing to satisfy $K*8$, we see that BERYL is also nonmonotonic in the sense that counterfactual consequences do not merely accumulate as the revising proposition is expanded. This is surely the more realistic state of affairs from a belief revision point of view.

Looking back to Example 2, as we acquire more information from a stronger revising proposition, ψ, certain counterfactual consequences of the weaker proposition, ϕ, cease to hold. Thus we have $\phi > \neg r$, but not $(\psi \wedge \phi) > \neg r$, even though ψ and ϕ are consistent with each other. Hence BERYL is nonmonotonic with respect to the revising proposition as well as with respect to the theory being revised.

PMA does not satisfy **K*8**, and PWA does so only if the order, $<$, defined over worlds is modular (Ginsberg, 1986). Cardinality generates a modular order, so Revise does satisfy **K*8**. In fact, Dalal (1988) shows that his system satisfies all eight of the Gärdenfors postulates.

The main difference between PMA and the other three systems is that it does not satisfy **K*4**, as the following example shows.

Example 3. In PMA, if we revise $S = \{p \supset q\}$ by p, then we get the following set of models: $\{[p, q], [p]\}$. $W_S = \{[p, q], [q], []\}$, and although $[p, q]$ is the closest model of p to itself and to $[q]$, $[p]$ is the closest model of p to $[]$. **K*4** is not satisfied, because the outcome is not a subset of $\{[p, q]\}$, the set of models of $S \cup \{p\}$. ||

Note that **K*4** is the postulate relevant to Example 1 concerning the 'Gärdenfors semantics.' Note also that **K*4** is a special case of **K*8**. However, unlike **K*8**, it is not a monotonicity condition.

Gärdenfors identifies a number of additional criteria for the classification of belief revision functions: the *preservation criterion* (**K*P**) and the *monotonicity criterion* (**K*M**). The former states that if ϕ follows from S and ψ is consistent with S, then ϕ will still follow from the revision of S by ψ. The latter states that if S and T are theories and T contains S, then the revision of T will contain the revision of S. We can show that the revisions sanctioned by BERYL are always preservative but not always monotonic. (**K*P** and **K*M** are translated into the present semantic notation in Theorems 5-8.)

Theorem 5. BERYL satisfies the preservation criterion, **K*P**, given as the following semantic constraint: If $S \not\models \neg\psi$ and $S \models \phi$, then $\psi > \phi$.

Proof. $S \not\models \neg\psi$ and $S \models \phi$ by hypothesis, so $W_{\{\psi\}} \cap W_S \neq \emptyset$ and $W_S \subseteq W_{\{\phi\}}$. But then $\psi(W_S) = W_{\{\psi\}} \cap W_S$, by Definition 6, and $W_{\{\psi\}} \cap W_S \subseteq W_{\{\phi\}}$. Thus $w \models \phi$ for all $w \in \psi(W_S)$, and it follows that $\psi > \phi$ by Definition 7. ||

Theorem 6 (Jackson, 1989). PMA does not satisfy the preservation criterion.

Proof. By counterexample. In PMA, it is not the case that $(\neg p \equiv r) > r$ with respect to the theory $S = \{p \equiv q, r\}$. The models of the revision are $\{[p, q], [r]\}$. Yet $(\neg p \equiv r)$ is consistent with S. ‖

It is easy to show that PWA satisfies **K*P** (see Definition 1). These results are not surprising, since **K*4** and **K*P** are equivalent in the presence of **K*2** (see Gärdenfors, 1988, p.158).

<u>Theorem 7</u>. BERYL does not satisfy the monotonicity postulate, **K*M**, given as the following semantic constraint: If $W_S \subseteq W_T$, then $\psi(W_S) \subseteq \psi(W_T)$.

Proof. By counterexample. Let $S = \{p \equiv q, p\}$ and let $T = \{p \equiv q\}$, so that we have $W_S = \{[p, q]\}$ and $W_T = \{[p, q], []\}$. Revising by $\psi = \neg q$, $\neg q(S) = \{[p]\}$, while $\neg q(T) = \{[]\}$. Hence $W_S \subseteq W_T$, but not $\psi(W_S) \subseteq \psi(W_T)$. ‖

<u>Theorem 8</u>. PMA satisfies **K*M**: If $W_S \subseteq W_T$, then $\psi^{PMA}(W_S) \subseteq \psi^{PMA}(W_T)$, where $\psi^{PMA}(W_S) = \cup_{M \in \text{Models}(S)}$ Incorporate($\{\psi\}, M$).

Proof. It is easy to see that $\psi^{PMA}(W_S) = \psi^{PMA}(W_T) \cup \psi^{PMA}(W_T - W_S)$, given that the Incorporate function computes closest worlds on an independent 'world by world' basis. ‖

Neither Dalal's Revise nor PWA satisfy **K*M**: use the counterexample in the proof of Theorem 7.

Table 1 summarizes our understanding of the relationships between the four systems. It does not feature **K*4**, since **K*P** and **K*4** are equivalent, given **K*2** (Gardenfors, 1988). All four systems agree on **K*2**, and on all other postulates mentioned in this section which are omitted from the table.

It can be seen that BERYL is closer than PMA or Revise to being a 'correction' of PWA, and we argue that PWA has good properties, other than its syntax-dependency. Preservation conserves information and lends stability to a belief revision function, but PMA lacks this property. Similarly, we argue that nonmonotonicity is an inescapable aspect of belief revision, both when expanding the theory to be revised and when strengthening the revising proposition.

However, we have seen that Revise *does* satisfy a particular monotonicity condition, namely that the revision of S by ψ increases monotonically as we strengthen ψ in a manner that is consistent with earlier, weaker revisions. Put another way, revising by $(\psi \wedge \phi)$ can never rule out any counterfactual consequences of ψ, so long as ϕ is consistent with the revision by ψ. In the following section, we give an example from the domain of diagnosis in which this condition is seems to be counterintuitive.

	PWA	BERYL	PMA	Revise
K*P	yes	yes	no	yes
K*8	no	no	no	yes
K*M	no	no	yes	no

Table 1. Comparison between PWA, BERYL, PMA and Revise on three postulates.

6 More on Revise and other related work

A significant difference between Winslett's Incorporation and Dalal's Revision is that Incorporation proceeds on a 'model by model' basis with no interference between models of ψ competing to be in the final revision on the basis of their closeness to different models of S. By contrast, Revision allows a model of ψ that is close to one model of S to oust another model of ψ that is close to *another* model of S. BERYL is somewhere between these two extreme positions. We allow one model of ψ that is close to a model of S to be kept out of the revision by another model of ψ if the latter is either a glb or an lub of the *same* model of S with respect to the world lattice while the former is not (see Definition 5, clause (ii), where we insist that $B_w(V) = \emptyset$ before we look for neighbours that are not glbs or lubs of w).

We argue that the Revise operator is less sensitive to the contents of S than BERYL's revision function, since not all worlds in W_S will necessarily have a neighbour in Dalal's revision. This is because it is only those worlds in $W_{\{\psi\}}$ which are closest to the *nearest* worlds in W_S which appear in the revision. Worlds in W_S which are any further away from $W_{\{\psi\}}$ do not influence the outcome, as the following example shows.

Example 4. Let $S = \{\neg q, \neg r, p \vee s, \neg p \vee \neg s\}$ and let $\psi = q \wedge (p \vee r)$. Thus $W_S = \{[p], [s]\}$ and $W_{\{\psi\}} = \{[p, q, r, s], [p, q, r], [p, q, s], [q, r, s], [p, q], [q, r]\}$.

Dalal's method produces the outcome $\{[p, q]\}$, since the ψ-world $[p, q]$ is just one step away from the S-world $[p]$. However, $[p, q]$ is not really close to the S-world $[s]$, because there is a closer ψ-world $[p, q, s]$. Thus the S-world $[s]$ is unrepresented in the revision. BERYL's revision contains [p, q, s] and [q, r, s], which are each neighbours of [s], as well as containing [p, q] — see Figure 3.   ‖

Thus the existence of the S-world [s] makes no contribution to the final outcome in Dalal's method, which is the same as if we were revising $T = \{p, \neg q, \neg r, \neg s\}$ by ψ. This is the sense in which Revise is less sensitive to the contents of S than BERYL, where $\psi(W_S) = \{[p, q], [p, q, s], [q, r, s]\}$ and $\psi(W_T) = \{[p, q]\}$. Such examples show that the two functions enforce different notions of minimality when computing revisions; it is worth attempting to explain this in more detail.

Syntactically speaking, Revise conserves more of S; from this point of view, it appears that BERYL gives up $(\neg p \vee \neg s)$ and $\neg r$ unnecessarily in Example 4. On the other hand, BERYL prefers to give up $(\neg p \vee \neg s)$ rather than admit $\neg s$; and gives up $\neg r$ in preference to deriving p from $\neg r$ and $(p \vee r)$. This minimizes change in a rather different sense, since $\neg s \longmapsto (\neg p \vee \neg s)$ and $p \longmapsto (p \vee r)$ but not conversely, so one could argue that losing the disjunction in each case is less of a revision than admitting the literal. More concisely, Dalal's method attempts to minimize change in the underlying contraction of S in the face of ψ, while BERYL attempts to minimize overall deviation from the contents of both ψ and S in the revision as a whole.

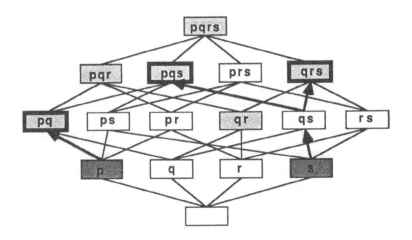

Figure 3. World lattice for Example 4; shading conventions as in Figure 2.

The difference between the two methods in practice can be illustrated by the following example.

Example 5. Consider the following simple diagnostic problem (from Jackson, 1990). Let our alphabet A be $\{d, f, g, r, s\}$, and let these letters have the following meanings: f = 'flat-battery', r = 'radio working', d = 'radio disconnected', s = 'car starts', and finally g = 'car is out of gas'. Also let

$$S^* = \{\neg r \supset f \vee d, \neg s \supset f \vee g\}$$

represent our diagnostic knowledge (to the effect that (i) a dead radio is caused by either a flat battery or disconnection, and (ii) failure to start is caused by either a flat battery or being out of gas), and let

$$S = S^* \cup \{r, s, \neg d, \neg f, \neg g\}$$

be the union of this knowledge with assumptions to the effect that there are no faults or symptoms present. Thus our diagnostic knowledge is protected, but the assumptions are not.

Now let $\psi = \neg r \wedge \neg s$ be an observation to the effect that the radio does not work and the car does not start. Then $(\neg r \wedge \neg s)(W_S) = \{[f], [d, g]\}$, and the models in the revision represent minimal explanations of ψ. $[f]$ represents the world in which a flat battery is the only fault, accounting for both symptoms, while $[d, g]$ represents the world in which the radio is disconnected and the car is out of gas (but the battery is not flat). Clearly, $(\neg r \wedge \neg s) > (f \vee (d \wedge g))$. In other words, the conjoined symptoms counterfactually imply the disjunction of the simplest alternative explanations that would account for them.

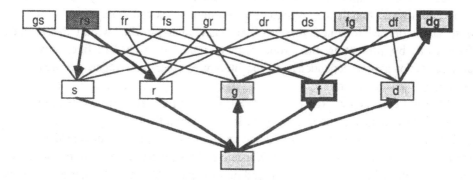

Figure 4. World lattice for Example 5; shading conventions as in Figure 2.

The relevant fragment of the world lattice for this problem is reproduced in Figure 4. [] is the closest world to [r, s] in $W_{\{\neg r, \neg s\}}$, but this world does not satisfy the protected propositions, S^*. The closest worlds to [] in $W_{\{\neg r, \neg s\}}$ that satisfy S^* are [f] and [d, g]. Note that Dalal's method would only produce [f]; the [d, g] diagnosis would be missing, because it does not represent a minimum cardinality change to [r, s].

In the last section, we pointed out that **K*8** insists that the revision of S by ψ must increase monotonically as we strengthen ψ in a consistent manner. Further, it is thanks to an insistence on minimum cardinality change that Revise satisfies **K*8**. But in the context of a diagnostic problem such as the present example, **K*8** means that observing additional symptoms consistent with the current state of knowledge will not eliminate any existing fault hypotheses. This is surely a counterintuitive state of affairs, constituting an argument against **K*8** and minimum cardinality. Inconsistency should not be the sole grounds for discarding hypotheses in this kind of problem solving. ‖

Thus, for applications of TMS that involve abductive reasoning, BERYL's revision function appears to be preferable to Dalal's. But there may be other applications where Dalal's notion of minimal change is more suitable than BERYL's. For example, when reasoning about action, it may sometimes make sense to minimize the actual *number* of changes, using a preference for minimal cardinality, although such a measure is somewhat representation-dependent.

Turning to other work, Nebel's (1989) account suffers from the same problems of syntax-dependency as PWA. If $S = \{p, q, p \supset q\}$ and $T = \{(p \wedge q), (p \supset q)\}$, then revising by $\neg p$ will produce different revisions in each case, even though S and T are equivalent. We argue that such approaches risk contaminating the semantics of logical operators with pragmatic considerations to do with which propositions 'belong together.' For example, to remove ($p \wedge q$) from T when revising by $\neg p$ removes q unnecessarily and founds the revision on a non-minimal contraction. If we want p and q to stand or fall together, then we can easily achieve this within the BERYL framework by protecting the proposition ($p \equiv q$). It is hard to find convincing arguments for syntax-dependency in the literature, other than vague gestures in the direction of psychologism.

Other writers, such as Rao & Foo (1989) and Fariñas del Cerro & Herzig (1988), revise only by literals, so their framework is less general than ours.

Finally, for an analytic review of some belief revision systems not considered here, the reader is recommended to consult Katsuno & Mendelzon (1989). In this paper, we have concentrated upon approaches based on or clearly related to counterfactual logic, but alternative approaches exist, *e.g.*, Satoh's (1988) revision operator for first-order theories which is based on circumscription.

7 Conclusion

Revision-based truth maintenance (RTMS) seems to have a number of advantages over justification- and assumption-based methods. Firstly, it computes the culprits responsible for contradiction in a knowledge base and excises them automatically in order to maintain consistency. We have shown that BERYL provides a semantics for such revisions which is entirely independent of the syntactic form in which the knowledge is stored. Secondly, RTMS can be systematically related to conditional logic, whose properties are well-known. In the Appendix, we show that BERYL satisfies an axiomatization of the counterfactual logic C (Lewis, 1973, Ch.6). Bell (1990) has recently argued that C is *the* basic logic of nonmontonicity; we will not recapitulate the arguments here as they are not central to our thesis. Finally, there seems to be no impediment to adding justifications or assumptions, if these are required by a particular application, although we have not explored this particular avenue at the present time.

BERYL has a number of advantages over alternative accounts of belief revision. Firstly, it is syntax independent, unlike PWA. This guarantees that inessential variations in the underlying knowledge representation do not affect the outcome of belief revision. Secondly, it is preservative, unlike PMA. This ensures that we do not lose beliefs unnecessarily when revising by information that is consistent with what we already know. The problem with PMA is that the more we revise, the more extant knowledge we are likely to lose.. The strongest alternative to BERYL is probably Dalal's method; we have seen that it offers a different notion of 'minimal change' which attempts to minimize the underlying contraction instead of minimizing the revision as a whole. We also saw that Revise is sometimes insensitive to the contents of the theory to be revised and that it satisfies a kind of monotonicity condition on the revising proposition. We saw that which notion of revision is preferred may depend upon the particular application of the TMS.

We have implemented BERYL (together with PMA and Dalal's method) within the lattice framework described in Section 3. The program transforms both S and ψ into a prime implicant representation, using the algorithm described in Jackson & Pais (1990). The models of S and ψ are easily derived from the prime implicants, and the closest neighbours are computed via a breadth-first search of the lattice based on Definition 5. This implementation is hardly efficient for large alphabets, although it is a useful tool for experimenting with different semantic revision functions. We have recently devised and implemented a syntactic revision method for BERYL which is more computationally feasible, but that is the subject of another paper.

Acknowledgement

This work was supported by the McDonnell Douglas Independent Research and Development program.

References

Bell, J. (1990). The logic of nonmonotonicity. *Artificial Intelligence*, 41, 365-374.

Dalal, M. (1988). Investigations into a theory of knowledge base revision: Preliminary report. *7th National Conference on Artificial Intelligence*, 475-479.

de Kleer, J. (1984). Choices without backtracking. *5th National Conference on Artificial Intelligence*, 79-85.

de Kleer, J. (1986). An assumption-based TMS. *Artificial Intelligence*, 28, 127-162.

Doyle, J. (1980). A truth maintenance system. *Artificial Intelligence*, 12, 231-272.

Fariñas del Cerro, L. & Herzig, A. (1988). An automated modal logic of elementary changes. In Smets, P., Mamdani, E .H., Dubois, D. & Prade, H. (eds.) *Non-Standard Logics for Automated Reasoning*, pp. 63-79, London: Academic Press.

Gärdenfors, P. (1988). *Knowledge in Flux*. Boston, MA: MIT Press.

Gärdenfors, P. & Makinson, D. (1988). Revisions of knowledge systems using epistemic entrenchment. *2nd Conference on Theoretical Aspects of Reasoning About Knowledge*, 83-95.

Ginsberg, M. L. (1986). Counterfactuals. *Artificial Intelligence*, 30, 35-79.

Harper, W. L. (1976). Ramsey Test conditionals and iterated belief change. In *Foundations of Probability Theory, Statistical Inference, and Statistical Theories of Science*, W.L. Harper & C. Hooker, Eds. Dordrecht: Reidel, vol. 1, 117-135.

Jackson, P. (1989). On the semantics of counterfactuals. In *Proceedings of the 11th International Joint Conference on Artificial Intelligence*, 1382-1387.

Jackson, P. (1990). Abduction and counterfactuals. In *Working Notes of AAAI Spring Symposium Series: Automated Abduction*, pp. 77-81.

Jackson, P. & Pais, J. (1990). Computing prime implicants. *10th International Conference on Automated Deduction*, pp.543-557, Berlin: Springer-Verlag.

Katsuno, H. & Mendelzon, A. O. (1989). A unified view of propositional knowledge base updates. *Proceedings of the 11th International Joint Conference on Artificial Intelligence*, 1413-1419.

Lewis, D. K. (1973). *Counterfactuals*. Cambridge, MA: Harvard University Press.

Martins, J. P. & Shapiro, S. C. (1988). A model for belief revision. *Artificial Intelligence*, 35, 25-79.

McAllester, D. (1980). *An outlook on truth maintenance.* Report No. AIM-551, AI Laboratory, MIT.

Pais, J. & Jackson, P. (1990). *Partial monotonicity and a new version of the Ramsey Test.* Submitted for publication.

Rao, A. S. & Foo, N. Y. (1989). Formal theories of belief revision. *1st International Conference on Principles of Knowledge Representation and Reasoning,* 369-280.

Satoh, K. (1988). Nonmonotonic reasoning by minimal belief revision. *Proceedings of the International Conference on Fifth Generation Computer Systems,* 455-462.

Winslett, M. (1988). Reasoning about action using a possible models approach. *7th National Conference on Artificial Intelligence,* 89-93.

Appendix

Here we show that our semantics for belief revision satisfies the axioms of the conditional logic C. In some places, we use a correspondence between the Gärdenfors postulates and various axioms of conditional logic (see Gärdenfors, 1988, Ch.7). Consequently, the proofs in Theorems 2 and 3 suffice for many of the axioms.

<u>Theorem 9</u>. The BERYL construction of Definitions 5-7 satisfies the nine axioms of the conditional logic C.

Proof. Let ψ, ϕ and χ be any propositions, and let $S \subset L$ be any theory.

A1. All truth functional tautologies. $\models \psi \supset \phi$ iff $W_{\{\psi\}} \subseteq W_{\{\phi\}}$ as usual.

A2. $(\psi > \phi) \wedge (\psi > \chi) \supset (\psi > (\phi \wedge \chi))$.
   If $w \models \phi$ and $w \models \chi$ for all $w \in \psi(W_S)$, then $w \models (\phi \wedge \chi)$.

A3. $\psi > T$. If $\models \phi$, then $w \models \phi$ for all $w \in \psi(W_S)$.

A4. $\psi > \psi$. This axiom corresponds to **K*2**.

A5. $(\psi > \phi) \supset (\psi \supset \phi)$. This axiom corresponds to **K*3**.

A6. $(\psi \wedge \phi) \supset (\psi > \phi)$. This axiom corresponds to **K*4**.

A7. $(\psi > \neg\psi) \supset (\phi > \neg\psi)$. $w \models \neg\psi$ for all $w \in \psi(W_S)$ iff $\psi(W_S) = \emptyset$.

A8. $((\psi > \phi) \wedge (\phi > \psi)) \supset ((\psi > \chi) \supset (\phi > \chi))$. This axiom corresponds to **K*6**.

A9. $((\psi > \chi) \wedge (\phi > \chi)) \supset ((\psi \vee \phi) > \chi)$. This axiom corresponds to **K*7**.   ‖

Note that **A7** does not correspond exactly with **K*5**. Thus we do not have a problem when revising an inconsistent theory, as we did with **K*5**. If $W_S = \emptyset$, then $\psi(W_S) = \emptyset$ for all ψ, so both $\psi > \neg\psi$ and $\phi > \neg\psi$ will hold for any ψ and ϕ.

Lecture Notes in Computer Science

Lecture Notes in Artificial Intelligence (LNAI)